REJOICE

A HISTORY OF THE PENTECOSTAL ASSEMBLIES OF ALBERTA
AND THE NORTHWEST TERRITORIES

ISBN 0-88925-434-6

Published by
The Pentecostal Assemblies of Canada
Alberta and the Northwest Territories (MacKenzie) District
11617 106 Avenue,
Edmonton, Alberta, Canada T5H 0S1

Printed and bound in Canada by
Friesen Printers
a Division of D. W. Friesen & Sons Ltd.
Altona, Manitoba R0G 0B0
Canada

Table of Contents

Dedication

REJOICE is dedicated to the ALBERTA PENTE-COSTAL PIONEERS, BOTH PASTORS AND PEOPLE.

Acknowledgements

The History Book Committee wishes to express their appreciation to the National Officers and Staff, Rev. R. W. Taitinger, Rev. Charles Yates and Mrs. M. Rodgers, for information from the Archives of the Pentecostal Assemblies of Canada, from The Pentecostal Testimony and from the Dominion Outreach; to the District Executive and Staff for information from District Bulletins and The Thrust, for guidance and financial care; to Rev. Paul Hawkes for information; to Northwest Bible College for the use of the John C. Cooke Library for research; to the Morsch Family for information and the use of Mabel Morsch's diaries; to Rev. Steve Holomis and Heritage Christian Assembly for the use of office space and equipment; to the Edwin Morsch Family for the use of their home and equipment; to the Vernon Robinson Family for the use of their home, and to pastors and congregations, who sent in histories or information.

The Committee wishes to express appreciation to those, who assisted in various ways to make this book possible. Among those are Mrs. W. F. (Sarah) Ball, Vida Bend, Mrs. D. N. (Kathleen) Buntain, Rev. and Mrs. J. C. Cooke, Mr. Roy Collis, Mrs. Beryl Day, Mrs. Bert (Eva) Dale, Miss Lila Dickinson, Mrs. Jean Dittman, Mrs. R. (Shirley) Drisner, Mrs. W. (Adeline) Emde, Rev. Greg Foley, Mr. Ron Foley, Rev. Edward Gaetz, Mr. Alfred Gill, Mrs. Maud Hill, Robertson and Elsie Howatt, Mrs. Nora M. Johnson, Rev. Norman Labrentz, Mrs. Bill (Bertha) Lagore, Rev. and Mrs. A. A. Lewis, Mrs. Georgina Maben, Clarence and Winnifred McAlister, Rev. David McAlister, Rev. Lorne McAlister, Rev. James McAlister, Rev. Clifford Nelson, Rev. and Mrs. Edgar O'Brien, Rev. and Mrs. Morris Olson, Rev. Mervin Peterson, Mrs. I. Roset, Rev. Jim Routley, Mrs. Art Sader, Mr. and Mrs. M. Shram, Mrs. O. H. "Bud" (Lois) Schneider, Mrs. Gilbert (Dorothy) Snider, Mrs. Philip (Mae) Snider, Mrs. Edina Sponholz, Mrs. G. Ryley (formerly Mrs. J. C. O'Brien), Kay Vaydick from the Northwest Territories Government office in Edmonton, Rev. and Mrs. Jack Field, Rev. and Mrs. E. W. Peterson, Evangel Pentecostal Assembly.

History Book Committee

J. Shirley Morsch, Editor in Chief
Agnes S. McAlister
Eileen P. Holomis
Edwin H. Morsch

This committee did much more than edit material sent in by churches and individuals. They did a great deal of research; had many, many interviews; wrote many histories and added to many other histories in order to compile as accurate a history of the Pentecostal Assemblies' churches, missions and district ministries in Alberta and the Northwest Territories (MacKenzie District) as possible.

The history, REJOICE, was commissioned by Rev. I. Roset, District Superintendent, and the District Executive of The Pentecostal Assemblies of Canada Alberta and the Northwest Territories (MacKenzie) District.

Others, who for a time, served on the committee were Rev. Kenneth Bunting, Assistant District Superintendent; Rev. R. J. White and Rev. A. Lindoff, District Presbyter at Large.

Edwin H. and J. Shirley Morsch with their son, Scott. J. Shirley Morsch (nee Johnson) graduated from Canadian Northwest Bible Institute in 1949; received her Ministerial Certificate for Women in 1952, while in home mission work; received her permanent teaching certificate from the Alberta Department of Education in 1960 and married Edwin Morsch in 1963. Edwin H. Morsch graduated from Canadian Northwest Bible Institute in 1949 and has worked for Woodward Stores for over 25 years. His co-operation and help have played an important role in the compiling of REJOICE.

Agnes S. McAlister (nee Leverth). Mrs. McAlister, widow of Rev. Harvey C. McAlister, was for years a very active lady minister, received her Deaconess Certificate years ago and was a school teacher for years. Her many years in the province made her a valuable resource person on the committee.

Eileen P. Holomis and Rev. Steve Holomis. Eileen Holomis attended a Saskatoon Business College and married Rev. Steve Holomis in 1953. Her stenographic skills have been a blessing both to churches, her husband and the History Committee.

Rejoice, my soul, within me!
For I want all to see
My heritage is one of praise,
My Father gave to me.

Rejoice, my heart, in worship,
Extol His name abroad;
For daily I commune with Him,
Creator, Father God.

Rejoice, my hands, in service,
For a servant I shall be
Not praise in words and prayer alone,
But rejoice in every deed.

Rejoice, my lips, my voice I'll raise
In song before my King;
My praise in melodies of joy
Eternally I'll bring.

Rejoice, my soul, within me
As I dance before my King;
I exalt the One who gives me life,
I rejoice in everything!

Rhonda Hoffman
(nee Holomis)
1983

Our Heritage

"REJOICE IN THE LORD ALWAYS: AND AGAIN I SAY, REJOICE." Philippians Chapter Four, Verse Four (Philippians 4:4).

OUR FAITH

We do have much for which to rejoice. We are happy because we have a loving God. He loved us so much, that He sent His only Son, God the Son, who is Jesus Christ, to die for our sins (John 3:16). Because Jesus Christ allowed Himself to be born of a virgin, then was tempted and yet was without sin, He was able to be our Saviour. He was the only one who could be our Saviour, the only one who could take the punishment for our sin. God sent his Holy Spirit to draw us to God. Romans 3:23 tells us that "All have sinned and come short of the glory of God." We were born with sinful natures, but God sent the Saviour. There is no peace like the peace that comes from knowing that your sins are forgiven. I John 1:9 tells us that, "If we confess our sins, He is faithful and just to forgive us our sins and to cleanse us from all unrighteousness." WHAT A GIFT!

As a testimony of our faith in Christ we are baptized in water. We need to tell others about this GOOD NEWS (Romans 10:9,10). We need to accept Jesus Christ as our own personal Saviour. He died for my sin and yours, then rose from the dead. After forty days, he ascended into heaven. Jesus Christ is the Healer (Exodus 15:26). Just as He healed the sick and performed miracles in Bible times, he is still able to do the same today (James 5:13-15). He has never lost His power. Whenever anyone receives a healing or a miracle, it is such an encouragement to believers. The Saviour has promised to come back for the believer. He is preparing a place in heaven for us (John 14:2,3; I Thessalonians 4:13-18).

The Lord will baptize the believer with the Holy Spirit with the evidence of speaking in other tongues (in a language the believer has not learned). We must ask the Lord for this experience, so that we may become more effectual Christians (Acts 1:8; Acts Chapters One and Two). When you receive the Baptism of the Holy Spirit, the Holy Spirit speaks through the believer in a language the believer has not learned. Notice how surprised the people were in Acts 2:8. The speaking in other tongues is the scriptural evidence of having received the Baptism of the Holy Spirit. It helps the believer to have more courage to live for God and spread the news that Jesus Christ is the Saviour and wants to help us every day of our lives. Because of this experience, the Pentecostal assemblies are really growing, especially where the Holy Spirit is invited to anoint the believers and the pastor.

EXPERIENCES THAT LED TO THE FORMATION OF PENTECOSTAL ASSEMBLIES

News that people were receiving the Baptism of the Holy Spirit, with the evidence of speaking in other tongues, created curiosity and interest. Those, who received this Baptism of the Holy Spirit were well aware that God is very real and powerful. Devout Christians wanted what was scriptural and this experience was scriptural. Quite a few received this experience in the United States and Canada.

Dr. Stanley Horton reported that his grandmother, Miss Clara Sanford (later Mrs. Elmer Fisher) who lived in Pennsylvania, received the Baptism of the Holy Spirit, with the tongues evidence, in 1880. His father, Harry S. Horton, received this same experience in 1906 in a meeting in the Winnipeg home of Mrs. Goldback. Both she and her daughter had been in the Azusa Street meetings. Later, H. S. Horton assisted A. H. Argue in Winnipeg.

This same experience was received by Rev. Elmer J. Seymour of Houston, who later went to Los Angeles to preach. He ended up preaching in a home at 214 Bonnie Brae Street, where on April 9, 1906 seven received this Baptism of the Holy Spirit, with the tongues evidence. Crowds gathered; some were converted. The home was too small for the group so services were held in the old Methodist Church at 312 Azusa Street, Los Angeles.

News of this Azusa Street Revival was spread far and wide by letter and paper. In Elmer Cantelon's

1

book, Harvester of the North, he reported that his mother, Mrs. Peter Cantelon, of the Manitoba Mather District near Cartwright, received the Baptism of the Holy Spirit in her own home in 1906.

In the Pentecostal Testimony of May 1956, Rev. G. A. Chambers reported that in 1906, he received the Baptism of the Holy Spirit in the home of Mr. and Mrs. Hebden, who also had received this experience. Among the others, who were at the prayer meetings there, was Daniel Awrey, who had received his baptism some years before.

Rev. Chambers recounted how he had heard a young girl prophesy in Latin (which she had not learned) to a lawyer, whom she told not to scoff but to go to the Upper Room, where he would meet God. This he did and was gloriously saved and filled with the Holy Spirit.

In the Pentecostal Testimony of May 1956, Rev. A. H. Argue tells how he went to Chicago, where a group of folk had received the Baptism of the Holy Spirit. While with them there in 1907, he too received this baptism. He returned home to Winnipeg and had services in his home. On May 2, 1907, three were filled with the Spirit. Soon they rented a hall for services. During 1907 and 1908, a great number received this experience, including a number of ministers and Christian workers. In A. H. Argue's paper, The Apostolic Messenger, November 1908 issue, he reported that by that time, many had received the Baptism of the Holy Spirit, according to Acts Chapter Two, Verse Four, in many countries — Arabia, Armenia, Australia, China, Cuba, Egypt, England, Germany, Holland, Ireland, Japan, Jeruca, Jerusalem, Norway, Persia, Russia, San Marcial, Scotland, Sweden, Switzerland, Syria, Tibet, Italy, New Mexico and Wales.

ALBERTA IS BLESSED

In 1908 there was an outpouring of the Holy Spirit in Calgary, Alberta.

George and Esther Taylor, who had received the Baptism of the Holy Spirit in Cartwright about 1909, moved to Red Deer, Alberta in 1911. Mr. Taylor, who had been an English Methodist Lay Preacher, was one to witness for the Lord. He told others about the Baptism of the Holy Spirit, which helped to form a base for Pentecostal services later on.

In 1912, a Victor Nysted arrived in Alberta. Because of his testimony of having received the Baptism of the Holy Spirit in Sweden, Rev. Elof Lindquist and Rev. Holm were the first to receive among the Swedish Christians in Central-Eastern Alberta. By 1922 at Metiskow, a Swedish Pentecostal Assembly was established. Services were conducted in Swedish.

As the news of the outpouring spread, more and more people would seek for the experience that brought such blessing to the believers. These groups were not legally organized but were a loosely knit fellowship with a common experience. It was later, that groups began to realize, that for purity of doctrine and form of church government, some legal organizing was needed. So eventually some of these groups joined the Pentecostal Assemblies. Some, who had not joined, asked Pentecostal Assemblies ministers to be their pastors.

In 1982, there were 92 Assemblies or Missions in this Pentecostal Assemblies of Canada District and Assemblies are still being added.

HISTORY OF THE GERMAN SPEAKING CHURCHES IN ALBERTA

The first Pentecostal ministers that preached in the German language in Alberta were: Reverend G. Schneider, Reverend W. Frederick, Reverend L. Posein, Reverend J. Schatkowski (known as "The Candy Man"), Reverend D. Baker and Reverend W. Kowalski.

The first Conference of the German Branch of The Pentecostal Assemblies of Canada was held July 8, 1940 in the Wiesenthal Church near Leduc, Alberta. It was there that Reverend Whilhelm Kowalski was elected as District Superintendent, a position he held until 1965. He was succeeded by Reverend Gustav Kurtz, who still serves as Superintendent of the German Conference.

In 1942 a Camp ground was purchased at Alberta Beach and every year since then, camp meetings have been held.

In 1960 the Alberta District of the German Branch had fifteen churches: Edmonton (two churches), Vega, Barrhead, Manola, Onoway, New Sarepta, Gardenview, Heimdal, Wiesenthal, Ferintosh, Millet, Thorsby, Ponoka, Medicine Hat, Calgary.

Due to the fact that many people left the farms and moved into the cities many of the farming community churches have closed. Thus in 1982 there were seven churches affiliated with the German Branch in the Province of Alberta.

The Southside Pentecostal Assembly is the largest congregation of the German Branch. This Assembly was organized on March 18, 1940. However its beginnings go back to house meetings beginning in 1930 and continuing until 1938 when a group of twenty-two believers purchased a lot on Ninety-Eighth Street and Seventy-Sixth Avenue for the sum of One hundred and twelve dollars and fifty cents and built a church costing two thousand one hundred thirty-nine dollars and twenty-nine cents. In 1950 a larger church was built on the same site. In 1956 the present building was built at Ninety-Ninth

Street and Eighty-Third Avenue and enlarged in 1970.

In 1976 the Southside Pentecostal Assembly mothered the Millwoods Pentecostal Assembly.

The senior pastors of the Southside Assembly were Reverend Daniel Baker (1944-1959), Reverend Wilhelm Kowalski (1959-1970), Reverend Gordon F. Rattai (1970-1977), Reverend Horst Doberstein (1977-   ).

Among those, who attended Bible College and/or entered the ministry (*), are Marga Algajar, Karen Bader, Ida Beier, Marlene Berg, Trudy Blum, Arnold Breitkreutz, Harold Breitkreutz, *Larry Breitkreutz, Ruth Breitkreutz, Elsie Daase, Elaine Doberstein, Larry Egert, Linda Eisler, Edwin Ehrenholz, Frieda Eisert, *Helmut Eisert, Hilda Fech, Allan Fitz, Harry Fitz, *Linda Fitz, Marilyn Fitz, **Stanley Fitz, Linda Folkman, Myrtle Garlock, Alice I. Gaucher, *Abe Guretzki, *Lucille Guze (wife of Reverend A. Sader), Fred Hildabrandt, Irvin Hilderbrandt, Lavon Hildebrandt, Sandy Hilderbrandt, Brian Hauer, Hilda Ickert, *Irene Isaac, Dennis Jacobson, Ernest Janke, Violet Jeschke, Frank Jensen, Dennis Jobs, *Otto Kakoschke, *Arthur Kalke, Frieda Kalke, Ursula Kakoschke, Marilyn Knakoske, Reinhold Komant, *Delilah Krieger, Emmi Krueger, Linda Kellert (now Milke), Lily Kolm, Lydia Kurtz, Raymond Kublik, *Reginald Kublik, Helga Kubitz, Eddie Kubke, Peter Kurney, *Norman Labrentz, Edward Laskowski, Gunther Laubenstein, Arnold Lotholz, Edith Lotholz, Judy Lotholz, Evelyn Malina, Frank Malina, Bill Marten, Dorothea Mangold, Robert Matz, Eric Milke, Erna Milke, Joseph Moech, Marlene Mohr, *Henry Miller, Wes Miller, Cecil Miller, Henry Miller, Marvin Miller, Gisela Molgahn, Dithmar Molzah (Gisela's brother), Arthur Muth, Hilda Muth, Ed Nerling, Ingrid Newbauer, Eli Numrich, **Eric Pahl, Albert Pohl, Allen Pohl, **Doris Pohl (wife of Reverend Gus Wentland), Ida Pohl, *Norman Pohl, Selma Pohl, Irvin Patz, Deloris Price, *Carolyn Rattai, Irene Rempel, Ruth Rebman, *Ed Rebman, **Audrey Rhiel, Betty Rhiel, Lois Rhiel, *Wally Rhiel, Erhardt Ritz, *Garry Rohr, *Rainer Rohr, Leona Rast, Sandy Rast (now Widmer), Karen Ritter, Reg Rygus, Phil Rohatynski, Gertrude Schulz, Charles Saunders, Adeline Sader, Elmer Schlender, Arthur Schlender, Evelyn Stoik, Trudy Stoik, Eileen Stoik, Eric Stoik, *Walda Schellert, **Paul Schellert, Betty Rejman, *Klaus Scheindl, Bernie Stein, Agatha Schmidt, Rudy Schmidt, *Ruth Schafrick, Dianne Steer, *Arthur Sader, *Bernard Schellert, Gottlieb Schell, Sherry Ann Snyder, Dave Tonn, *Erna Tonn, Gerhold Tonn, Esther Tews, Harold Tischer, Helmut Tonn, *Erica Tonn (wife of Reverend Wally Rhiel), Karen Tonn, Marlene Tonn, Werner Trapp, Hildagart (Hilda) Trelenberg, Inez Wentland, **Gus Wentland, Dianne Witzke, Edeltraut Zieman. Missionaries who were/are on fields outside Canada are double starred (**).

HISTORY OF THE SLAVIC CHURCHES IN ALBERTA

Rev. Karp Hrycauk was converted at Christmas time in 1920 and was filled with the Holy Spirit in 1928, while in the Ukraine. That same year, 1928, he came to Canada to live. He endeavored to start services, wherever he stayed. He did carpentry work to support himself. His method was to go into a town or district, have services in homes with the aim of winning souls for Jesus. As soon as he had a nucleus of believers, he would appoint a deacon, whom he left in charge of the group of believers. This deacon would keep in touch with Rev. Hrycauk, asking for help whenever he had a problem. Among the places, where he had services, were Rife (L. Krawchuk and John Harbarenko were converted.), Brosseau (He gathered nine families together. Mike Twerdy and Mr. and Mrs. William Melnychuk were saved. William Melnychuk became the next preacher.), Glendon (By 1931, there were twenty-seven families in the church. Mr. Kryzenowsky was the deacon in charge.), Iron River (Deacon Kalinski was in charge.), Bear Trap (News of a wonderful answer to prayer opened a door there. A lady in this district received a wonderful answer to prayer, too. After some services there, three German families, nine Ukrainian families and two Polish families were saved. Deacon Sader (father of Art, Ray, Adeline, Eileen, Helen and Edith) was the best deacon, so said Rev. Hrycauk. John Harbarenko, while in Glendon won Pearl Bidolack to the Lord. She moved to St. Paul, where she was so active for the Lord that she gathered a nucleus together that eventually became the St. Paul Church.).

Rev. Hrycauk had services in Vilna, Beaverdam, Pakan and Thorsby (Deacon Miller was left in charge).

In 1930, a Ukrainian or Slavic Conference was held with Rev. Hrycauk as Superintendent. He continued as Superintendent until 1940, when he appointed William Melnychuk to succeed him. Brother Melnychuk served as Superintendent until his death. In 1947, they joined in fellowship with The Pentecostal Assemblies of Canada, when their own Western Slavic Branch was formed. George Derkatch, who had really pressed for this affiliation, became the Secretary-Treasurer. Nick Tomen was also on their executive. English and German Pentecostal ministers ministered in their churches from time to time.

Among those, who attended Bible college and/or entered the ministry (*), are Gladys Arychuk, Gloria Balehowsky, John Balehowsky, Norman Balehowsky, Doreen Bespoyasny, Helen Botha, *Michael Brandebura, *Anne Burma, *George Derkatch, Nina Davidiuk, Werner Engler, Cassey Ewanciu, Nancy Ewaschuk, Leonard Gavronsky, Ken Haopniuk, *Steve Holomis, *Eunice Hunka, **Jack Hunka, Rhonda Kalinski, *Peter Kerychuk, Evangeline Krawchuk, *Nina Krawchuk, Madeline Krochmal, *Dan Knol, *Walter Knoll, *Michael Kutney, Lena Mandrusiak, *William Melnychuk, Nicholas Revega, Kay (Kathleen) Rubilak, Louis Sabatier, John Strilesky, Doris Suprovich, Mary Swekla, *Ann Twerdochlib, Lucy Twerdochlib, Jean Twerdy, Ernest Twerdy, Nettie Twerdy, Cornel Woycenko, Florian Woycenko, *Nick Wynychuk, Sharon Zukiwsky.

There still are churches, who have services in Ukrainian, but more and more are using more English. They still have the inside track when it comes to ministering to Slavic people. There is a special bond among the Slavic people.

Farewell to Our Pastor

No, it is not good-bye, just a whispered, "God
  Bless,"
A hand-clasp, a smile and a prayer
That God will be with you each step of the way,
And guide you with tenderest care.

You have loved us, and fed us from God's Holy
  Word,
Have wept when the waters were deep,
Nor faltered when God whispered, "Lovest thou
  Me?
Feed my sheep, feed my lambs, feed my sheep."

No, it is not good-bye, but a low whispered prayer
That ever and always you'll find
The years be as fruitful, the friendships as true
As those you are leaving behind.

Then Onward! Press Onward — the goal is in
  sight,
The battles of life almost won,
A harp and a mansion, a robe of pure white,
And the Father's clear ringing, "Well done!"

Fern Williams Brewer
from "Beyond the Blue"

Printed with permission from Fern Williams Brewer of Lacombe, Alberta.

Assemblies in Alberta

AIRDRIE
FELLOWSHIP BIBLE CHAPEL

In the summer of 1978, the Pastors of First Assembly, Calgary, Rev. Jack Keys and Rev. Ken Bombay, considered starting a church in Airdrie. After much prayer and consideration and a six-month-internship at First Assembly, Harvey and Arlene Trauter moved to Airdrie to pioneer this work in a town of 6,000. Feeling confident that this was God's will, the Board of First Assembly decided to support this work completely for one year, then the support would be cut in half the following year, then again cut in half the following year, then all support was to be cut off. This way the church would not have to worry about their financial position and the pastor could devote full time to ministering. The church began with three families from First Assembly, Mr. and Mrs. A. Allison, Mr. and Mrs. H. Smith, Mr. and Mrs. F. MacLean. On October 30, 1978, the first board meeting was held. Pastor Keys, Harvey Trauter, R. Neubauer and J. Cumming were present. The name of Fellowship Bible Chapel was chosen and November 19, 1978 was to be the opening Sunday Service. 100 people attended the first service. The First Assembly Singers sang. The gym of the Airdrie Elementary and Junior High School was the home of this church until the late spring of 1980.

The church began with one Sunday School class, Morning and Evening Services. The growth of the church moved slowly with visitors coming out occasionally. Home Bible Studies were started, also an Outreach night. The three founding families, Pastor and Mrs. Trauter went door to door introducing the church to the people of the community. Three ladies from Bible college had a successful Kids Crusade, which added many children to the Sunday School. Now there were three Sunday School classes. For two Sunday nights during the summer, special Drive-In Services were held. Special singing groups participated. A crusade with Jim Raddatz was held and the film, "The Cross and the Switchblade," was shown. A successful Christmas Program was held and 1979 proved to be a year of many outreach activities.

By March 1980, things began to happen. Other families joined the church and some were saved in the church. In the fall, five were baptized in a makeshift baptismal tank.

On May 21, 1980, the church purchased a triple-width Atco Trailer from the Government for only $9100.00. God performed a miracle by supplying this. The unit had been up for bids three other times for as much as $40,000.00. A bid was made for $9100.00, but the deposit cheque for 10% had not been enclosed. Pastor Trauter was phoned saying the bid was incomplete but if they would bring in the money, the unit would be theirs. Now a place was needed to put the trailer. After Pastor Trauter met with Frank DeFehr, it was agreed that a piece of Rockyview Industries Land could be leased for $1.00 a year. This was also agreed to by the town. The unit was moved from Fish Creek to Airdrie. Major work converted the trailer into a sanctuary seating 100 plus five classrooms. On July 27, 1980, at 3:00 P.M., these facilities were dedicated to the glory of God. District Superintendent, Rev. Ivar Roset, officiated at the dedication. Rev. Jack Keys of First Assembly was the guest speaker.

On October 23, 1980, the first business meeting was held with nineteen members. A local church constitution was adopted and three men elected to the board. In December 1980, the church again held a Sunday School Christmas Program at the George McDougal High School with 250 people in attendance.

On February 22, 1981, two Morning Worship Services were started. The Scout Hall just north of the church was rented to expand the Sunday School Classes. Looking back, it is evident that God has led and blessed this church.

BARRHEAD
GLAD TIDINGS PENTECOSTAL
ASSEMBLY

Glad Tidings Pentecostal Assembly was started in April 1961, by a group of people who came from the German Pentecostal Church. The desire of this group was to establish an English speaking Pentecostal church in Barrhead.

The first service was held in the Banquet room of Stehelin High School on April 9, 1961, at 2:00 P.M., with Reverend C. A. McClain as speaker.

On April 17 an organizational meeting was held in the basement of the old Barrhead High School. Reverend S. R. Tilton, District Superintendent for Alberta; Reverend R. J. White, District Presbyter; Reverend J. C Cooke, President of the Northwest Bible College; Reverend A. McClain; Reverend W. Pipke were present at this meeting. Altogether there were seventeen adults in attendance. After some discussion it was decided that an English Pentecostal Assembly be opened in Barrhead and that it be affiliated with the Pentecostal Assemblies of Canada. Reverend Angus McClain was called as pastor.

On May 10, 1961, another business meeting was held. The Local Church Constitution was adopted. Three board members were elected — Mr. Julius Maser, Mr. Heinz Steinbrenner, Mr. Oswald Kryger. Mr. Julius Maser was Secretary-Treasurer as well. Charter members of this assembly were Mr. and Mrs. Julius Maser, Mr. and Mrs. James Penner, Mr. and Mrs. Oswald Kryger, Mrs. Doris Schneider, Mr. and Mrs. Heinz Steinbrenner, Mr. and Mrs. Frank Kristel Jr., Mr. and Mrs. Ewald Assenheimer, Mr. and Mrs. Manny Shulz. This first group consisted of thirty-five adults and children. Sunday School was started on April 16, 1961. In August of that same year there were seventy in Sunday School.

The Banquet Room in the Stehelin School soon became too small for the growing congregation. Plans were made to have their own facilities. In June 1961, a large lot was purchased, costing one thousand dollars. This was made possible by the help of the Minute Men of the Alberta District of the Pentecostal Assemblies. The construction of the church began in August 1961. Most of the building was done by volunteer labor, except for plumbing, heating and stuccoing. The cost of the building was twenty thousand dollars. A loan of eight thousand dollars was obtained from the National Office. The church was thirty-two feet by sixty feet with a full basement containing Sunday school rooms and a lower auditorium. The first service was held on December 16, 1961. On February 18, 1962, the church was dedicated with Reverend S. R. Tilton and Reverend R. J. White in attendance.

In those first years, there were financial struggles to pay outstanding bills, but God was blessing. In March 1963, Evangelist Eunice Meyer held special meetings in the Assembly. Seventeen people received the baptism of the Holy Spirit.

Reverend Norman Labrentz became pastor of the church in 1966. On Sunday December 21, 1969, Reverend C. Yates was present at the Mortgage Burning Ceremony. This was a great day of rejoicing for the Assembly.

In 1970 two more lots were purchased, one for the parsonage, the other to be developed as a parking lot. Pastor Labrentz resigned in 1970.

In February 1971, Pastor Rueben Drisner arrived. A three-bedroom parsonage was built in 1972, under the capable hands of Reverend Drisner. Another pastoral change came in 1974, when Pastor Victor Munshaw was called. He pastored for three years. At a Sunday night baptismal service, Reverend Ivar Roset ministered the Word. A young man gave his heart to the Lord. He, too, wanted to be baptized in water. Twelve candidates were baptized that night.

In October 1977, Reverend Hector McDonald came to pastor. Growth continued until the need for larger facilities became evident. Extension and renovations were expected to cost one hundred and ten thousand dollars, however the actual cost became one hundred thirty-three thousand and thirty-nine dollars and thirty-five cents. Donations of labour by professionals and volunteers along with memorials helped to make possible the fine facilities of Glad Tidings today. Dedication was held June 1, 1980, with an overflow crowd in attendance.

In Conference 1981, Pastor McDonald reported they had had a crusade with Reverend Otto Kakoschke in the Spring, followed by another crusade with Evangelist Eunice Meyer in the Fall. Many were saved and filled with the Holy Spirit in these meetings. At the beginning of March 1982, Reverend and Mrs. Hector McDonald moved to St. Paul.

The Gladtones, Al and Vivian Sloboda, originated from this assembly.

In about twenty years of existence, this church has made great strides for the furtherance of the Gospel.

Pastor J. Anonby has been called to pastor this Assembly.

Among those, who attended Bible College and/or entered the ministry (*), are Linda Assenheimer, Joyce Breitkreitz, Lorraine Breitkreitz, Alma Carruthers, Ingrid De Ruigh, *John Drisner, *Helga Engler, Martin Engler, Mildred Engler, Larry Kryger, *Lori Grace Labrentz (married Monty Williamson), Ingrid Miller, Wayne Miller, Harold Schiewe, *Ron Steinbrenner, Eric Stoik, Betty Wiebe, Linda Wiebe, Wilfred Wiebe.

BENTLEY
BENTLEY CHRISTIAN CENTER

Mrs. Carrie Erskine, of the Bentley area, received the Pentecostal experience in British Columbia in 1928. The first Pentecostal preacher was Reverend John Wood. Services were held in Durham School. A. Dalby and A. Christianson, Pentecostal lay preachers from Calgary, commuted to Bentley for Sunday services for a few years. Services were held in the Durham School, then in the Bert William's Hall. In 1931, Lennox Smith, Miss Maisie Coulter (now Mrs. A. A. Lewis) and Jack Field each served as pastor for a few months.

The early preachers stayed with the Blish or Morsch families.

October 11, 1931, Reverend John McAlister, Pentecostal Assemblies of Canada Alberta District Superitendent, met with the Bentley group of Pentecostal believers. They decided to become the Bentley Pentecostal Assembly, affiliated with the Pentecostal Assemblies of Canada. The first board members were J. M. Erskine, E. H. Morsch B. Sc., and E. C. Rud. A. Dalby was asked to be pastor. The first church families were J. M. and Carrie Erskine and daughter, Dorothy; Mrs. John Blish and Lily; Mrs. Rachael Petry, Gordon, Leslie, Grace, Bertha; Edwin and Mabel Morsch with Lillian, John, Edwin, Alberta; Ernest and Marie Spycher, Arnold, Chris,

Group in front of the Pentecostal Assembly.

Godfrey, Freda, Ernest; Mrs. Chaland, Vera and Irene; Mrs. Kelso; Mr. and Mrs. E. C. Rud, Alfred and Irma; Mr. and Mrs. Gelin and Effie. Services were held in the Bert William's Hall for about two years.

After the Dalbys left, local people filled in until the next pastor came, who was Dorothy Erskine. She was followed by Clare and Alice Richardson. John

Morsch remembers being really impressed with one of Clare Richardson's sermons. Next came R. M. McCallum, who also had services in Lockhart and Meadow Brook Schools.

While Pastor and Mrs. Ian Presley (1934-1935) were there, the Pentecostal Assembly's first church building of their own was built by themselves. The church was dedicated December 4, 1935 by Reverend G. R. Upton, Alberta District Superintendent. Young People's meetings were held in different homes. During Pastor Presley's ministry, there was an outreach ministry — Sunday School in Aspen Beach and Gull Lake Schoolhouse during the months of June, July, August and the first Sunday of September.

Young People's Outing, probably in the Rocky Mountain House area.

While Hugh Fraser (1936-1940) was pastor, local assembly people added two-story living quarters to the north end of the church.

Reverend and Mrs. Arthur Sayer and Lillian arrived in 1940. The church enjoyed real growth. In 1944 the parsonage was built and the sanctuary was extended into the old living quarters increasing the seating capacity. Pastor Sayer passed away in May of 1946.

Pastor and Mrs. N. E. Britton (1946-1947) followed Sayers. At this time, the basement was put under the church.

Various supply pastors came until 1949. Pastor and Mrs. Henry Lindberg (1949-1950) came after the pastor graduated from Canadian Northwest Bible Institute. During their ministry, Freda Spycher organized and the church aired the children's radio program, Savior's Air Corps, over CKRD Red Deer, for over two years.

Under Reverend and Mrs. E. W. Peterson (1950-1967) the church enjoyed much growth. The Sunday School peaked over two hundred many times, when the Village of Bentley had a population of about five hundred. There was a large youth group. Many of these young people left for Bible College, University, to find work in other places. They were really missed. During the Peterson's ministry, an addition was made on the west side of the church and the front to accommodate the growth.

Reverend and Mrs. A. A. Lewis pastored from 1967 to 1972. They worked to build up the church.

Ernest Spycher Sr., Murray Bigam and Edwin H. Morsch Sr. were made Honorary Board Members for the rest of their lives because of extended service on the church board. Mr. Morsch was secretary-treasurer for 35 years.

Reverend and Mrs. Rosswell Olson came from 1972 to 1974. Reverend Olson was known to be a good Bible teacher. Following his Bentley ministry he joined the staff of Northwest Bible College, Edmonton, Alberta.

Reverend W. D. Lewis and his wife, Pattie, (1974-   ) have endeared themselves to the church. Their new church, Bentley Christian Center, was dedicated May 22, 1977. Because the local church people donated money and help, it cut the cost of the church considerably. In 1979, this church opened their own Christian day school. To increase the size of the sanctuary and accommodate the school, a large addition was made, including a gymnasium. This was usable in September 1980. The school has a capacity for one hundred students. In the 1980-1981 term the school had an enrollment of sixty-six. At the time of printing the church is debt free. Congratulations are in order.

Savior's Air Corps — Mrs. Sanders is at the piano. Far Right: Leader, Miss Freda Spycher; Pastor Henry (Lindy) Lindberg.

For varying numbers of years, this church has had various outreach programs. Pastor Hugh Fraser and young people, including John Morsch, held services in Sylvan Lake. Sylvan Lake soon had another church, a Pentecostal Church, with its own pastor. Branch Sunday Schools were held at Aspen Beach,

Gull Lake; Chappel School, Forshee; Stephenson School, west of Bentley; Gilby; Blindman School near Blackfalds and all were staffed by Bentley Church folks. Street meetings were held on Main Street. Drive-In Services were held at Gull Lake by The Sanders and Freda Spycher. Sunday School Bus service was given for some time. Edwin Morsch Sr., Norman Wheeler and Edwin Morsch Jr. were among the bus drivers. Folks from the church helped a great deal in the development of Sunnyside Pentecostal Camp on the north shore of Sylvan Lake. For years, the Women's Ministries group has helped missionaries, provided some of the needs of the H. H. Williams Memorial Hospital in Hay River, North West Territories and more. Today the church has Bible Study Groups in areas where their students live. In September 1982, Sunday morning service outreach was started in Rimbey. The service staff commutes from Bentley.

Sunday School in 1958.

Among those who attended Bible College and/or entered the ministry(*), are Joyce Bigam (now Mrs. Mike Shram), *Norman Blish, Larry Bigam, Audrey Carruthers, *Dwain Carruthers, Elaine Carruthers, *Ruth Carruthers, Jean Cox, Angie Curtiss, Bert Dale, *Tommy Davies, *Dorothy Erskine (married to Reverend Lindgren), *Betty Evernden, Carol Goertzen, Garth Gorskey, Bill Gyori, John Gyori, *Hazel Hawkings, *Laurie Hueppelsheuser, Linda Larsen, Edwin Morsch, *John Morsch, Ruth Nelson, *Grace Petry, *Norman Petry, *Lillian Sayer, *Freda Spycher, *Olive Vold (married to Reverend Jack Whitesell), Margaret Wheeler, *Jack Whitesell, *Eileen Murray (married Rev. Jack Field), *Dorothy Betty Huckle (married Jack Telman), *Hilda Collis (wife of Rev. John Wood).

Bentley Christian Center really loves to be of service to the Bentley area.

BLACKFALDS MARANATHA ASSEMBLY

Reverend George MacKenzie, a former pastor of

Red Deer Christian Centre, began a work in Black-falds. They became affiliated with the Pentecostal Assemblies of Canada in 1982.

BONNYVILLE
LAKEVIEW GOSPEL CENTRE

Lakeview Gospel Centre was founded in the early seventies, when several Christian families had a vision for their community. Rev. Nick Wynychuk was the first pastor when the group, with a membership of twenty-three, became affiliated with the Pentecostal Assemblies of Canada under the name of Lakeview Pentecostal Tabernacle.

Land was purchased at the Lakeside. On October 3, 1971, an exciting sod-turning and site dedication service was held. On June 1, 1972, the assembly was able to hold services in their new church. Though it was not fully completed, they worshipped there while it was still under construction.

The Lakeview Gospel Centre

The church was erected by the men of the founding families. The ladies helped with the painting. Other volunteers helped, too. Some Edmonton trades people donated their time and assistance as well. Among the founding families were Pastor and Mrs. Nick Wynychuk, Mr. and Mrs. Tom Antoniuk, Mr. and Mrs. Stan Omilion, Mr. and Mrs. Steve Kalinski, Mr. and Mrs. Nick Gavronsky, Mr. and Mrs. Jon Zaboschuk, Mr. and Mrs. Emile Sabatier, Mr. and Mrs. Bill Woycenko, Mr. and Mrs. Louis Sabatier, Mr. and Mrs. O. Petry, Mr. and Mrs. Alvin Tollefson, Mr. and Mrs. Zaboschuk Sr., Mr. and Mrs. Gavronsky Sr.

The dedication service was held April 21, 1974, with Rev. C. Yates, then District Superintendent, and Rev. Ken Bombay as special speakers.

On May 1, 1975, Rev. Gus Rankel became the pastor and in his one year of ministry the church saw spiritual growth. After Rev. Rankel left, the church was served by Rev. and Mrs. Floyd Schwindt, also by

laymen from the church — Tom Antoniuk and Louis Sabatier.

Rev. Peter Hubert, with his wife and three daughters, came to pastor the congregation on March 1, 1977. On October 30, 1977, the church celebrated with a Mortgage Burning Ceremony, at which Rev. Ivar Roset ministered and the Sneed family sang.

The name of the church was changed to Lakeview Gospel Centre in March 1978.

Choir on Dedication Day, February 7, 1982.

A forty-two passenger Sunday School bus has been purchased in an endeavor to minister to the needs of the community.

Over the past five years about 90 people have been baptized in water. There have been spiritual and emotional healings in peoples' lives and families. Pastor Hubert is still pastoring here and has a continued vision for the Bonnyville area.

A new addition and extension to the sanctuary was dedicated on Sunday, February 7, 1982.

The Lakeview Gospel Centre has blessed the community of Bonnyville, and may it continue to do so until Jesus comes.

Among those, who attended Bible College and/or entered the ministry (*), are Cyndy Gavronsky (now Mrs. Nadon), *Stephen Gavronsky, Earl Matichuk, John W. Petry.

BURDETT
BURDETT FULL GOSPEL CHURCh

The Burdett church started in 1939 with a group meeting for prayer and Bible study in the homes of N. F. Edlund, August Johnson and Henry Lane. A Brother Moss dropped into the Lane home one evening and stayed to conduct services over the winter months. The fall of 1940, the following young people left for Bible school in Saskatoon: Grace and George Johnson, Woodrow and Doris Edlund and Henry

Osterhouse, who had been staying at the Lane home. They returned in the spring and brought a number of students with them. They obtained jobs in the district and helped with the services that summer. These, who came, were Harold Barry, Bill Churchill, Ruth Engloff and Evelyn McCullum (nee Murdock).

In the summer of 1940, the old Morman church was purchased. A church was organized with the help of Ernest Hawtin and Albert Schindel, two graduates of Bethel Bible Institute in Saskatoon. Miss Edina Harding (now Sponholz) assisted in the musical area.

The first pastor after organizing, Stanley Gomph, arrived in 1941 and stayed with the Lanes. He received only small collections for his wages.

Pastor and Mrs. Bill Larson came in 1943. A house was rented for a parsonage. Pastor and Mrs. Ken Bunting served from 1944 to 1945. Evangelist Edward Gaetz, with the assistance of Sister Edina Harding, held a campaign and also a few services in neighboring Bow Island.

Brother John Martins pastored from 1947 to 1948. The school was then purchased and moved into town. The pews and piano were acquired from the Nemiskam Church, which was closed.

Although there was no pastor for a short while, there was revival and several made decisions for the Lord. Brother and Sister Bob Oldridge pastored from 1949 to 1950. At this time living quarters were added to the back of the church. Miss Edina Harding supplied for approximately two months in 1950. She was followed by Mr. and Mrs. Gordon Mast for four months, then there was no pastor for a while. Brother John Erhardt came occasionally for a time.

Brother and Sister Hubert Rosenke pastored from 1953 to 1960. Many improvements were made on the building during this time. New pews were built by Brother Rosenke and Brother Ron Lane, a member of the congregation. Brother and Sister Housworth pastored for approximately six months in 1960, Brother and Sister Pennington for about six months in 1961, Brother and Sister Osterhouse from 1961 to 1964, Brother and Sister Ian Lockie from 1964 to 1967. A further addition was made to the parsonage during this period. The next pastors were Brother and Sister Keith Evans (1961-64), Brother and Sister Jack Hood (1972-75), Brother and Sister David Shoop (1975-77) and Brother and Sister David McAlister (1977-80).

Others, who attended Bible college, are Brian Lane, Charlene Lane and Wesley Lane, who married Carol Kiffiak.

This assembly joined the Pentecostal Assemblies of Canada during the time Rev. S. R. Tilton was District Superintendent, which was from 1952 to 1968. The exact time is not known.

CALGARY
ABUNDANT LIFE CENTRE

The Abundant Life Centre began September 12, 1982. Reverend and Mrs. Jack Keys are pioneering this assembly. Ken Jasper is the assistant pastor.

The services are held in the Annie Foote Elementary School in the Temple District of north-east Calgary. The church office is located at Fifty-second Street and Marlborough Drive.

Reverend and Mrs. Keys pioneered the Idylwylde Assembly in Edmonton and also pioneered Lacombe, before going as missionaries to the West Indies, where they pioneered several churches. For quite a few years, Reverend and Mrs. Keys successfully pastored First Assembly, Calgary. Reverend Keys will be on Home Missions for the first year.

CALGARY
BEDDINGTON PENTECOSTAL CHURCH
(Formerly Capitol Hill Pentecostal Church)

In 1956 the Eighth Avenue Church, Calgary's only Pentecostal Assembly of Canada Church at the time, built the original Capitol Hill building to serve Calgary's North Hill. Several families — including the Bob Conns, Garry Feils, Shirley Graham (now Mrs. Jim Kane), Fred Holdsworths, Henry Leinwebbers, Maurice Madges, Al Matsons, Ron Moores — accepted the financial and program responsibility of furthering this witness, formed the initial nucleus, and agreed to repay Eighth Avenue twenty-five thousand dollars for the church building. Soon Capitol Hill became an active church serving a growing Calgary.

Original Capitol Hill Pentecostal Church

Rev. James Hazlett served as pastor for the first year, followed by the Reverend Charles Yates, who served as pastor from 1957-1968. During that time the church realized consistent growth, not only from people moving into Calgary but through penetration of the community and an active bus ministry.

Dr. Harry Faught assumed the pastorate of Capitol Hill in 1968 and continues as senior pastor in the Beddington Church. In 1969 an addition was opened, doubling the size of the Capitol Hill Church building, providing much needed Christian education and office space. In 1973 some families left or took a leave of absence from Capitol Hill, to assist the District in the establishment of a church in Marlborough. Capitol Hill continued to grow with increased attendance, enlarged outreach, missions involvement and expanding budget, until in 1978, the decision to relocate was taken.

Chorale that was active in the early nineteen seventies. Back Row: Carmen Ryall, Bruce Huekstra, Dorothy Goodhew, Kay Tyerman, Maurice Glover, Glen Bradley. Middle Row: Raymond Gjesdal, Gertrude Ryall, Carol Bradley, Marie Gjesdal, Bunny Wilcox, Olga Glover, Wayne Meyer. Front Row: Pianist, Dr. H. Faught; Director, Betty Funk; Organist, Janette Olson.

Through the years Capitol Hill has become known as a centre of Bible preaching, with a strong program of music for adults as well as children, active Women's Ministries, Men's Fellowship and youth groupings. For years a bus ministry was maintained in the Forest Lawn area and a summer boys' and girls' camp held at Canmore, Alberta. Capitol Hill was the first Canadian Church to have a Missionettes program — at that time the American program. This group was directed by Shirley Kane.

Capitol Hill always supported and made a large contribution to the District ministry. Mr. Bill Fraser was one of the original founders of Sunnyside Camp and served as Camp Manager for at least ten years. Mr. and Mrs. Fraser recently celebrated their sixty-fifth Wedding Anniversary. Les Inkster served as Men's Fellowship Director and Director of the Banff Men's Retreat for a dozen years. Maurice Glover has been serving as District Men's Fellowship Director for the last six years. Reverend Charles Yates left the pastorate of Capitol Hill to assume the Superintendency of the Alberta District.

Beddington Pentecostal Church opened in March 1981.

Beddington Pentecostal Church, with sanctuary and Christian Education facilities for one thousand people, opened in March 1981. Formerly known as Capitol Hill, the congregation relocated to the extreme north centre of Calgary, for greater opportunity of expansion and outreach. Several of the Capitol Hill original group continue to share in the ministry of the present Beddington Church. Ron Moore was chairman of the Beddington Church Building Committee.

Pastor Faught serves on the District Executive, on the Executive of the Sub-Arctic Mission and teaches at Northwest Bible College. The church looks forward to a fruitful ministry in the new Beddington area.

Among those, who attended Bible College and/or entered the ministry (*), are *Richie Haward, Cheryl Harding, Colleen Kifiak, Darlene Kifiak, Doug Craddock, Kerry Ek, Doug Madge, *William (Bill) Olson, Betty Olson, Jacqueline Skelton (now Mrs. Vern Seib).

CALGARY
CALGARY CHRISTIAN CENTRE
(formerly Montgomery Pentecostal Tabernacle)

Harry Nettleton, a Western Pentecostal Bible College graduate, and his wife, Beth, rented a small house in the Montgomery district. There in the early spring of 1952, weekly Bible clubs and Sunday school grew to a group of forty. With the prayerful guidance of Pastor John Watts and the Eighth Avenue congregation, the Nettletons purchased the old school — four old army buildings joined together. The Montgomery Assembly held their opening service February 15, 1953. Jim Henderson was one of the first board members and May the first secretary-treasurer. One of the first Sunday school superintendents was Sister Lorna Dittman. The Women's Mission Council was formed in October 1953, with May Henderson as president.

By September 1955, the church was self-supporting. Then Pastor and Mrs. Nettleton left to pioneer the work in Peace River. Reverend and Mrs. Ross Pennoyer with Ron and Wayne arrived to pastor in October 1955. The Christ's Ambassadors grew greatly. Len Egley and Glen Williams were two of the first presidents. Jack Kuhn was their first member to attend Bible college. June 1964 the Pennoyers left for Red Deer.

In 1964 the assembly received the title for their land from the Eighth Avenue church for the amount of two thousand five hundred dollars. Eighth Avenue church paid the four thousand dollars remaining.

In August 1964 Pastor and Mrs. Lyle Preston arrived with Garry and Brian. They ministered until June 1966. That same month Rev. and Mrs. Ken Bunting arrived. Rev. Bunting and the board realized the need for a new building. With much volunteer labor, the church was ready. This lovely new church was dedicated March 30, 1969. Pastor Bunting conducted the first baptismal service.

From Peace River on November 28, 1971, Pastor and Mrs. Dave Lagore with Robert, Debbie and Kenny arrived. Rev. and Mrs. Lew Larson assisted them for some time. The Montgomery assembly outgrew their church so relocated at 5300 53 Avenue N.W., Calgary. This was renamed Calgary Christian Center. This is a thriving assembly. Their staff includes Gordie and Kathleen Lagore; Pastor George and Gwen Lagore, who heads their Foothills Academy and Acts Leadership Training School; Pastor Ron and Cheryl Goodhew; John and Norma Broughton; Doug Smith; Harley Torgerson.

Among those, who have been part of this church family, were/are Grandpa and Grandma Lee, Doug and Verna Marsten and family, the Howats, Petermans, the Norrises, the McIntoshes, the Browns, the Heerschops, the Stan Troddens, the Andersons, the John Kuhns, the Giesbrechts, Brandsgards, the Besseys, the Fons, the Larry Troddens, the Tony Kuhns, the Batleys, the Dittmans, the Gordon Terrys, the Irvines, Terril Sterling, the Golds, the Gibneys, Ernie Mueller, the Jack Elliots, the Osmonds, the Scotts, Lorne and Bev Terry, Wesley Bilowus, the Tsirouplases, the Gauvreaus, Evelyn and Sandra

Elless, the W. Elliotts, the Josephsons, the R. Troddens, the A. Rasmussens, the Mitchells, the Hughes, and ladies, Evans, Kinsel and Switzer.

CALGARY
CHINESE PENTECOSTAL CHURCH

In 1959 a store front was rented in Chinatown to reach the Chinese people of the city. Reverend John Kong had only two families at the beginning the Seto family and another family who have since passed away. They held services in this store front for about one year, then they moved into a bigger store front. Here they conducted their services for about one year and a half. The fire department declared the building unsafe, so a building program was started in the spring of 1963. That year they moved into their new church at 127 Second Avenue, South East, Calgary.

Later the church was enlarged and another building added to it.

By Christmas 1980 they had built a second new sanctuary right next to the existing building which is now used for Christian Education and youth activities.

Reverend John Kong is a very busy pastor. He is a Commissioner of Oaths and works with the Immigration and Government Affairs to assist new Chinese to settle in Canada. Many of these refugees were/are Chinese from Viet Nam.

In 1982 his church had an attendance in the neighborhood of three hundred. With their outreach to others, this Chinese church is an inspiration to other Chinese christians in Canada.

In 1969 the Pentecostal Dominion Outreach reported, "Progress is the note sounded in a report from the Chinese Pentecostal Church in Calgary. 1968 was a year of victory. The church continues to give and to send out tracts to all the Chinese in Canada, endeavoring to lead them to Christ.

God had given this congregation many professional people in recent years. There are medical doctors, a druggist, nurses and a number of engineers. Above all, all these people are christians, who take time for God."

CALGARY
FIRST ASSEMBLY
(Pentecostal Tabernacle of Calgary but now referred to as First Assembly)

This First Assembly had a very unique beginning. Calgary was the place of the first known outpouring of the Holy Spirit in Alberta, which took place in 1908. Among those, who received the Baptism of the Holy Spirit, were Mr. and Mrs. Kelly, who were "Jesus only" people. They were the parents of

Early Days. Left to Right: Lady, Rev. R. E. McAlister, Rev. Walter McAlister, Mrs. Harvey (Ethel) McAlister, little Eileen McAlister, Rev. Harvey (Uncle Harvey) McAlister, Lady.

Lillian, Alice, Norman and Grace. Mr. and Mrs. Ramsbottom may have been among this group who received or joined a little later. It is not known how many received the Baptism of the Holy Spirit in 1908. About 1912 Mrs. Winnie Hughes and Mrs. Knight began attending.

Early assemblies or groups were not part of any larger organized groups in the beginning. They fellowshipped with other groups as they too received this same Baptism of the Holy Spirit. This Calgary group was no different.

Around 1917 or 1918 Doctor Lillian Yeoman and Nurse Amy Yeoman had services in their home. They too were Spirit-filled. Doctor Yeoman, always precisely on time, would enter the service room and begin playing the piano and praising the Lord. About this time Mrs. Harry Annis and children (Maud later Hill, Harry, Dorothy and James) attended when they could. Later after moving into Calgary from the farm, they attended regularly. Others, who attended then, included Mr. and Mrs. Reid, Mr. and Mrs. Tuff, Doris Inskster, Ruth Chamberlain.

When the Yeomans left, Reverend Harvey McAlister, called "Uncle Harvey" by many, came to pastor. He was brother to John and R. E. McAlister. (There was his nephew, Reverend Harvey McAlister, who also became a preacher in Alberta.) Services were held in various homes (Chamberlains, Spencers, Trevettes and others). In 1919 Mrs. Bruehlman with Wilma, Marguerita, Nelly, and Mr. and Mrs. Orr and son began attending services.

Later services were held in halls — hall in the Armor Block, Kickman Hall (next to Hunt's

Olivet Sunday School Picnic

Boneyard and across from the Lighthouse Mission) — until the old Olivett Baptist Church on Fourteenth Avenue and Ninth Street South-West (referred to as the Fourteenth Avenue Church) was purchased.

Those ministers, who followed Reverend Harvey McAlister, were Reverend Merrin, Reverend Percy Wills, Pastor Gordon, Pastor Pilky, Reverend Billy Steinberg (Fourteenth Avenue Church), Reverend George Schneider (-1926).

Among those, who attended the Fourteenth Avenue Church, were Mrs. Ida Elizabeth Fraser and her son, Bill Fraser. Bill Fraser came in 1923 when Reverend Steinberg was pastor. Bill Fraser was to be very active in the church on Eighth Avenue. Then he and his wife joined Capitol Hill Church which later became the Beddington Pentecostal Church. In 1982, he and his wife were both eighty-nine years old. In 1923 Miss Mabel Watson was saved at a Doctor Charles Price meeting in Calgary.

Hear **Evangelist A. H. Argue**
OF WINNIPEG, AT THE
Calgary Pentecostal Tabernacle
928 EIGHTH AVENUE WEST
OLD-FASHIONED GOSPEL MEETING STARTS APRIL 30
MISS ZELMA ARGUE, a gifted Trombonist and Song Leader will assist her father throughout the campaign

A Business Man with a Message for Business Men

SUBJECTS FOR THE FIRST WEEK:
SUNDAY—"The Age Terminus, is it in sight?"
MONDAY—"And When shall these things be?"
TUESDAY—"Jerusalem and the Jews"
WEDNESDAY—"The World's Greatest Message"
THURSDAY—"Divine Healing Service"
FRIDAY—"The Sky Shout"

Miss Zelma Argue
SUNDAY SERVICES:
10.30 a.m. - 7.30 p.m.

Rev. A. H. Argue
WEEK NIGHTS:
8.00 p.m.

1933 Evangelistic Meetings with A. H. Argue and his daughter, Zelma Argue.

Early in 1927, Reverend John McAlister and Walter McAlister held some evangelistic meetings. The meetings were well attended. About April 1927 this fine assembly was organized with the Pentecostal Assemblies of Canada. The meeting place was called a mission. They were reported to have had a splendid orchestra. For about a year they met in an upstairs hall in the Miriam Block, the corner of Eighth Avenue and Third Street South-West and across from where the Eaton's Store was built.

Among the early mission families were Jack Anderson; Mr. and Mrs. Harry Annis with Maud (now Hill), Harry, Dorothy, James; Mrs. Bell; Mrs. Helen Black; Mrs. Carpenter; Mr. and Mrs. T. Allan Christensen; Mr. and Mrs. Coulter with Maisie (wife of Reverend A. A. Lewis), Vera, Hazel (wife of Reverend E. Opheim), Mervin; Mr. Debnam with Bob and Winnie (and later Mrs. Debnam); Mrs. Falls with Eleanore, Lorna, Vivian, George and Jack; Mrs. Fraser and Bill; Mr. and Mrs. French and Lindsay (They grew flowers to always have flowers in the church); Mrs. Gaetz with Selma, Emma; Minnie and Gladys Green; Mrs. Mary Hill with Leonard; Doris and George Inkster with Norman, Leslie and Opal; Mr. and Mrs. Robert Mains; Fred Nichol; Mrs. Pearson with Bengta; Millie Peters; Mr. and Mrs. Gerald Smith; Mrs. Ada Smythe; Miss Merla Wells; Mr. and Mrs. Jack Williams with Gwen and Bert; Mr. and Mrs. John Williams. (Lipperts came later).

Then they moved nearby to a larger basement hall at 407A Eighth Avenue, South West, in the same block across from Eaton's Store.

In the spring of 1929, under Reverend Hugh McAlister's ministry, the Pentecostal Tabernacle of Calgary was built at a cost of twelve thousand dollars. The address was 928 - Eighth Avenue, South West. It was dedicated on May 26, 1929. Reverend Harvey McAlister was the guest speaker; Bill Dutton was the guest pianist; the Lethbridge orchestra joined the Tabernacle orchestra for the day under the leadership of Stanley Newby, the Tabernacle orchestra leader.

Top Row: Rev. J. M. Watts. Third Row: Mrs. J. M. Watts, Johnnie Watts, George Watts. Second Row: Mrs. P. S. Jones, Dorothy Anne Watts. First Row: Rev. P. S. Jones.

Those, who were added to the families at the Eighth Avenue Church, the Pentecostal Tabernacle of Calgary, were Howard Gay; Rose and Howard Grant;

Mr. and Mrs. Gray with Alfred, Joy, Allen; Mr. and Mrs. John Huckle; Mr. and Mrs. Robert Hurst with Margaret; Mr. and Mrs. Jean Hurst with Hazel and Shirley; Mr. and Mrs. Frank McLachlan; Mr. and Mrs. Roland Moore, Art and Roland (twins) and Gwen; Stanley Newby; Mrs. Peel with Robert (Bob) and John; Fern and Jake Shantz with Wilda, Dorothy (Wilda and Dorothy sang duets), Orville and Hugh; Mr. and Mrs. George Hislop (Georgian nee Leibrock, was an excellent violin soloist); Mr. and Mrs. H. F. Toothe with Leora, Eileen, H. F. (Bud) who became a gifted pianist; and others.

In 1940, the Tabernacle was over-crowded, so an extension was built on the back to increase seating by one hundred sixty. The extension plans were designed by J. J. McLeod of Edmonton. The extension was dedicated Easter Sunday, March 23, 1940, when Reverend G. R. Upton was pastor at the time. That day John Peel gave an interesting, evangelistic address in the open session Sunday School.

Under the ministry of Reverend Kenneth Bombay, a new church was built and dedicated in November 1968. The name of the church was not officially changed but the new church is referred to as First Assembly, or First Pentecostal Assembly. The congregation out-grew this building as well — nine hundred to a thousand people — so for years they held two Sunday morning services. Property was bought in Strathcona Heights with a plan to build when able. The Sunday evening services became over-crowded too, so in September 1979, a second Sunday evening service was held in a rented place in an area close to the property purchased. The pastors, Reverend Keys and Reverend Bombay, took turns speaking in this second service. This Strathcona evening service was discontinued in May 1981, due partly to understaffing.

Under the Pentecostal Assemblies of Canada the First Assembly pastors have been Reverend H. J. McAlister; Reverend and Mrs. Clare Scratch, who was Alberta District Superintendent for some months before they resigned to become missionaries to China; Reverend Leonard Palmer; Reverend and Mrs. G. R. Upton, who began the radio broadcast, Glad Tidings Gospel Hour; Reverend Flemming May; Reverend and Mrs. J. M. Watts, who were great promotors of Sunday School and Youth activities; Reverend and Mrs. R. E. Davis; Reverend Kenneth Bombay, a dynamic speaker, who loves the moving of the Holy Spirit; Reverend J. A. Keys and co-worker Reverend Ken Bombay, who loved to keep a church growing in God and in numbers; Reverend and Mrs. Alvan Lewis, who have already won the respect of First Assembly, and Reverend and Mrs.

Les Markham, returned missionaries from Thailand, are assisting.

There are a number of beginnings in First Assembly. The Sunday School and Christ's Ambassadors (Young People's) meetings and Women's Groups all began when Reverend and Mrs. Hugh McAlister were pastoring. In 1940, the library originated in the Young Men's Sunday School Class with Bob Peel and Hugh McCullock in charge. The Women's Missionary Council originated in the Young Ladies' Sunday School Class with Mrs. H. L. Toothe as the teacher. In 1941, the Ladies' Quilting Circle was organized. There were and still are many busy workers at First Assembly.

Outreach of the Pentecostal Tabernacle of Calgary

In the early thirties, there was an outreach into West Calgary. Sunday School and/or services were held in Springbank area, Bowness, Silver Springs, Wellington Hall. Among those, who were in charge of these services were Allen and Eva Christensen, Mr. and Mrs. E. A. (Ted) Tobin, Jerry and Mary Wilson. (Mary Wilson's maiden name was Jobson). Allen Christensen and Andy Dalby commuted for weekend services in Bentley.

In 1938 the Lighthouse Mission on the east end of

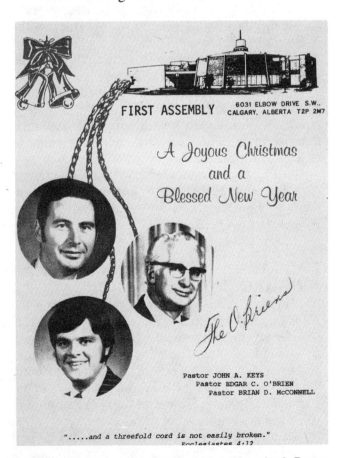

FIRST ASSEMBLY
6031 ELBOW DRIVE S.W.,
CALGARY, ALBERTA T2P 2M7

A Joyous Christmas and a Blessed New Year

The O'Briens

Pastor JOHN A. KEYS
Pastor EDGAR C. O'BRIEN
Pastor BRIAN D. McCONNELL

".....and a threefold cord is not easily broken."
Ecclesiastes 4:12

Christmas Greetings from Pastor John A. Keys (top), Pastor Edgar O'Brien (right) and Pastor Brian D. McConnell.

Eighth Avenue was opened. This served folks in a very poor central area. Miss Audrey Hutchinson (now Mrs. Allen Taylor) remembers that as a teenager, she had appreciated the opportunity to help to minister there. This was open for forty years, then the building was sold.

For many years, the Glad Tidings Gospel Hour over CFRN has been a blessing. Sylvia Jorgenson and Gladys Tuff sang on the first broadcast. The Tabernacle telecast, Pentecost Presents, has been aired since 1969. It too has proved a blessing. It was and still is an avenue of service for singers and musicians.

The Tabernacle has also mothered other congregations. In 1955 the Pentecostal Tabernacle of Calgary's forward-looking board, E. P. Holmes, R. M. Campbell, E. F. Grant, J. S. Garden, G. K. Hislop and W. L. Fraser, together with Pastors J. M. Watts, P. S. Jones and H. W. Nettleton made plans to build and then had the new branch church (Capitol Hill Pentecostal Tabernacle) built. The sanctuary held about four hundred people. When appealing for funds, Mr. W. L. Fraser, who was speaking for the board, said, "I hope to live to see eight branch churches dotting the residential areas in this city."

The Tabernacle assisted in the establishment of the Ogden Pentecostal Assembly, the Calgary Chinese Church and the Fellowship Bible Chapel in Airdrie.

The Tabernacle gave its blessing to about twenty couples forming the nucleus of the Neighbourhood Church and to work with Reverend and Mrs. Gerald Johnson.

When the Tabernacle, now referred to as First Assembly, grew so much that they had two Sunday morning services for years, twenty-two acres of property was bought for a future Strathcona Heights Assembly. Because of the over-crowding at First Assembly, the board looked for a meeting place for a second Sunday evening service out towards the Strathcona Heights property so that part of the congregation could worship and set the ground work for the new Strathcona Heights Assembly when it's built. This second evening service was held in Mount Royal Ford Theatre Auditorium with some two hundred in attendance for a few months, then to St. Matthews United Church. These services were staffed by Pastor Keys and Pastor Bombay at alternate times as well as Assistant Pastor Ron Michalski on occasion. Blaine Eagle, music director, had a choir and King's Kids (children's choir). They had a nursery. Junior Worship service was also held. Wednesday evenings were set aside for Leadership Training Course and New Life Adult Bible Study. Strathcona had its own Women's Ministries, too. For some time

Calgary has also supported native works in Kenya and Liberia. From the Bible School student list you will notice its contribution to the ministry, including foreign missions. What a vision First Assembly has.

The new senior pastor is Reverend Alvan Lewis (1982-   ), with his co-pastor Reverend Les Markham (1982-   ).

Among those, who attended Bible College and/or entered the ministry(*), are **Irene Ashley, *Billy Bennet, **Irene Boris (Registered Nurse), Doug Burns, *Sandra Charette, Margaret Christensen, *Mr. and Mrs. T. Allen Christensen, *Shirley Cook (wife of Reverend Norman Pohl), Victor Cooper, Leigh Coppin, *Joyce Coppin, *Maisie Coulter (wife of Reverend A. A. Lewis), *Vera Coulter, *Hazel Coulter (wife of Reverend E. Opheim), Diana Cutforth, *Mr. and *Mrs. Andy Dalby, *Bill Dogterom, Jan Dogterom, Gordon Duncan, Wayne Dyck, Jack Falls, **Elsie Feary (later Blatner), **Thomas W. Fodor, **Rae Garden, *Bill Garden, Rose Gardener, Larry Gauvreau, Brian Gilliland, Rudy Heideberg, **Doctor and **Mrs. Pat Higgins, John Holmes, *Peter Hudel, Audrey Hutchinson (now Mrs. Allen Taylor), *Roberta Irvine, *Ken Jasper, *Calvin Keys, *Dan Keys, Karen Keys, *Pamela Keys (wife of Dan Keys), Kathy Keys, *Shirley Knight (Registered Nurse, and wife of Reverend Rueben Drisner), John Kowalchuk, Laurie Kowalchuk, Mavis MacKenzie, *Louann (Jo) McArthur **Irene Megyesi (wife of Reverend Lyle Horrill), Vandale Megyesi, *Jenny Nash (wife of Reverend Anthony Nash), Mavis Norstrom, *Dorothy Plastow (now Mrs. Roy Sorenson), **Robert (Bob) Peel, **Avis Poppelwell (later Mrs. Mitchell), *Madeline Rhodes (Registered Nurse, now Mrs. Bill Widmer), Don Robertson, Terri Robertson, Rainer Rohr, Marilyn Schultz, Rudolf Schmidt, Harvey Snider, Jim Steinke, John Sweeney, *Ivy Stickel, Don Taylor, Rob Taylor, *Ian Tegart, *Mrs. Margaret Ann Tegart (nee Rhodes), *Ross Tegart, **Mr. and Mrs. P. Thunberg, Stan Trodden, Karen Turner, Larry Warkentin, Melody Wayne, Harold Wells, Lila Wells, Paul Willms, Beatrice Young (Registered Nurse). Missionaries who were/are on fields outside of Canada are double starred (**).

CALGARY
MARLBOROUGH PENTECOSTAL
CHURCH

Services for the new Marlborough Pentecostal Church in north-east Calgary commenced September 9, 1973 in the Bob Edwards High School. Former missionaries and evangelists, Reverend and Mrs. Eugene Johnson, were appointed by the Alberta District to pastor this work. Two years prior to this, the Alberta District had proposed a church in this district and four double lots had been purchased. Six existing churches in Calgary co-operated in promoting this assembly and encouraged families to help establish the work. Some of the founding families were Reverend and Mrs. M. Olson, Mr. and Mrs. Todd Brown, Miss Grace Edler, Miss Mary Edler, Mr. and Mrs. David Knight, Mr. and Mrs. Manuel Olson, Mr. and Mrs. Talmage Rancier, Mrs. Esther Stickle, Mrs. Larry Zaychkowsky.

A building program was begun in October 1973. The assembly moved into their new church on June 9, 1974 when a parade of Sunday School teachers, students and boy scouts of the Marlborough community joined in the march from the school to the new church building — this was the first church building in the Marlborough district. It was dedicated on September 15, 1974.

In August 1975 Pastor and Mrs. Gerald Jeske came to minister in Marlborough.

In the spring of 1976 the first Sunday School bus was purchased.

The second phase building program began in October 1977 and was in use by February 1978.

The Sunday School and morning service attendance has shown a steady increase over the years.

At the showing of two films, "A Thief in the Night" and "A Distant Thunder," for a period of three evenings over a weekend, sixty souls found the Lord Jesus as their personal Saviour.

Gerry Leipert and his wife assisted the Jeskes from July 1978 to June 1979.

Pastor Eli Chiarelli and his wife, Elsa, and their three children, Corinne, Gary and Gina, came to pastor in October 1979.

Among those, who attended Bible College, are *Ivy Stickel (Valedictorian, Northwest Bible College), Virginia Knight (Olson), Randy Galusha, Pam Knight, Bruce Ganske.

CALGARY
NEIGHBOURHOOD CHURCH

Reverend Gerry Johnson began pioneering the Neighbourhood Church in September 1978. Services and family night are held at Nickle Junior High School in Lake Bonavista. The pastoral and administrative offices are in a new building in Midnapore.

Sunday February 14, 1982 was farewell day for Pastor Wes Komant. He had served with Pastor Johnson since the beginning of the assembly.

Pastor Johnson received Home Missions support for the first year, then the assembly was self-sustaining financially. Between one hundred and fifty and two hundred people attended Neighbourhood Church.

Eighteen acres of property have been purchased. Two attempts have been made to proceed with the building program but the door has been closed each time. The church design, twenty-two thousand six hundred square feet, will seat approximately eight hundred.

Pastor Johnson resigned in the spring of 1982 and has accepted a pastorate in Ontario.

Reverend and Mrs. Ed Pahl from Maple Ridge, B.C., have accepted this pastorate.

CALGARY
NEW LIFE COMMUNITY CHURCH
(Formerly Ogden Pentecostal Assembly)

This assembly started with a Sunday School in the Ogden Legion Hall on November 30, 1958 by Reverend and Mrs. George Corris. Reverend and Mrs. R. Drisner were asked to take charge of the Sunday School when Pastor Corris resigned and moved to Cold Lake.

The Sunday School knew consistent growth in spite of the fact that the Legion Hall wasn't an ideal setting for spiritual ministries. In spite of the lack of the traditional setting for spiritual ministry, God blessed. Soon a short morning worship service was added for the Sunday School staff and some of the parents, who attended the adult Bible class conducted in an apartment across the street from the hall.

It soon became obvious that the community needed and was responding to this ministry. Something had to be done to acquire more suitable facilities. But how? There was no supporting church membership. Those who helped in the Sunday School were members of other churches in the city. The District wasn't able to give much assistance. It would have to be entirely a venture of faith.

In the spring of 1963 Pastor Drisner acquired a partially built house at the end of Twenty-second Street near Seventy-eight Avenue. Across the avenue was an open and unsightly gravel pit. Between the house and Seventy-eighth Avenue there were five twenty-foot lots. This area didn't appear to be a very good location for a church. But God impressed upon Pastor Drisner that this should be the site. Inquiries were made. They discovered that three of the lots were owned by the city, one by the Canadian Pacific Railway and one by a former Alderwoman who had bought the lot so she could run for the office of city counsellor. They learned that they would have to consolidate the entire five lots before they would be allowed to build. The city was prepared to sell their three lots for two hundred and fifty dollars each. The Canadian Pacific Railway wasn't particularly interested in selling their lot. After much prayer and correspondence, by the fall of 1964 the five lots had been purchased for just over eleven hundred dollars. The District gave a grant of one thousand dollars to help pay for the property.

Now a building was needed to accommodate the Sunday School and allow for future growth. This would cost approximately fifty thousand dollars. A loan of five thousand dollars was received from the Pentecostal Assemblies of Canada Pension Fund. The assembly decided to build the church themselves with volunteer help from the churches in Calgary. They would build as funds allowed. The building was to be a simple structure of concrete blocks, laminated beams with wood decking, twenty-four hundred square feet. After the building plans were approved the sod-turning took place in May of 1965. Much of the material was purchsed at half price. It was estimated it would take two thousand hours of volunteer labour to complete the superstructure and basement auditorium and classrooms. By the end of 1965 the superstructure was completed. In the spring of 1966 work began on the lower auditorium and the landscaping. The work was completed by fall and it was a great day when the Sunday School moved into their own building.

Ogden Pentecostal Assembly with Rev. R. Drisner's home right next door.

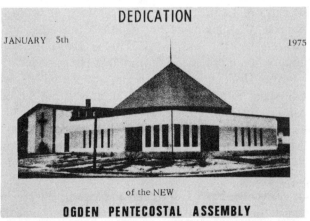

Dedication of the new Ogden Pentecostal Assembly, January 5, 1975.

It was now possible to enlarge the church program. Evening services were started. By 1967 they had outgrown the lower auditorium facilities and were forced to complete the upstairs. This took another year of volunteer labour and it was completely finished for dedication on November 6, 1969. This was eleven long years of perseverance from the time the first Sunday School was held in the Legion Hall.

Pastor Drisner was told by some it couldn't be done. The building now stands in Calgary attesting to the fact that with God all things are possible. The entire project cost fifteen thousand dollars.

When the Drisners resigned, Reverend and Mrs. Steve Holomis came as the first full-time pastors. Pastor Drisner worked as a carpenter and his wife, Shirley, as a nurse at the General Hospital, while pastoring and building the Ogden church.

January 5, 1975 was a long awaited day for the Pastor and congregation of the Ogden Pentecostal Assembly in Calgary. It was dedication day of the second new sanctuary. The dedication service was led by Pastor Steve Holomis. Reverend Robert Taitinger, General Superintendent, was the guest speaker and Reverend Ivar Roset, District Superintendent, led the Act of Dedication. Good wishes were brought from the city by Alderman Harry Huish. Guest soloist was Les Halliwell.

The new church has a seating capacity of three hundred and fifty and is fan-shaped giving the congregation a sense of being close to the platform. It was decorated with blue carpeting, royal blue velvet drapes for the background to the platform area, dark walnut pews and pulpit, roof of natural cedar decking. The lower auditorium was carpeted throughout. The church was built totally by volunteer help with Pastor Holomis as general contractor. The assembly realized a fifty percent saving on the total cost of construction. The previous building became the Christian Education wing, giving a total of ten thousand square feet of floor area. Kitchen, offices and washroom facilities and nursery were also completed. A grand piano and Conn organ were purchased for the assembly. Pastor Holomis and congregation praise God for all that He provided.

Wee College was started and a bus ministry established. Two lots east of the church were purchased for a parking lot.

Pastor Holomis resigned in 1976, when he joined All World Crusade as Associate Director to Don Schellenberg, Director and Founder of All World Crusade.

Reverend Peter Cuke became pastor in July 1976 and at the time of printing is still the pastor. The name was changed from Ogden Pentecostal Assembly to New Life Community Church.

Some of the original families who helped were Allan and Audrey Taylor and family, the Galbraiths, Dave Cunningham, the Warnkeys, Dave and Ruth Neustaedter.

CALMAR
CALMAR CHRISTIAN ASSEMBLY

The Calmar Christian Assembly had its beginning when in July 1948 the Thorsby Pentecostal Church decided to help two young ladies start a work in Calmar. Miss Alice Shevkenek and Miss Katherine Thiessen, who had a proven ministry and had conducted a Daily Vacation School in Calmar with good success, undertook the challenge.

This church was opened as an independent church and later became affiliated with the Pentecostal Assemblies of Canada.

A group of believers gathered for two years in the

Miss K. Thiessen

old United Church until 1950, when the congregation felt they needed a church home of their own. The congregation was blessed with believers being added to the church.

Bible student, Grace Veale, assisted for two years as her studies permitted. After seven years of pastoring Calmar, the pioneer workers resigned.

Reverend and Mrs. G. Veale came to pastor in August 1955. They were pleased with the little church and the well kept grounds. Mrs. Ruff and family, and the Summers family were part of the Assembly. The church had a comfortable suite in the basement for the pastor's living quarters. They soon learned to put a good supply of water in the fridge which made it almost drinkable!

They had one family who were not members but attended at times. Their daughter was always in Sunday School and some years later she became their daughter-in-law. Her parents kept them supplied with eggs, chicken, vegetables and sometimes bread and pastries. The Veales resigned in 1958.

Miss Alice Shevkenek

The assembly was without a pastor at different times.

Pastor David Michie and his wife pastored from June 1967 to May 1971. There were about five attending when they came and through visitation and picking up children the number grew to forty.

Others who pastored were G. Harding, Mr. and Mrs. Dave Shoop, Mr. and Mrs. Del Duncalfe, Mr. Duval.

The Duncalfes report an average of thirty people on a Sunday morning. They have a group of twelve young people and four have come to know the Lord as personal Saviour.

Among those, who attended Bible College and/or entered the ministry (*), are *Paul Dyck, Max Fedina, Mark Gunsch, Judy Ruff, Paulette Ruff.

The Summers Family with Rev. and Mrs. R. G. Veale.

Congregation 1971

CAMROSE
CALVARY PENTECOSTAL
TABERNACLE

Early nineteen hundred and thirties Harvey and Clarence McAlister had home or school meetings north of Camrose. Around that time Brother and Sister Will McPherson opened services in a former Lutheran Church. They resigned to pastor Killam.

The first services were held at the Langbell home. Then the Cottage School was rented for evening services. In 1934, the people moved to the church at 5211-Fiftieth Avenue. It was rented from the Seventh-Day Adventists for about seven years. Rent was nine dollars a month. The building was bought for the rent paid plus one thousand dollars. The church was used until the end of March 1977. Some of the founding families were the Langbells, Champs, Alfred and Opal Madison, Conrad and Verna (nee Langbell) Johnson.

The Assembly moved to Our Lady of Mount Pleasant School until the end of June 1977. Then they moved to the Masonic Hall and then to Sifton School until October 1977.

The sod-turning for the new Calvary Pentecostal Tabernacle took place on Easter Sunday, 1977, the new location being 4820-Sixty-Fourth Street. Easter Sunday 1978, the church was dedicated. The business meeting to sell the former church was held October 18, 1976. On January 29, 1978 the assembly moved into their present sanctuary.

Some of the pastors were Will McPherson (1934), John Wood (1935); Victor Graham (1941); Ruth

Nystrom and Hazel Coulter (1936) (Ruth married Gunnar Gulbransen and Hazel married Eugene Opheim); Series of meetings with Gunnar Gulbransen and Marvin Forseth (1939); B. Leonard conducted campaign, many were saved and healed (1941); Severt Amundson (1940); Lee and Gladys Prest (1946); John and Ida Cooke (1948-1950); Lucy Hardy and Emma Hemke; Mel Delgetty; Ken Bunting; Freda Schindel and Mae Crowell; Mr. and Mrs. Norman F. Langford; Mr. and Mrs. Wendal Lewis; Reg Carbol; Lindy (Henry) and Doreen Lindberg; Eugene and Hazel Opheim (1950-1955); Reverend and Mrs. M. Olson (1955-1963); Reverend and Mrs. Steve Holomis (1963-1966); Ervine Fuhrman; Ed. Rebman; Pastor and Mrs. Ken Roset, who are the present pastors (1982).

In the fall of 1948 John and Ida Cooke were asked to pastor Camrose. There was no place for them to live and very little support. Mrs. Cooke was offered a position in the Verdun School, grades one to seven, in the Wetaskiwin School District. Each morning Brother Cooke drove Mrs. Cooke to school, and then in the afternoon he would go to the school to pick Mrs. Cooke up, a total of sixty-four miles a day. Some days it meant shovelling through snow drifts and arriving at the school to find that the school furnace had not been lit because it was too cold for the janitor to get there.

The assembly did not have a place for the Cookes to live, so in return for a two-roomed suite to live in, Mrs. Cooke looked after a rooming house of twelve rented rooms, cleaning the halls and bathrooms and washing all the bed linen. Many times the cleaning and washing had to be done after teaching all day. The biggest task was drying the sheets. In twenty and thirty degree below weather, the sheets were frozen stiff before the clothes-pins were fastened on the line.

Sunday mornings Mrs. Cooke took the car and gathered up children for Sunday School. The attendance tripled.

A very dear friend, Doctor Bierstein, made it possible for the Cookes to purchase a comfortable house through his Housing Development, which they moved into in 1949.

The principal of the Camrose High School, Charlie McCleary, asked Mrs. Cooke to teach a special Grade Five class in the Camrose High School. Mrs. Cooke had the privilege of reading the Word of God to these children every morning. Ronald Marken was one of the students. His writing was atrocious. Mrs. Cooke persuaded him that he could develop his hand-writing. He tried. His parents were astonished and proud. Ronald became a Professor of English in the University of Minnesota.

What a success story about a boy that really tried, by giving his best.

Mr. Alex Setterlund was over seventy years of age and unable to read. One day he prayed the Lord would teach him to read. The Lord directed him to John, chapter seventeen. He began to read with painful effort. As he read on, word by word, with great effort, he suddenly realized that he could read, a life-long dream had been fulfilled. The Holy Spirit not only taught Brother Setterlund to read but he found the Lord Jesus Christ as his personal Saviour.

In the fall of 1949, Reverend D. N. Buntain invited the Cookes to return to Northwest Bible College in Edmonton.

During the ministry of Reverend and Mrs. M. Olson, a basement was put under the sanctuary and many improvements were made.

During the ministry of Reverend and Mrs. Steve Holomis, Sunday School rooms were built in the basement and rugs laid. Daily Vacation Bible School was conducted each year. An organ was purchased for the church. Dial-A-Meditation was started; many were helped and encouraged spiritually. The morning service was broadcast over CFCW about every two to three months. During the week, each pastor in the City of Camrose was given broadcast time of one-half hour. This also took place about every two to three months as it had under Rev. Olson. For some time, Pastor Holomis also had an evening gospel sing every Sunday evening over CFCW. Pastor Holomis resigned to become the first full-time Christian Education Director for Alberta.

Among those who attended Bible College and/or entered the ministry(*) are Beryl Berg, Rusty Berg, Margaret Lahofer, Linda Gaye Larson, Glen McBride, *Grace (married to Reverend Len Schmautz), *Ann Setterlund (married to Reverend Howard Lund), *Ken Olson.

CHERRY POINT
CHERRY POINT GOSPEL MISSION

Cherry Point is a small community near the mighty Peace River. The church there was independent before 1955. In the period following Alex Stone held services. For some time there was no pastor. Ed Fredrickson, a local farmer and holder of Certificate of Recognition with the Pentecostal Assemblies of Canada, pastored this small assembly for many years and resigned as pastor in March 1982. Mr. and Mrs. Fredrickson gave years of faithful service. The Labrentz Group held tent meetings at Cherry Point in the summers of 1974, 1975, 1976, 1977 and some other summers. Beside adult services, there were children's services.

At the time of publishing, the supply minister is

Jim Gamble, who drives out from Dawson Creek to minister on Sundays and whenever he is needed.

This assembly is one that was part of the British Columbia District for a time because of its remoteness in our province. Dawson Creek has been an encouragement to them and the fellowship was appreciated.

CLARESHOLM
CLARESHOLM PENTECOSTAL ASSEMBLY

In the early part of 1925, prayer meetings were held in the home of Mrs. May Thomas, who led the services assisted by Mrs. Elizabeth Curtis. In May 1925, a baptismal service was held when five people were immersed by Rev. R. Reynolds. The formation of the church was in July 1925 and it was known as the Claresholm Tabernacle. In August of that year he conducted another baptismal service when eleven people were baptized. Rev. and Mrs. Rufus Reynolds became the first pastors. Services were held in the I.O.O.F. hall until September 1925, when the congregation bought the Beaver Lumber Hall on Railway Street. There were living quarters for the pastor upstairs. This building was dedicated December 6, 1925. On April 17, 1930, the church was registered as the Claresholm Tabernacle.

Mrs. Thomas in front of the mission.

Several ministers filled the pulpit in the early years among whom were R. C. Moreash, Gus Batkie and Klyber, Rev. and Mrs. Swanton, Rev. Atkinson, Rev. and Mrs. Cecil Cobb and Mrs. May Thomas, resident, who filled in between pastors.

In March 1935, Rev. H. F. Hargrave held three weeks of meetings. Many were saved and thirteen people were baptized in water.

The next pastors were Rev. and Mrs. Andrew Dalby (1936-1940), Sivert Amundson (1940-1942) and Victor Graham (1942-1943). In 1943 Rev. and Mrs. Arden Lewis came to minister. During their ministry in 1946, the church building was moved from Railway Street to 47th Avenue. A house was purchased in Champion and moved in beside the church. This became the manse. In 1946 Rev. and Mrs. Eugene Opheim came to pastor. A funeral chapel and residence on Second Street and 48th Avenue was bought in 1949. The former church and manse were sold.

On January 9, 1950, the name of the church was changed to Faith Temple. Later in 1950, Rev. and Mrs. John Peel began their ministry. The interior of the church was then remodelled, including a bigger platform. Rev. and Mrs. R. J. White came to minister in 1953. At this time the building of a Sunday School hall was commenced to accommodate the growing departments of the church. This was completed during the ministry of Rev. and Mrs. Harvey C. McAlister, who came in the late fall of 1956. In 1960, Rev. and Mrs. Elisha Asselstine accepted the pastorate and ministered until 1964 when Rev. and Mrs. Lyle Horril came to fill the pulpit. They remained until 1968 when they were accepted as missionaries to Uganda.

Rev. and Mrs. Cobb

On May 15, 1968, the name of the church was changed to Claresholm Pentecostal Assembly. They again felt the need of a larger church facility so a decision was made to build. In 1969, during the ministry of Rev. and Mrs. Angus McClain, the old church was demolished and the Pentecostal Church from Coaldale was purchased. On the old church site, a full-sized basement was poured. However, after a heavy rainfall, the mud pushed in the south cement wall so it had to be redone. Eventually the church was moved on to a full sized basement. The first service in this building was held in December 1969.

From 1970 to 1972, Rev. and Mrs. Bill Lewis ministered to the Assembly followed by Rev. and Mrs. Kenneth Bunting from 1972 to 1979. There was a mighty move of the Holy Spirit in February and March of 1974 which affected and stirred the whole community. During this revival, Evangelist Robin Thomas conducted two weeks of special meetings. Many souls were saved, filled with the Holy Spirit and were baptized in water. A number of young people felt the call of God upon their lives and attended Bible school. Several are now in full time ministry.

In 1977, extensive renovations were done inside the church including new upholstered pews. The seating capacity was increased by two-thirds. A remodelling Dedication Service was held in November of that year with Rev. Angus McClain as guest speaker. Rev. Richard Cooper was called to pastor the church in 1979.

Pastor Opheim and Congregation in front of the Pentecostal Tabernacle.

The departments of the church have been very active over the years. The Women's Ministries were organized while Rev. and Mrs. Arden Lewis were pastors. Mrs. Cook, the Provincial Director, came to assist in their first meeting. During the time of Rev. and Mrs. Peel, a young women's club, The Gleaners,

was instituted and continued for about twelve years. Under the direction of Mr. Earl Sargeant, a Boy's Club was also started at this time and is still a very vital part of the church. The girl's club, now known as Missionettes, has had many years of outreach to the young girls of the community. Men's Fellowship has functioned from time to time. The young people have regular weekly meetings. Beside the regular prayer meeting of the week, there is a Tuesday morning Ladies' Prayer and Bible Study.

Claresholm church finished in 1972.

Among the founding families in 1925 were Harry Thomases, J. M. Soby, Ed Schrams, Eric Harveys, Tom Bensons, J. Hillerudes, Morrows, Mrs. Foss, Mr. Heyland. Other families, coming in later, were Trotters, Allards, W. Sinclairs, F. MacLochlands, Ruth Hinkles, John Findleys, Mrs. Messerli, Mrs. Ringrose, Mary Symonds, Harry Taitingers, whose son, Bob, became General Superintendent of The Pentecostal Assemblies of Canada.

Among those who attended Bible Collge and/or entered the ministry (*) are *George Ayres, Linda Benson, Gary Benson, *Stewart Coutts, *Laura Skoye now Dietrick, Debbie Floen, Karen Floen, Valerie Floen, *Cindy Garber now Layne, Kurt Garber, Laverne Hinkle now Pachal, Hans Inniger, Wayne Hillendorf, Allan Hillendorf, Twila Dawn Pachal now Wyton, John Prusak, Rory Ryan, *Dean Steel, *Ken Stange, Susan Stange, Joyce Schram, *Paul Slemming, *Bernadine Sergeant (Mrs. Larry Trodden), Deanna Sinclair, Cheryl Scholler (nee Van Dellum), Gene Scholler, *Robert Taitinger, *Mary Lou Taitinger (wife of Reverend Dale Carpenter), *Gary Taitinger, Valerie Wood.

COALHURST
PENTECOSTAL ASSEMBLY

Before 1917, Mr. Simonette, a layman from the Lethbridge Pentecostal Tabernacle, canvassed the Village of Coalhurst with little success until he came to the Johnson residence. There he found a desperate need in the home so he prayed for God to intervene. God answered his prayer. As as result Mother Johnson was the first to accept Christ as her Saviour. The Johnson Home became the meeting place for many cottage prayer meetings. A number were saved and filled with the Holy Spirit.

Later house meetings were held in the Fred Smith home. There was beautiful fellowship among the early Christian group. Among the early people, who attended these meetings, were Mrs. Johnson and Lillian, Mr. and Mrs. Fred Smith, Mr. and Mrs. John Holmes, Mr. and Mrs. William Borrows, Mr. and Mrs. Nesbit. These folk were all sympathetic to the Baptism of the Holy Spirit experience.

Coalhurst was a coal boom town. Salaries were good. Coal was cheap.

The Simonettes still came out from Lethbridge for services. Coalhurst had its share of mining accidents. One victim of a mine accident was Sam Kendrick, who was badly injured. His wife was also very ill. Mrs. Simonette came to the Kendrick home to talk to Mrs. Kendrick about the Lord. Both of the Kendricks came to the meeting in the Smith home. That February 14, 1918 meeting was to change their lives. That night when asked if he was saved (converted), Sam Kendrick said that he didn't know. He then proceeded to list the things he did — smoked, drank, played cards and more. After Brother Simonette explained the way of salvation, both Sam and his wife, Ethel Kendrick, accepted Christ as their personal Saviour. Later they both received marvelous answers to prayer, which were so encouraging to their group of believers.

The Assembly grew in number. The Lord prospered them so much so that they gave financial gifts to the Lethbridge church, which was rather small at that time. This Lethbridge church had shared their faith in Jesus Christ and their knowledge of the Baptism of the Holy Spirit. So it was that the folks in Coalhurst wanted to share too.

As more and more received the Baptism of the Holy Spirit, the more the group rejoiced. Not too long after their conversions, Sam and Ethel Kendrick received the Baptism of the Holy Spirit. The Kendricks home was added to the list of places, where services were held.

About 1920, the Assembly bought Ernie Pitt's one-room butcher shop. After cleaning the shop and papering the walls with plain blue paper, church furnishings were added — benches, some with backs; a pot-bellied stove or heater; a table for a pulpit. Coal was cheap so they were able to keep nice and warm. Later the benches were replaced by chairs for fifty cents each. Winnifred McAlister (nee Kendrick) remembers a grease spot on one wall. It was the spot where the sausage machine had been in the days of the butcher shop. The grease came through the wallpaper. This church held about fifty people. During Sunday school the classes were held in the corner areas of the church. Mrs. Johnson was one of the faithful Sunday school teachers.

When Mrs. McGuiness, who suffered from arthritis, was no longer able to come to service, the folks had prayer meetings in her home. Mrs. McGuiness also received the Baptism of the Holy Spirit.

Frances and John (who ran the mine engine) Holmes had a daughter, Dorothy, who later married Ole Austring. (Later they were the pastors at Brocket.)

About 1921 on Sunday afternoons, Mr. Kendrick drove to Lethbridge, brought the preacher (layman or minister) to his home in Coalhurst for supper, then to evening service. After the service, he took the preacher back to Lethbridge. The roads were not very good — dusty, narrow and, if it rained, very muddy and slippery. Among those, who came to preach, were Lethbridge Pastor John McAlister, Sam Fredrickson, Bill Manley and others. Among those, who were saved around this time, was a Reverend Evans. He, too, received the Baptism of the Holy Spirit.

About 1930, the Assembly outgrew the butcher shop building so they used a local vacant United Church. Brother R. Martin McCallum pastored here.

In 1932 Winnifred Kendrick moved to Edmonton for Nurses' Training. Her parents, Sam and Ethel, moved to Edmonton in 1933.

The Coalhurst Assembly was under a unique arrangement with the Lethbridge Pentecostal Tabernacle. Coalhurst had its own pastor but the pastor of the Lethbridge Tabernacle was the chairman for Coalhurst as well. In 1937, Pastor S. Fredrickson served under the chairmanship of Rev. George Bombay of Lethbridge. The services were still in the United Church. In November 1937, Sister Beulah Hamilton was installed as Deaconess/Pastor. She was also the Sunday school superintendent and Charlie Wesselman was the assistant superintendent. That year the Assembly purchased the United Church, in which they had been meeting. Sister Hamilton resigned in June 1938, so Brother Good from Lethbridge preached each Sunday. In January 1940, the chairmanship of the church was changed from Lethbridge to the local layleadership in Coalhurst. At that time, Brother Bill Dutton, a railroad engineer working out of Lethbridge, was pastor and Brother William Borrows was chairman. In February 1941, both offices were amalgamated into one under Brother Dutton. In May 1941, Miss Edina Harding, a new graduate of Bethel Bible Institute in Saskatoon, Saskatchewan, became the pastor/chairman. She was assisted by Elsie Abrahamson (now Gray) and May Crowell (became Mrs. Gusella) of Mayton. A number were filled with the Spirit during her service here. A baptismal service was held in the river bottom backwater near the Lethbridge bridge, which no longer exists. About 1943, a country house was bought and moved into Coalhurst. This became the parsonage. Miss Harding resigned in May 1945.

Pastor John Erhardt served as pastor/chairman from January 1946 to September 1947. Brother James Robertson pastored until January 1951. Rev. and Mrs. N. F. Peace pastored from January 1951 until February 1952, when the church was destroyed by fire one windy day. On September 30, 1951, Harvest Festival Services were held in Coalhurst. There were morning, afternoon and evening services. Those, who took part that day, were Rev. W. F. Peace, host pastor; Mrs. W. F. Peace, Reverend Allen, Reverend Erhardt as speakers; Sunday school children from Coalhurst, Mrs. Allen, the Erhardts and Mrs. Peace sang or recited or performed monologues. The church was packed for the festival. It was a real blessing to all who attended from the surrounding areas. From January to September of 1951, thirty-two were saved and eight were baptized in water.

Although Brother Peace resigned, he was asked to remain until a replacement could be found. Rev. D. N. Buntain served as chairman of the assembly until Reverend and Mrs. Charles D. Howey arrived in June 1952 and served until May 1956. Men from Lethbridge preached in the services until Pastor and Mrs. Norman Labrentz arrived in November 1956 and served until December 31, 1958.

Brother Charles Wesselman served the church in various offices. He served as Sunday school superintendent for thirty years. In January 1959, Brother Lewis Varty became the pastor. Among others, who pastored, were Pastor and Mrs. Henry Conrad. Pastor Conrad pastored both Coalhurst and Vulcan at the same time.

The Lethbridge Canadian Pacific Railway Yards are, at the time of publishing, moving out to between Coalhurst and Kipp. More houses are being built in Coalhurst so the future holds good prospects for Coalhurst and the Pentecostal Assembly there.

Among those, who attended Bible college, are Edwin Wiebe and Violet Wiebe.

COLD LAKE
FULL GOSPEL CHAPEL

In 1953, Mr. and Mrs. George Gullackson and their three children (Glen, Lorraine and Paul) arrived in the Cold Lake area. As there was no Full Gospel work there, they started a Sunday School in the Cold Lake School. In about two years, a fine Sunday School was established with about forty-five or more children (native and white) in attendance.

They purchased two lots in a good residential area and within a year the church was built. They used an oil stove for heat. Outside toilets were provided. They then started services as well as Sunday School. Even though the building wasn't always too warm in the cold winters, they were happy and had many wonderful times in the Lord there. Mr. and Mrs. Harry Taitinger were living in Cold Lake at this time and were pillars in the church. Several evangelists held services, when souls were saved and filled with the Holy Spirit.

Sunday School Picnic at the Gullackson Farm in 1955.

In 1956, a little girl was born into the Gullackson family named Bonnie. Mr. Gullackson worked as a carpenter in the large air base, which was the main source of employment in Cold Lake at that time. Many people came here to work and when certain jobs were finished they moved elsewhere. Among these labourers and Air Force Personnel were many fine christians, who came and helped in the Full Gospel Chapel.

In 1960 when Gullacksons moved to B.C., Mr. and Mrs. George Corris took over the pastorate until 1962. After they left Mr. and Mrs. Ken Richardson were in charge for six months, then Mr. Thompson, who was in the Air Force at the Cold Lake Air Base, held the church services for several months. Mr. Bud MacLean was pastor for a while and was followed by Mrs. Gladys Prest.

The Gullackson family had returned to Cold Lake, and once again they took over the Lord's work in the Gospel Chapel. Mr. Gullackson worked as a carpenter at the Air Base to help support the Gospel work. There was a need for a larger church with better facilities so all the church offerings were put in a building fund, except for what was needed for upkeep of the church and for visiting missionaries and evangelists. However, Mr. Gullackson was laid off from his job at the Air Base and went north to find work. In his absence for several years, during the summers, Bible Students and laymen conducted the services. Mr. Bernard Holmstrom pastored from 1970 to 1972. After he left, the Gullacksons again pastored the church, and the building of the new church began. While the new church was being built, services were held in the Gullackson home. In 1973, they moved into the new church, which was dedicated in 1974.

New Full Gospel Chapel

In 1977 Mr. and Mrs. Randy Harriman became the pastors for one year. They were followed by Mr. Warren Clark who was there for six months. Mr. Westmore Cowpersmith also ministered here from time to time. Mr. Anderson was then appointed to fill in until the present pastors, Mr. and Mrs. Barry O'Coin, arrived. The Lord is blessing the work in the Cold Lake area and the work of God is going forward.

Among those, who attended Bible College and/or entered the ministry (*), are *Harvey Lehsner (Grande Centre) and Diane Smith.

DRAYTON VALLEY
DRAYTON VALLEY PENTECOSTAL TABERNACLE

In 1960 Reverend S. R. Tilton, District Superintendent, was approached with a request from a few families to open a church in Drayton Valley to provide Pentecostal fellowship. The request was looked upon with favor by the District. Two young ladies, Misses K. Thiesson and A. Shevkenek, who had returned from missionary work in the Far East, volunteered to accept this missionary venture.

For the first year, the services were held in the Legion Hall. The second year, they had the use of the memorable portable tabernacle. This was a new concept for opening churches in new places. Unfolded it would seat about one hundred people. It had church windows, organ and what was required for a meeting. Folded up it could be transported to where ever it was needed next.

Some of the founding families were Summers, Staroziks, Topstads, McDonalds, Anhorns, Mrs. June Falls.

In 1960 Mrs. June Falls organized the Women's Missionary Council in the assembly.

It was during this second year that the church received a major spiritual uplift. Several families experienced the grace and blessing of God in salvation, healing and the infilling of the Holy Spirit. An adult baptismal service was held in Pigeon Lake where six people were baptized.

Now it was time to have their own church. Construction began in the fall of 1961. Many volunteers from Drayton Valley and neighboring churches came to help with their expertise and labour. Among these were Bill Lagore, Al Carruthers, Al Forsythe and Ernie Peterson. These men would come with a group from their church to build on a Saturday or a holiday weekend. The basement was ready for occupancy in 1962. In 1963 they were able to use the upstairs sanctuary.

This same year, 1963, Miss Thiessen resigned because of ill health; Miss Shevkenek resigned to resume overseas missionary work. Pastor and Mrs. Art Sader and family came to Drayton Valley to minister. There was still much work to be done on the building. Cupboards were built in the suite in the basement. The upstairs sanctuary was drywalled and tiled. Cement sidewalks were poured. Pastor Sader also taught Business Administration part time in the High School. In 1964 he resigned to take further studies at the University of Alberta.

Reverend and Mrs. Harvey McAlister and family were in charge of several Sunday services, until Miss Hilda Mueller became interim pastor. Reverend L. Kokot was then called to take charge of this work. He moved with his wife and family to Drayton Valley in January 1965. The work on the building was finally completed. On May 30, 1965, the official dedication was held. Reverend Kokot ministered until 1967.

In 1967, the Assembly had drive-in church services and Daily Vacation Bible School.

Reverend Roy Kemp from Manitoba accepted the call to minister. He pastored the assembly three and one-half years before he was elected Christian Education and Youth Director for Alberta. The next pastor was Reverend Ken Smith from Saskatchewan. During his ministry, the parsonage was constructed. After three years another change of leadership took place, Reverend and Mrs. H. Osterhouse came to minister in the fall of 1973. In November 1975, Evangelist Eunice Meyer conducted meetings for a week, when ten people received the Baptism of the Holy Spirit. At the end of June 1977, the Osterhouses retired from pastoral service. They were followed by Reverend G. Giles, who came to Western Canada from Newfoundland to engage in Bible college teaching. Reverend Giles was followed by Pastor and Mrs. Calvin Reid.

In 1980, Pastor and Mrs. Ben Sieppert came to Drayton Valley. In the 1982 Conference, Pastor Sieppert reported that God was blessing the Assembly.

Among those, who entered Bible college, are Allan Starozik, *Ed Summers and Sandra Summers.

DRUMHELLER
ELIM PENTECOSTAL TABERNACLE

The first Pentecostal services were held in an old hall in South Drumheller and were conducted by the Rufus Reynolds family in the summer months of the early twenties. In 1925 Hazel Murner (Mrs. Jim Raisbeck) and Lila Robinson (Mrs. John Chapman) held services in a hall above a grocery store on the corner of Third Avenue and First Street. After some time these meetings were discontinued. Then around 1931 a Pentecostal family, the Simonds, moved to Drumheller and began holding meetings in their home. Mr. Simonds was a railroad engineer. Later along with the son-in-law, Reverend C. K. S. Moffat, they held services in a scout hall.

In 1932 Miss Vera Coulter and Miss Alice Richardson came as pastors of this congregation, which now moved back into the hall above the store. A fire destroyed this place and everything was lost, so they moved back into the Scout hall. During this time souls were saved, among whom were Mr. and Mrs. S. R. Tilton and Mr. and Mrs. N. Langford.

Dedication of the upper sanctuary of Elim Pentecostal Tabernacle on August 29, 1948. Platform People. Left to Right, Back Row: Brother A. MacKinnon Sr., Charles Howey, Rev. D. N. Buntain, Rev. C. Myhre. Front Row: Bud Toothe, Pastor and Mrs. H. C. McAlister, Mrs. C. Myhre, Miss Eunice Meyer, Mrs. H. Rosenke, Mrs. D. N. Buntain, Rev. H. Rosenke, Brother H. H. Crowell, Brother Knud Peterson.

Both Mr. Tilton and Mr. Langford became ministers and served as pastors and evangelists in the Pentecostal churches. Reverend S. R. Tilton was the District Superintendent for Alberta for many years. The McKinnons and Raisbecks were some of the families in this early church which now felt the need of their own place of worship. They purchased a building which had been a feed store, a hospital during the flu epidemic, also at one time a morgue. This was renovated into a soul-saving lighthouse in this mining town of Drumheller.

From 1933 to 1936 several men of God (Eddy Scratch, Hargraves, Walter Frederick, Jack Field) were ministering as pastors of the church.

In 1936 Reverend and Mrs. A. A. Lewis (1936-1941) felt the call of God to pastor this congregation. Many souls were saved and filled with the Holy Spirit, among these were Mrs. Edna Walker, Mrs. Parge, Fern and Pete Petersen, and they are still a part of the Pentecostal congregation in Drumheller. Also, during an evangelistic campaign held with Miss Evelyn Olson from the United States, the Jack Crowell family were saved. They were farmers and shortly after their conversion a hailstorm destroyed their crops. This was rather discouraging for new believers but their trust was in God. The grain grew again and that fall they reaped a good harvest.

Brother J. Crowell and Brother P. Petersen were members of the deacon board for many years.

During the ministry of Reverend and Mrs. Jim Routley (1941-1946) the present church building was started and the services were held in the basement.

In 1946 Reverend Harvey McAlister and family came to minister in the Drumheller valley. The church was completed and dedicated to the Glory of God August 29, 1948. They also continued holding certain Sunday afternoon meetings in the Verdant Valley Schoolhouse. Weekly Bible Clubs were conducted in Drumheller, Nacmine and Midlandvale. Miss Dorea Lindskoog and Miss Anne Twerdoclib came to assist in the children's work. Reverend Charlie Howey also came to help in the ministry. A special evangelistic campaign was held in East Coulee with Evelyn Glosser and Leila MacIntosh. Several souls were brought to the Lord. Reverend Howey continued this work for some time. In 1950 the McAlisters left to begin a work in Stettler. Miss Edina Harding and Miss Irene Ashley pastored the work in 1951. In 1952 Reverend and Mrs. Gilbert Rowland and family were called as pastors. They laboured faithfully until 1957.

Reverend Edgar and Iva O'Brien and small daughter, Patricia, arrived in Drumheller one hot and dusty Friday in July 1957.

The famed "Dinasaur Trail" although only a dust, mud and gravel road at the time, caught the imagination of O'Briens. Giving God credit for the inspiration, he soon mustered the assistance of local contractors, businessmen and officials. Before the year was out, he had dedicated "The World's Largest Little Church". The slogan "Seating ten thousand — six at a time," aptly suggests its miniature size.

Frustrated by apparent Sunday evening apathy and the heat, the Church Board approved a plan to conduct the seven o'clock evening services "Drive-in" style — come-as-you-are and let your car be your pew. Although unheard of before in western Canada, it soon gained interest and attendance grew from an initial twenty to over two hundred. So popular was this summer series that it continued through the nine years of the O'Brien's ministry here. Other ministers continued the same summer outreach.

Rev. and Mrs. E. C. O'Brien, Patricia and Gregory

The arrival of a local radio station provided a challenge. Gaining a month's free broadcast time gave Reverend O'Brien time to secure local sponsors for the international "Revivaltime" broadcast. From its very beginning, the weekly broadcast was supported entirely by contributions of the radio audience. Pastor O'Brien became so apt at cuing in local announcements and dubbing in special local music, that he soon had a regular evening broadcast of his own. Pentecostal Hymntime became a regular feature that often extended into all night gospel music marathons.

It naturally followed that a church with radio broadcasts should also publish its own magazine, so an eight-page glossy called "Gospel Echoes" was published. Again it was the local business community that supported the nine years of publication by their small ads and sponsorships. Although regular subscriptions never exceeded two hundred, there were numerous times that every household in the Drumheller Valley was personally visited and delivered the magazine by the pastor and his wife.

"Community Pulpit" was a winter project that parallelled the summer "Drive-in-Church." The local theatre became the Sunday afternoon meeting place for hundreds from up and down the valley as the Pentecostal congregation hosted guest speakers, singers and musicians for the good of the entire christian community. Sought after preachers, beyond the financial reach of the local congregation, were often brought to Drumheller for these monthly specials through those long winters.

As attention and interest increased, so did attendance and conversions. The old parsonage was used for classrooms created by an ever-growing Sunday School.

The Sunday School Annex also served as a fellowship hall and youth center. Even then, a nearby vacant store was location for the midweek Pentecosal Crusaders, which enjoyed a healthy and active existence. While pastoring Drumheller, Reverend E. C. O'Brien was assisted for short periods first by Reverend Laurie Hale and then by Larry Remple.

In 1966 the O'Briens moved to Calgary. Reverend and Mrs. Jim McAlister were interim pastors until Reverend and Mrs. L. Carbert arrived in September of that year. During the next five years souls were saved and bodies healed. Reverend Carbert had an all-night Gospel radio program.

Reverend and Mrs. M. Wall and their two boys came to Drumheller in August 1971 and ministered there until the fall of 1980. The sanctuary was enlarged and a very attractive entrance and foyer were added. Reverend James Smart, who was Assistant Pastor for four years, was also a counsellor in the Drumheller Institution. Reverend Wall counselled as well.

An interesting incident happened to Reverend Charles Yates while he was interim pastor in Drumheller at a time when the old parsonage was at the back of the church lot. He decided to explore the basement which was only a hole under the parsonage. As he opened the door he reached for what he thought was the light chain, but it was only a cobweb. Down he went to the bottom! Perhaps at that moment only his dignity and pride suffered, but to add to this his wife called, "Are you hurt Charles?" Rising above these things, Reverend Yates is now the General Secretary for the Pentecostal Assemblies of Canada.

From the early years of the church, there are many who will not be forgotten: Grandma Raisbeck, Grandma Jones, the MacKinnon family, Mrs. Parsons, Mrs. Bennet, the Tiltons, Petersens, Crowells, the Parge family, the Walkers, the Toughs, the Percy Robinson family. Some have moved away, others promoted to Glory, but several are still part of the church in Drumheller.

Among those, who attended Bible College and/ or entered the ministry (*), are Lawrence Brown, Ron Mepham, Vernon Robinson, Mary-Jo Rowbottom, Linda Sargent, Sandi Stockall, Dennis L. Walker, *Melva Tough (Mrs. Ross Pennoyer).

Reverend Virgil Lawrence came to pastor in January 1981. His wife and two children joined him on weekends until school was out. Then they moved to Drumheller. The church has seen souls saved.

EDMONTON
CASTLE DOWNS PENTECOSTAL CHURCH

In 1964 or 1965, Reverend Karp Hrycauk held services in a rented place on Jasper Avenue and ninety-second Street, Edmonton. The congregation was Ukrainian. About a year or two later, this group purchased a little Lauderdale Baptist Church located just south of 132 Avenue on 101 Street, for eight thousand dollars. Here Reverend Hrycauk was assisted by John Shabak. Reverend Hrycauk left in 1966 or 1967. Brother Shabak filled in until Brother

Northside Pentecostal Church

Melynkne from Hope, B.C. came to pastor. Then Michael Kutney, Superintendent of the Ukrainian Youth, became pastor.

Some of the Lauderdale families were Mr. and Mrs. John Shabak, Mr. and Mrs. Joe Machocal and family, the Basuiks, the Frank Kuzyk family.

Under Michael Kutney's leadership, this congregation built a new church, Kensington Assembly of God. By this time everything was more or less in English. Some of the early families here included John Polachuk, the Arychuks, the Hastmans, the Ray Wills, the Corny Funks.

Other pastors here were Interim Pastor Dan Knoll, Colin Wellard and his wife (about two years), then Lawrence Aksenchuk who came in September 1974. Under Lawrence Aksenchuk, the name of the assembly was changed to Northside Pentecostal Church. This church was sold and the congregation moved to Castle Downs Shopping Centre about September 1979. A new church was built at 9949-169 Avenue, Edmonton, at a cost of nearly one million dollars. The sanctuary holds five hundred and twenty-five people.

On March 8, 1981 Castle Downs Pentecostal Church was dedicated. Greetings were brought from Jan Reimer, City of Edmonton Alderman; Henry Woo, Government of Alberta M.L.A.; Orville

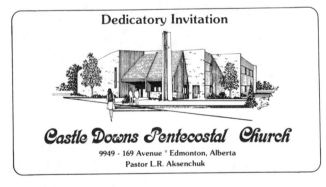

Dedicatory Invitation

Castle Downs Pentecostal Church
9949 - 169 Avenue ° Edmonton, Alberta
Pastor L.R. Aksenchuk

Dedicatory Invitation for the Castle Downs Pentecostal Church Dedication on March 8, 1981.

Williams, Northwest Bible College Alumni; John Dixon, Genstar Developments. Jack Telman, musical director, played the organ. The address was given by Reverend Robert Taitinger, General Superintendent of the Pentecostal Assemblies of Canada. The Act of Dedication was performed by Reverend Ivar Roset, Alberta District Superintendent.

Reverend Aksenchuk resigned June 1982. At the time of writing, Reverend Ross Pennoyer has accepted the call to pastor.

EDMONTON
CLAREVIEW ASSEMBLY
(Formerly Beverly Pentecostal Tabernacle)

About 1955 Reverend M. Gardziliwich first held services in Beverly area homes and then, on Sunday afternoons, in the Maranatha Christian Reformed Church at 11905-47 Street, Beverly. As Reverend Gardziliwich recalled, those, who assisted him, were Mr. and Mrs. Tony Shykowski, Jack and Stella Chetek (Stella was the pastor's daughter), Lawrence Denisuik, Peter Pawluik, Mrs. M. Beliski, Mr. and Mrs. J. Stayko, Jacob Shykowski, John Perch, Mrs. Wanchulak, N. Soltis. Services were conducted in the Ukrainian language and the Assembly was registered with the Western Slavic Conference of the Pentecostal Assemblies of Canada.

Beverly Pentecostal Tabernacle

In 1957 the construction of the church began at 11901-50 Street in Beverly to the east of Edmonton, in fact just across the street from Edmonton. In April of that year while standing in the basement excavation, Reverend Gardziliwich heard a voice say, "Why aren't you working?" He replied, "How can I, if I don't know where to start?" This led to an atheistic, retired-carpenter neighbor becoming the director for laying the foundation of the Beverly Pentecostal Tabernacle. As the construction progressed, more people attended the services. Miss Sadie Chetek organized the Sunday School and was its first superintendent from 1958 to 1962.

As more people came, many could not understand the Slavic language. So to meet the needs of the English speaking people, Reverend Paul Kerychuk became assistant pastor in 1961.

Reverend Kerychuk had been active in the St.

Albert area. He brought with him Walter and Mary Aksenchuk, Mike and Elsie Aksenchuk, Paul and Mary Krawchuk, Mike and Eileen Kochan, Mr. and Mrs. Irvine Fester, Mr. and Mrs. C. Woodcock, Joe Lachine and Vicki Ewasiuk. Later that year, they were joined by Walter and Lydia Steinke, Walter (Micah) and Elsie Kozak, Ben and Elsie Kozak, Mike and Nancy Kozak, Mike and Angelina Chetek, and Henry Macioha, who came to know the Lord, while Evangelist Eunice Meyer was holding revival meetings.

The young people's department was established in 1961. The first executive was Walter Aksenchuk (president), Irvine Fester (vice-president), H. Macioha (treasurer) and Vicki Ewasiuk (secretary). This department was active and helpful in the church.

During the first year, Pastor Kerychuk was not given a salary. During the second year, he was given a small salary. To meet his financial needs, he also worked for Sears.

Paul's wife, Margaret, was active in the musical area. His son, Larry, is known for his football career with the Edmonton Eskimos and the Winnipeg Blue Bombers. He was also very active with Athletes in Action and other groups to promote the Gospel among athletes. In 1981 Larry became youth pastor in Tommy Barnett's church in Phoenix, Arizona. Michael, who was the joker in the family, finally settled down to become an effective preacher. He pastors in Preston, Arizona. The family took an active part in the church.

Left to Right: Rev. Gardziliwich, Joe Shykowski, Rev. Paul Kerychuk (at the Pulpit), Rev. Smolchuk, Rev. C. Yates, Norman Filtz at the tenth anniversary service in 1971.

By 1964, the services were totally in English, so the church registration transferred from the Western Slavic Conference to the Pentecostal Assemblies of Canada. Reverend Gardziliwich still took care of the older Slavic-speaking people while Paul Kerychuk pastored the English speaking congregation. In 1967

Reverend Norman Filtz assisted Pastor Kerychuk. Walter Knoll was a student pastor. Paul Kerychuk left in 1970.

In 1970 Joe Shykowski, a graduate of Northwest Bible College, became Interim Pastor. Both Joe and his wife, Jeanette, have been very active in the church.

In 1972, Reverend Magnus Borsheim became the first full-time pastor on salary plus a parsonage. During his seven years as pastor, he was assisted by a number of young men for varying lengths of time — Assistant Pastors: Len Rosenfeldt (1974-1976), Lloyd Kupka (1977-1978), Bob Bidwell (1979-1981) and Student Pastors: Alwyn Coleman, Allan Bartlett, Steve Gavronsky, Peter Hudel.

In 1976, the Beverly Pentecostal Tabernacle purchased one acre of land in the Clareview District of Edmonton, because there was not suitable property in Beverly. The Clareview Assembly was the new name for this Assembly when they moved to this new location of 4925-134 Avenue. The new building was built by volunteer help under the leadership of the general foreman, Ben Kozak. Dedication Day was May 15, 1977.

Sod-Turning Ceremony for Clareview Assembly. Left to Right: Rev. A. Lindoff; Rev. C. Yates; *Henry Macioha; Assistant Pastor, Rev. L. Rosenfeldt; *Ben Kozak; *John Albiston; *Joe Shykowski; Rev. I. Roset; *Mike Chetek; City of Edmonton Representative; Pastor, Rev. M. Borsheim. Board Members' names are starred (*).

Reverend Gardziliwich purchased the Beverly Tabernacle for the Slavic people and registered it with the Western Slavic Conference.

Reverend Borsheim left November 11, 1979. Bob Bidwell and Student Pastor Hudel filled in while waiting for the new pastor to come. Reverend and Mrs. Lyle Horril arrived in December 1979. Bob Bidwell assisted and was youth director as well until June 1981. Howard Bishop became the Assistant Pastor and youth director in November 1981. The wives of the pastors, assistants and student pastors are very helpful, too.

One of the members, Ben Kozak, is very thankful for God's care.

The church family increased so much, that expansion was necessary. The expansion building was started in 1982.

This Assembly has enjoyed the blessing of God.

EDMONTON
EDMONTON CENTRAL
PENTECOSTAL TABERNACLE

In 1917 in the home of Mr. and Mrs. Edgar Taylor, Edmonton Central Pentecostal Tabernacle had its beginning under the leadership of Rev. John McAlister (1917-1919). He had some revival meetings with a group of Holiness Movement believers (David and Matilda McAlister with Pearl, May, Clarence, Harvey C. and Marjory; Mr. and Mrs. Edgar Taylor with Lillian; Mrs. John (Alice) McAlister with Hugh, Lila and Walter). A number of them received the Baptism of the Holy Spirit. Rev. R. E. McAlister installed John McAlister as pastor of this group. Alice, his wife, was a deaconess. In those early days, Mrs. Eleanore Rutter, the Houghton Family and the John Kennedy Family joined this group of believers. In 1918, an auditorium in the Powell Block, at 95 Street and 114 Avenue, was used for some time as a place of worship.

The Edgar Taylor Home

Rev. Hugh M. Cadwalder of Texas became the pastor in 1919. In 1920, Evangelist C. O. Benham and Evangelist Jack Saunders were tremendous blessings to this early assembly. There were wonderful conversions, marvelous healings and precious baptisms. The sanctuary of the church, probably the church at 11412 93 Street, was enlarged by taking down partitions and still the church was packed for services. On March 21, 1921, Samuel and Elizabeth Hamilton, with Mae and Marie, came to the church after hearing the news of the healing of a certain man, whom they knew well. In 1921, a minister, Philip Snider, married Mae Hamilton. Philip filled in for Rev. Cad-

walder, while he was away. From April 1 to July 15, 1922, the longest revival in Edmonton was held in the Empire Theatre. Among the speakers were May Fry, Jack Saunders and a Brother Munro. Bill Dutton from Lethbridge was the pianist. His excellent playing added much to the services. The moving of the Holy Spirit was very evident. The altar was filled every night. Rev. Cadwalder had a very fruitful ministry during this time, but resigned in 1922.

Others, who ministered in the 93 Street church, were Rev. Elmer L. Hoff (1922-23); Rev. Walter E. McAlister and his wife, Ruth (nee Manley), (1923-24); and Rev. Hugh J. McAlister with his wife, Jean, who was a pianist (1924-27).

Church Picnic at the South Side Park. Present is the core of the Ninety-Third Street Church.

Among those, who were added to the congregation, were Dagny Suvan, the Suvan Family; Mrs. Barnes and her two sons; Mr. and Mrs. George Taylor and Family (George was a very happy, active member); Robert and Mary Heslep with Ruth, Lonny (Scotty), Hazel and Audrey; Victor and Irvin Graham; Mrs. Castor; Grandma Neely; The Hamiltons; Mr. and Mrs. James Shedden with Stanley, Frank, Don and Ernest (from 1921 or 22); Shedden's daughters, Madie and Vivienne (from 1924).

Under Rev. Hugh McAlister (1924-27), the Ninety-third Street Church was sold and the Assembly moved to the basement in McDougall Court, across from the MacDonald Hotel. The exact date of this move is not known.

In 1925, Dr. Charles Price had marvelous services in the Edmonton Arena. Many were converted, including John J. McLeod, and others were healed. His services created quite a stir. Sadie M. McLeod, a Pentecostal missionary to Hong Kong, remembers the McLeod Family would take a lunch along when they left at four o'clock and traveled to the Edmonton Arena by streetcar for the evening service. On the way home from the meetings, people would sing hymns in the streetcars.

In 1927, Mrs. Fry and Miss Hazel May held some special services. Mrs. Ruth Dickinson received the Baptism of the Holy Spirit in one of those services. Through this experience, the whole William (Bill) Dickinson family came into the Assembly. In 1927, Mrs. Jean Boyle was saved. She said there were good little meetings then. There were prayer meetings in the Morris home with Jean Boyle and Mrs. Avery in charge.

The Tabernacle on 108 Street.

In the Young People's minutes of January 3, 1930, the Assembly was referred to as **Bethel Pentecostal Assembly**. Later in 1931, it was called **Edmonton Pentecostal Assembly**.

Others, who ministered in McDougall Court, were Rev. Allan S. Ellis (1927-30), Rev. W. R. Collings (1930-31), and Rev. Clifford Nelson (1931-37).

Among those, who were added to the congregation during the McDougall Court times, were William (Bill) and Ruth Dickinson with Lila, Vivian, Vernon, Olive, Roy and Jim; the Colin Campbell Family including Gordon, Kenneth and R.; Brother and Sister Jim Morris with Jean, Ruby, Mac, Hobert, Irene, and Iris; Brother and Sister John (Jack) Pike Sr. with Dorothy, Violet, Marjorie and John Jr.; the J. D. McSwains, who were great for entertaining; Brother and Sister Richardson with Clare, Maxine, Bob and Alice; Miss Ella Wheeler and her mother; the Kings; Mrs. Jean Boyle; Mr. and Mrs. Ryall with Carmen, Vera and Marguerite; Mrs. Zelkie; John J. and Sadie Jane McLeod with Anna, Henry, Edith, Sadie and Mildred.

In February 1932, Rev. and Mrs. W. C. Nelson moved the Edmonton Pentecostal Assembly to an upstairs auditorium in the Bell Block, where there were eighteen windows to let the daylight and the sunshine in, which was not the case in the basement of the McDougall Court. At that time, the Army and Navy Store was in that same block on 101 Street.

The Assembly bought the Eighth (108) Street property for five thousand dollars. According to Brother Nelson, the building permit, for the Tabernacle built there, was the largest permit issued in the City of Edmonton in 1932. Under the ministry of Brother Nelson and skills of Brother J. J. McLeod with many volunteers, the Edmonton Pentecostal Tabernacle was built in three months at 10047 108 Street. The sanctuary seating capacity was about five hundred fifty. This Tabernacle was dedicated in July 1932 with Rev. Donald Gee of Scotland as guest speaker. One lady remembers that her parents pitched their tent just north of the Tabernacle for their accommodation, while attending the dedication and services. Other out of town guests stayed in homes. It was indeed a time of rejoicing.

In 1933, Rev. W. C. Nelson originated the radio broadcast, Evening Evangels, over CJCA, later over a small station, which became CFRN. The broadcast over the years had two other names, Morning Evangels and Evangeltime. This broadcast continued over CFRN Edmonton until April 27, 1981. At that time, CFRN changed its programming so Evangeltime was discontinued.

Others, who ministered in the Pentecostal Tabernacle, were James Swanson (1937-38), who, in 1920, had a business in Edmonton, then had a business in Lethbridge, married May Scratch and became a Pentecostal Minister; Rev. Willis G. McPherson (1938-40), who saw the Sunday School increased from one hundred thirty-eight to two hundred thirty-eight and the crowds in the services increased so it became necessary to install one hundred new seats; Evangelist Evelyn Olson (1940), who filled in until December 15; Rev. Tom Johnstone (1940-42); Rev. Rourke for a few months in 1942; Rev. A. Mallory (1942-44), whose assistant for one year was Mark Buntain; Rev. Willard C. Pierce (1944-45); the Rev. Dr. D. N. Buntain (1945-55) with assistants Rev. J. C. Cooke (1946-47), Paul Cornish (1947-48), Bob Taitinger (1948-55); Rev. R. W. (Bob) Taitinger (1955-69).

One of Brother Buntain's favorite hymns was We Shall Shine as the Stars of the Morning. He always said, "God will look after any church that puts Missions first." His motto was "The supreme task of the Church is the evangelization of the World." He was very missionary-minded and also loved the moving of the Holy Spirit.

Rev. Buntain put feet to his vision of an Alberta-based Bible college, Canadian Northwest Bible In-

Montrose Branch Sunday School. Front Row, Left to Right: Bertha Motz (now Mrs. Bill Lagore), Ruth McAlister, Eileen Sader (now Mrs. W. Rimer), Evelyn Olson, Charlotte Erbacher, , Helen Erbacher. Second Row: Far left, Mrs. Shmautz. Left to Right, at far right: Ray Sader and Bill Fawcett. Third Row: Second from the left is Adeline Sader.

stitute, and opened it on October 4, 1946. It was housed in the Edmonton Pentecostal Tabernacle and it was a blessing to both the congregation and the Province of Alberta.

Under the Ministry of the Buntains, the church began a period of unprecedented development in the entire church program. The Sunday School, which averaged one hundred fifty to one hundred seventy-five, reached four hundred in attendance. The Tabernacle service attendance and membership increased so much in five years that it was necessary to enlarge the Tabernacle by adding a foyer, offices and increasing the sanctuary seating capacity to seven hundred and fifty, which of course was done. The assembly continued to grow.

Rev. R. W. Taitinger married Miss Shirley Mae Johnson on June 5, 1954. The Taitingers have three children, Renae, Rick, and Richelle, who were all born in Edmonton.

Rev. Taitinger assisted Reverend Doctor Buntain from 1948 to the time of Dr. Buntain's death. During the two years prior to this death, Brother Taitinger assumed more responsibility. On September 28, 1955, he was inducted as pastor in a special service conducted by Rev. John Watts, acting on behalf of the District. "Rev. J. E. Purdie D.D. conducted his induction in a most impressive manner."

In 1960, the Pentecostal Tabernacle's name was changed to Edmonton Central Pentecostal Tabernacle, which is usually referred to as Central Tabernacle.

Because the congregation had grown so, the property at 107 Avenue and 116 Street was purchased for $70,000. Then they built the first Tabernacle on that site. This Tabernacle with a sanctuary capacity of one thousand cost four hundred thousand dollars. It was dedicated October 4, 1964, with Phil Gaglardi as guest speaker.

At the Tabernacle's Fiftieth anniversary, in 1967, twelve of the fifteen former pastors were present. Twelve hundred people were fed downstairs. Three hundred pumpkin pies were served. It was a refreshing time.

1978 Garden Party for Sadie McLeod, shortly before she returned to Hong Kong that year. Front Row, Left to Right: Miss Blanche Pardo, Lila Dickinson, Clara McIlwain, Selma Sproule, Lillian Kuhn, Mrs. J. J. McLeod, Evelyn Shedden, Jean Boyle, Axie Benson, Irma Strandberg, Jane Taitinger, Miss Sadie McLeod. Second Row: Vivian Turner, Mary Twerdy, , Alice Kerber, Florence Lange, Mrs. Anderson. Shirley Morsch, the Hostess, took the picture.

Mrs. Shirley Taitinger was very active at Central. She put her musical talents to work. She organized Melodettes (a triple trio), played the piano for many a service and accompanied soloists and a number of musical groups.

At the 1962 National Biennial Conference, R. W. Taitinger was elected to the General Executive and, at the 1968 Biennial Conference, he was elected General Superintendent of the Pentecostal Assemblies of Canada. Rev. and Mrs. Taitinger were entertained at a farewell dinner on January 5, 1969. This much-loved family left for Toronto shortly after. Rev. Taitinger then assumed the office of General Superintendent.

During Rev. Taitinger's ministry in Central Tabernacle, his assistants were Rev. George Smith (five and a half years), Rev. Murray Dempster (three and a half years), Bob Muir (two years), James Thomas, Colin Wellard, Rev. Clifford Nelson.

Rev. George C. Smith followed Rev. Taitinger as pastor. Rev. George Smith (1969-78), his wife, Barbara, and children, Mark and Becky, arrived in January 1969. Sister Smith was an excellent pianist and organist.

Under Rev. Smith's ministry, the pyramid-style sanctuary, seating two thousand, was built just south of the Tabernacle at 11605 107 Avenue. The two buildings are joined by a tunnel. The old Tabernacle was changed somewhat to increase classroom space, more office space, a fairly large chapel on the main floor, but retaining the fellowship hall, kitchen, nursery and chapel in the basement. The new sanctuary building also included nurseries, washrooms, an office and choir room. The new sanctuary was dedicated on April 23, 1972.

Central Village, a senior citizen complex, was built in 1972 and is owned by the Pentecostal Benevolent Association. This complex was made possible by a generous contribution along with a long-term, low-interest mortgage from the Federal Government Canada Mortgage and Housing Department. This Pentecostal Benevolent Association, also, manages Central Manor (1976), another senior citizen complex, which is owned by the Provincial Government of Alberta. The Board of the Edmonton Central Pentecostal Tabernacle is also the Board of the Pentecostal Benevolent Association. There are programs, meetings and outings for the seniors. These two complexes are within walking distance of Central Tabernacle.

Edmonton Central Pentecostal Tabernacle

While Rev. Cal Ratz was assisting Rev. George Smith, he organized the Church Life Training Centre. Its first semester began in January 1976. Tabernacle folk were offered courses to help equip them for more effective ministries in Central, home, hospitals, work or wherever there was a need. Al Kiffiak was the Registrar. One of the courses offered was the Shepherding Program. The Shepherding Program was tried for a while.

Rev. Ratz established the Neighbourhood Bible Studies. These Studies involved discussion of the assigned Scripture studied and conversational prayer.

Bible Study Leaders and Hosts were trained in a class that met during the Christian Education Time on Sunday mornings. The content of the studies were discussed. Methods and presentations were given. In one particular Neighourhood Bible Study group, members were able to minister to two widows, who lost their husbands while part of the group. Efforts were made to win others to the Lord. One of the ladies, who speaks Ukrainian, was able to lead the mother-in-law of one of the widows to the Lord. Another lady quietly gave her heart to the Lord during one of the group's prayer times. A very special bond developed in this group. Other groups experienced blessing and bonding, too. This program is still in operation at the time of publication.

Rev. George Smith's assistants and student pastors were B. Lee Bell (Business Administrator), Warren Benson, Laurey J. Berteig (Music), Greg. R. Foley, Rev. Gerald A. Johnson, Gregg Johnson, Rev. Brian D. McConnell (Music), Rev. W. Clifford Nelson, Rev. Calvin C. Ratz, Glen L. Rutledge (Music), Rev. Robert J. Smith, Rev. August H. Stiller, James R. Thomas, Mr. Paul Shank (Ranch), Gordon Wiebe, W. Laird Bell (Ranch).

Under Rev. George Smith, television ministry was used as an outreach. The radio ministry was also continued.

Rev. James M. MacKnight (1978-82) with his wife, Margaret, and son, Mark, arrived in August 1978.

Under Rev. MacKnight's ministry, a television studio was installed in Central Tabernacle. The television program, 60 Minutes with Central, is produced in Central Tabernacle by our own television crews. The results of this television ministry have been very heart warming. Many have been helped.

1981 Staff at Central Tabernacle. Back Row, Left to Right: Warren E. Benson, Dan R. Shedden, Greg R. Foley, James M. MacKnight, Laurey J. Berteig, Ron G. Orr, Mark J. MacKnight. Front Row: Donna Cornish, Cathy Nordstrom, Ruth Milliken, Ruth Rome, Shelley Walters.

Evangeltime, Central's radio program, was produced until April 27, 1981.

Just east of the pyramid-style sanctuary, a large multi-purpose room was added and dedicated January 18, 1981. It is usually referred to as the new prayer room. It is used as a prayer room, classroom, et cetera.

On November 18, 1979, Lila Dickinson was honored for thirty-five years of service as church secretary. She has since worked part-time.

Rev. MacKnight's assistants and student pastors were Rev. Rosswell F. Olson, Rev. Cameron Stevenson (from January 10, 1982), Rev. Cal Ratz, Gregg M. Johnson, Rev. Warren E. Benson, Rev. B. Lee Bell (Business Administrator), Rev. Ron G. Orr (Business Administrator), Rev. Greg R. Foley, Mark MacKnight, Brad Eastman, Cam Milliken, W. Laird Bell (Ranch), John R. Carson (Ranch), Laurey Berteig (Music), Dan R. Shedden (Music).

Rev. James MacKnight's last Sunday as pastor was November 28, 1982. The Tabernacle's Farewell Dinner for the MacKnights was held November 29, 1982.

Rev. Robert H. Johnson became the next pastor.

Edmonton Central Pentecostal Tabernacle congregation has been pastored by six General Superintendents of the Pentecostal Assemblies of Canada. These ministers were Rev. Walter E. McAlister (Pastor 1923-24, General Superintendent 1952-62), Rev. James Swanson (Pastor 1936-38, General Superintendent 1934-36), Rev. D. N. Buntain (Pastor 1945-55, General Superintendent 1936-44), Rev. Tom Johnstone (Pastor 1940-42, General Superintendent 1962-68), Rev. R. W. (Bob) Taitinger (Assistant Pastor 1948-55, Pastor 1955-January 5, 1969, General Superintendent 1969-82), and James M. MacKnight (Pastor 1978-82, General Superintendent 1983-   ).

For a long time, it has been very evident that God has used both men and women to make Central Tabernacle's congregation a very strong, active church. Among the many men, who were faithful in prayer and support, were/are John McAlister, David McAlister, Edgar Taylor, George Taylor (who loved to witness and work in the prayer room), Harry Cornish (elder), Albert Gaetz (elder), Norman Thompson (elder), Clarence McAlister (elder), John J. McLeod (builder and prayer warrior). Among the many women, who brought blessing and help to many, were/are Mrs. Axie Benson, Mrs. Jean Boyle (leader of the Ladies' Prayer Band for many years), Mrs. Olga Albrecht, Mrs. Lillian Petry, Mrs. Ruth Dickinson, Mrs. J. J. (Sadie Jane) McLeod (who helped many in need and also knitted about five hundred sweaters for needy children in Hong Kong),

Mrs. Jane Taitinger (who, herself, received a marvelous answer to prayer), Mrs. G. Maynard, Mrs. Mary Heslep, T. Kemp, Mrs. Ona, Mrs. Poulton, Mrs. Verna Evans, Mrs. Lena Albiston, Mrs. W. E. Nobles. The Women's Missionary Council (later known as Women's Ministries) have ministered to many at home and abroad. In 1982, Miss Ruth Ada Heslep became the leader of this group. There have been various groups for outreach over the years, for women, men (Men's Fellowship) and for both (Pentecostal Teachers' Fellowship, a group of Pentecostal school teachers from different assemblies in Edmonton and area, who, for a few years, helped a number of foreign university students and also tried to encourage missionaries involved in school work).

Children's groups that were/are a blessing included Crusaders and Cadets. Alberta Onciul, a Crusader Leader for years, became the Provincial Crusader leader. Boys' groups have ranged from Crusaders, Venturers, Sea Scouts, Cubs to Christian Service Brigade.

Youth Ministries began at least as far back as 1929. The earliest Young People's minutes are dated January 3, 1930. The 1930 officers elected were President, Miss Clara Worthington, who became the wife of Gerry McIlwain; Assistant President, Clarence McAlister; Ushers, Brother McKenzie and Brother Snowball; Leader of the Thursday Evening Prayer Meeting, Brother Clarence McAlister. The Young People's group became known as the Christ's Ambassadors in 1943 and in 1982 was known as the Youth Department, which included a Junior High School Group, a Senior High School Group and Young Adults. One of their young people, Rev. Greg R. Foley, became one of their student pastors, then a youth pastor, and in 1982 became the National Youth Director.

Central Tabernacle was the first church to have Wee College, originated by Mrs. M. (Joyce) Shram. Mrs. V. (Grace) Robinson, who taught in the college from its beginning, became the director at Central when the Shrams moved away. For more details, see the Wee College Report under Church Ministries under District Officers and Ministries.

One unique area of our Sunday School year, are the school-year length mission studies, which are usually taught once a month. In the fall of 1969, Rev. Robert Smith gave opportunity for mission studies to be written and taught in Central's Sunday School. By about January 1970, the first studies were begun. At the time of publishing, two of Shirley Morsch's mission studies, The West Indies (from January 1970, except for the 1971-72 term) and Liberia (from 1974), are still being taught. Many, many children have been won to Christ during her mission study classes. A love for missions is developed, too.

Music has long been a part of Central's services. About 1930, Miss Madie Shedden, directed the very first choir of Central Tabernacle, then known as Bethel Pentecostal Assembly. Among others, who followed as choir directors, were Hilda Smith; Clarence McAlister, who was also Rev. Buntain's Radio Music Director; Ernie Shedden and later Music Ministers. In 1982, the Tabernacle choir was known as the Festival Choir. Among the early junior choir directors were J. Shirley Johnson and Mrs. Jeanne Mack, who directed children's choirs for many years. The childrens choir groups later included the Choristers, Praise Singers and Cherub Choir. These childrens choirs and the youth choirs have warmed the hearts of many who have heard them sing.

The first orchestra was organized under Stanley Shedden, its first conductor. Clarence McAlister followed as the next conductor. In 1982, Central's bands included a Concert Band, Concert Brass, Special Recording and Performing Groups, a Senior Bell Choir and a Junior Bell Choir. Central Tabernacle also has the Central School of Music.

Among Central Tabernacle's pianists and organists have been Jean McAlister, Lillian Petry, Mrs. Dorothy Plastow, Don Miller, Rev. R. J. Muir, Colin Wellard, Mrs. Shirley Taitinger, Mrs. Barbara Smith, Mrs. Joanne Lantz, Miss Marlene Borsheim, Herb Ehrenholz and Miss Shelley Walters.

Central Tabernacle has done much in mothering assemblies in Edmonton by direct involvement, by giving their blessing for people to leave to form the nucleuses for new assemblies, by some members forming part of a board to help a particular assembly in its early time, and by financial gifts or loans. In spite of all this, Central has grown to the point that by 1982, their usual Sunday morning service attendance was about fifteen or sixteen hundred people.

Central has long been a very missionary minded assembly, not only giving of their own people for missionary service but financially as well.

Central Tabernacle's outreach also included a radio broadcast for many years and television programs. In 1982, the telecast, 60 Minutes with Central, proved to be of great benefit to many.

In the nineteen thirties, Central's young people and the Four Square Folk became involved in Jail ministry. Mrs. Jean Boyle was one, who ministered in the city jail for forty-six years. She was leader of that group for most of that time. This group included people from Central and other churches in the city.

The Christian Education Hour, formerly known as Sunday School, has played a very important role in educating the whole family in the Word of God.

Among the Superintendents of the Christian education Department were Clarence McAlister, John (Jack) Pike Sr., Albert Gaetz, Walter Zieber, Rev. Robert Smith, Peter Welychka and Ruth Rome. Among those, who have taught in our Sunday School for many years, are Florence Lang; Mrs. McSwain; Clara McIlwain; Olive Morsch; Ruth Heslep; Joyce Heslep; Shirley Morsch; Lillian Petry, a widow, who rounded up over forty to come to Sunday School with her and also visited the absentees of this group; Alice Kerber, who was also involved in the Sunday School Bus Ministry. Rev. Robert Smith was great for Sunday School promotion.

For many years, Central Tabernacle had branch Sunday Schools, usually held in schools. Among those Branch Sunday Schools were the west-end one that eventually ended up as the Gospel Centre Pentecostal Church; Montrose; Prince Charles; Brightview and Canora, which were begun by Mrs. J. C. (Ida) Cooke because of the concern she had for a student in Brighview School. These schools were staffed by many people from Central Tabernacle.

Birch Bay Ranch, which consists of twenty-six acres of land by Cooking Lake, was donated to Central Tabernacle by Sam McCaughey. The Ranch was and is a blessing to many young people and children. Ranch Directors to date have been P. Shank, W. Laird Bell and John R. Carson. In the summers of 1981 and 82 alone, five hundred and ninety-eight children and young people were won to the Lord. The Pentecostal Benevolent Association is in charge of Birch Bay Ranch.

Among those from Edmonton Central Pentecostal Tabernacle, who attended Bible College and/or entered the ministry (*), are Rita Aeichele, Glen Albright, Lloyd Albright, Larry Alexander, Bietta Anderson, Margaret Anderson, Cindy Baur, *Terry Baur (wife of Rev. B. Glubish), Gordon Beck, Jeffrey Beck, *Warren Benson, *K. Howard Bishop, Sal Biondolillo, Don Bjorgen, *Spencer W. Bradbury, Marlene Borsheim, *Fulton Buntain (saved at the Tabernacle after Mark Buntain had preached), Walter Busenius, *Jean Campbell (wife of Rev. H. McAlister), Paul Campbell, Verna Caswell, *Paul Cornish, *Marion Cornish, Robert (Bob) Cornish, Zoly Csontos, Jim Cumming, Sadie Cummins, Linda Derpack, Lorie Derpack, *Bob Derval, Frank Drader, Doug Drisner, Debbie Devlin, *Lila Dickinson, Brad Eastman, Ruth Eastman, **Mary Edler, *Gisela Ekstrom, *Robert Eckstrom, Mrs. Charlotte Fleet, Barb Foley, *Greg Foley, Ron Foley, Doreena Fothergill, Ralph Frank, *Lil Freund (wife of Al Goodzeck), *Doris Gaetz (wife of Rev. James Tyler), *Kenneth Gaetz, *Margaret Gaetz, Gordon Gee, Maxine Glanville, *Brian L. Glubish, Jean Graham,

Lorne Gray, **Jean Grieves (wife of Rev. Robert Peel), Walter Gunther, *David Haimila, Don Hall, Bill Hallson, Jeffrey Hanson, Jennifer Hanson, Gretel Harke, *Mrs. Rod Harrington (nee Marge Kerber), *Rod Harrington, Connie Hastman, Joyce Hastman, Paul M. Hay, *Robertson L. Howatt, *Mae Hamilton (wife of Rev. Philip Snider), *Dan Havens, *Stewart Heffel, Helen Hein, Marcia Hodges, *Jack Hood, Sharon Hunter, Edith Hunter, Gary Javorsky, **Cheryl Ann Johnson, *Dyllis Johnson (wife of Rev. Wayne Walters), *Elsie B. Johnson (wife of Robertson L. Howatt), *Gregg Johnson, *J. Shirley Johnson (wife of Edwin H. Morsch Jr.), Terry Jones, **Helen Emma Keller, *Lloyd Ketchum, Gail Kinsella, Randy Kinsella, **Ivan Kirsch, Candace Komant, *Selma Komant (wife of Cecil Sproule), *Wes Komant, **Kenneth Korol, David Krawchuk, Debbie Krawchuk, George Labercane, *Mr. and *Mrs. Garry Lafebvre, *Stan Lagore, *David Lagore, *Virgil Lawrence (married Nina Krawchuk), *Henry Lindberg, *Doreen Lindberg (wife of Henry Lindberg), Valerie Lohrer, **Wilda Lund (Mrs. Joseph Dragatis), June Mac-Rae, Darlene Martz, John Martz, Lily Martz, Armen Maser, *Elizabeth (Betty) Maser (wife of Rev. David McAlister), **Ruth Maser (wife of Mel Friesen), *David McAlister, **Lila McAlister, (wife of Rev. James Skinner), *Hugh McAlister, *Walter McAlister, *Harvey C. McAlister, *Perle McAlister, *Lorne McAlister, Mrs. McDonald, *Norma McLeod, *Mildred McLeod, **Sadie M. McLeod (Missionary to the Orient for over thirty-five years), *Yvonne McLeod (wife of E. I. Wood), **Dan McTavish, Gene (Jean) Melnychuk, Karen Melnychuk, Glynda Meister, Dave Miller, Edward Miller, *Cameron Milliken, Lorraine Minix, *Irene P. Morris (wife of Rev. Wendell Lewis), Jean Morris, *Olive Morsch (wife of Rev. John Morsch), *Ruth Morsch R.N., *Hilda Mueller, *Minnie Mueller, John Mulko, Harold Murphy, *Neil Muth, *Anthony Nash, *Mrs. A. Nash, Brian Nelson, *Violet Nelson (wife of Herman Strom), *David Nesbitt, Palle Nicalajsen, *Ruth Nystrom (wife of Rev. Gunnar Gulbransen, *Pat Opheim (wife of Rev. Don Argue), **Mervin Opheim (now Peterson), *Olive Opheim, *Marlene Osterman (now Zimmerman), Janice Paulsen, Frank Pap, Karen Park, Leona Pettigrew (wife of Cliff Eagle), Marjorie Pike R.N., *Violet I. Pike (wife of Rev. T. Edward Crane), Carol Pipke, Brian Proch, John Purich, *Ed Rebman, Stella Reddekopp, **Frieda Regehr, Mrs. Ryta Relf, Roly Relf, Joan Raynolds, *Glenn Rhind, *Alice Richardson (wife of Rev. Fred Dobson), *Clare Richardson, **Maxine Richardson R.N., Geoff Robertson, Steve Robertson, Terri Robertson, Dallas Sader, Daryl Sader,

Norma Schoenleber, Ingrid Schulz, Glen Shaw, *Ernie Shedden B.A. LLB., *Mary Shram, *Dan Shedden, Sharon Shields, Anne Shykowski, Richard Simpson, *Debbie Smith (wife of Rev. Bob Bidwell), *Coreen Smith (wife of Agape Force Member, Gabriel Arosemena), Robert Smith, Sharon Smith, Sydney Smith, *Gilbert Snider, *Sherry Ann Snyder, Dianne Sonnenberg, Elsie Steinke, Ken Steinke, Ron Stojan, Allan G. Starozik, John Strilesky, *Marsha Sullivan, *Ken Sumners, *Ruth Sumners, Donna Suprovich, Doris Suprovich, Mary Swekla, *Mrs. Shirley M. Taitinger (wife of Rev. R. W. Taitinger), *Lillian Taylor (wife of Rev. Hugh Fraser), **Virginia Thompson R.N. (wife of Rev. Jess Lynn), *David Tonn, Arlene Vaxvick, Byron Waterhouse, Karen Walker, Shelley Walters, *Wayne Walters, Carlton Whiteside, *Barbara Wicks, Gordon Wiebe, Ruth Wierschke (now Milliken), *Ella Curtis Wheeler (wife of Rev. Gordon Allen), Jim Willford, **Ruth Williamson, *Beatrice Wilson, Emilie Wolfe, Marlin Wolfe, *Greg Whyton. Missionaries for fields outside of Canada are double starred (**).

The influence of Central Pentecostal Tabernacle people reaches far and wide and, with God's help, will continue to do so.

© Copyright by J. Shirley Morsch 1982

EDMONTON
EDMONTON CHINESE PENTECOSTAL CHURCH

In January 1978, the Pentecostal Assemblies Alberta District Executive made an agreement to purchase the Gospel Temple located on the corner of 95 Street and 103 Avenue, Edmonton. Miss S. M. McLeod, missionary to Hong Kong, and Reverend Cal Ratz, a former missionary to Hong Kong, gave advice and help as requested. This new small congregation began having services early in 1978. They enjoyed the purchased church facilities.

Besides reaching out to the Chinese residents, they also ministered to the needs of many Vietnamese Chinese people.

In 1979, Mohan Maharaj was appointed as their "Honorary Pastor." William Wai, student of Northwest Bible College, assisted in this church from 1979 until the spring of 1982, when he graduated from college.

Since the congregation was too small for the church, the building was sold in July 1980. A house was rented to store the church furniture and as a place to hold services. Later, though they still rented the house, they used the Alex Taylor Elementary School for services for a little over a year.

Sharon Butt assisted in 1981 and 1982, while she attended Northwest Bible College. Pastor John Kong, of the Calgary Chinese Church, came to preach, encourage and advise as requested. Sometimes, his youth choir came to minister. While home on furlough in 1982, Miss Sadie McLeod was a blessing to this congregation. She was able to minister in a number of services.

The congregation purchased the Edmonton Bible Presbyterian Church at 11310-101 Street, Edmonton and moved into the church in May 1982. The name of the church is the Edmonton Chinese Pentecostal Church.

This group of Chinese Christians are looking forward to more growth under God's blessing.

EDMONTON
EVANGEL PENTECOSTAL ASSEMBLY

In 1974 at Sunnyside Pentecostal Camp, District Superintendent, Rev. Charles Yates, met with Seffron and Eleanor Drisner, Ray Sader and Lena Lehman to discuss how they felt about the future. It was decided to have a meeting in Ray Sader's home. There were twenty-six plus Rev. Yates and Rev. Lindoff (District Presbyter). They decided to begin a new church. A temporary board was elected to work with Rev. Yates until a pastor was found. This board consisted of Seffron Drisner, Ray Sader and Ed Lasner. Rev. Yates would be available for advice. Speakers were arranged for the time before a pastor was elected.

In August 1974, this church group chose the name, Evangel Pentecostal Assembly. Rev. A. L. Lindoff was asked to be the pastor. The Lord had prepared the Lindoffs for this position months ahead. He had resigned from Medicine Hat early in 1974, because they felt it was God's time for them to leave. They did not know where they would go. When he was asked to be pastor, they knew this was the place for them.

The first services were held August 11, 1974 in St. Stephens United Church with an attendance of fifty-eight in the morning and an attendance of seventy-one in the evening. This church was used for morning and evening services for the rest of August. In September 1974, they held Sunday School and Morning Service in Forest Heights Elementary School and Evening Services in St. Stephen's United Church. In September 1975, Bill Dogterom became assistant pastor.

The founding families included Seffron and Eleanor Drisner and family; Frank and Myrtle Jensen; Ray and Elizabeth Sader and family; Connie Beger, Irma Beger; Ray and Leila Newman; Albert and Erna Pohl and daughter; Ed and Helen Lasner and family; Harold and Ruth Greet; Tom and Ruth Raisbeck; Chester and Irene Marchuk; Ken and Karen Bedwell; Albert and Alma Schaber; John Martens; Eileen Smith often came; Emerson and Ella Cook.

The Idylwylde Pentecostal Tabernacle was sold and moved to Olds, Alberta, to be the new church there. The sod-turning ceremony was held February 12, 1978. The new church was built and dedicated November 19, 1978.

The special music was lovely. The dedication was led by Reverend I. Roset and Reverend A. Lindoff. Reverend Charles Yates was the special speaker.

The first board members were Ray Newman, Seffron Drisner, Ray Sader, Chester Marchuk, John Martens.

Pastor Craig Pitts and his wife, Dorothy, arrived in June 1979. The church continued to grow in numbers to the point, where in February 1980, two morning services were held and have been to the time of publishing this book. The Assembly is considering enlarging their facilities.

Rev. Keith Smith arrived to become the assistant pastor. He and his wife, Esther, and little son came in September 1979. The much-loved Pastor and Mrs. Pitts left for ministry in Ontario in July 1981. Rev. Keith Smith became the Pastor in August 1981. Rev. Keith Smith is giving good leadership. The Assembly does enjoy the blessing of God.

Among those, who attended Bible college, are Byron Ball, Julian Brown, Doug Drisner, David Dutka, Peter Erends (Idylwylde), Bill Huget, Margaret Rose Korol, Val Marchuk, Don Muth, Donna Muth, Nelson Newman, Dale Plante, Daryl Sader, Ken Steinke, Esther Schwindt, Richard Van Dewark.

EDMONTON
GOSPEL CENTRE PENTECOSTAL CHURCH

In the late nineteen twenties and thirties, young people from the Edmonton Pentecostal Tabernacle (now Central Pentecostal Tabernacle) came out to the Jasper Place area to conduct Sunday school. Tony Nash with his banjo, Clarence McAlister with his guitar or accordion and others came. They all worked together. They sang and played to make Sunday school a very delightful time. Harvey McAlister came part of the time, since he was usually busy with other ministry. He played a guitar and a coronet. These Sunday school services were held in the McDonald, Cummins or Clement homes.

Among those, who attended in those early days, were Florence Lang, Sadie Commins, Isabel Ament, Anne Ament, Bluebell Ament. The young people carried on until May 1941, when Deaconess Sadie McLeod took charge. At that time, the retiring Sun-

1930 West End Pentecostal Branch Sunday School. Back Row: Third and Fourth from the Left are May McAlister (now Mrs. Jim Henderson) and Grandma MacDonald. Front Row: Harvey C. McAlister with his trumpet.

day school superintendent was Clarence McAlister. These young people, who came out from the Tabernacle, had done a good job.

Miss McLeod conducted Sunday school, visited and, as she worked, felt that there should be church services in Jasper Place, which was just west of Edmonton. After renting Mr. Case's Meat Market, she and other young people cleaned and furnished it for the opening of the West End Mission at Stony Plain Road and 149 Street. The opening took place on February 1, 1942 with Sunday school at 3 P.M., Sunday evening service at 7:30 P.M.. The services continued at those times from Sunday to Sunday. She also conducted Thursday evening services at 8 P.M.. Mildred McLeod, Miss McLeod's sister, played the organ. Doris Gaetz helped, too. Both these girls were from the Pentecostal Tabernacle in Edmonton. Rev. Tom Johnstone, then pastor of the Tabernacle came for the opening and also once a month for communion. Miss McLeod left in September 1942 to attend the Toronto Missionary Medical Institute (now the Mission Health Institute) to prepare for missionary service. Mr. Henry Curry was left in charge of the work. He continued for a short time.

Ed and Violet Crane took charge and had Sunday school and possibly services, in late 1942 in the Crestwood Community Hall. Miss Sadie McLeod was in charge again from January to September 1947. J. Shirley Johnson helped here. The Sunday school was held in the Crestwood Community Hall. After Miss Mcleod left for China to be a missionary there, June Miller conducted Sunday School in the Community Hall. Mr. Henry took charge for the summer of 1948 but was unable to because the Crestwood Hall burned down. Central had purchased two corner lots at 148 Street and 100 Avenue earlier, but had not used them to this point. After the fire, Sunday school was held in an old red brick school house, just north of this property. In 1949, the Pentecostal Tabernacle

West End Mission Invitation. Deaconess S. M. McLeod was Pastor.

moved an old army barracks building onto one of the lots. They dug a cellar for the furnace. In 1949, Miss June Miller was appointed Alberta District Sunday School Supervisor (Director) and became pastor of Jasper Place (later called Jasper Place Gospel Centre). Forty people in the Pentecostal Tabernacle paid two dollars a month for June's salary as pastor of Jasper Place. Elsie Johnson kept the books for the collection and salary to June. June used her tithe to buy her District Sunday School supplies. In October 1951, undergraduate Dale Carpenter and his wife, Mary Lou, took over the leadership of Jasper Place Gospel Centre. They had Sunday school and morning worship services. In May 1952, just after graduation, Dale and Mary Carpenter were appointed pastors of this church. The church grew in the Lord and in number during their ministry. They ministered until the spring of 1955. During Carpenter's time, a basement was put under the building and a pastor's suite built in the basement.

J. Shirley Johnson (now Mrs. E. H. Morsch) and Sadie M. McLeod, just before Miss McLeod left as a missionary to China.

Among those, who attended about this time, were Mrs. Ethel Murray and her family, Sadie Commins, Orville and Marjorie Williams and family, Robbie and Elsie Howatt (Elsie's maiden name was Johnson), Archie and Helen Robinson (Helen was a very good pianist) and family, Gordon and Peggy Tremblay and family, Mrs. Whyte and family.

During the summer of 1955, the congregation enjoyed the ministry of Rev. James Beam. In the fall, Rev. and Mrs. J. C. O'Brien came to pastor. Their two ambitious sons were a real blessing to their parents. The O'Briens served faithfully for almost fourteen years. Under their ministry, a new church was built on the same location in 1963.

Rev. and Mrs. I. Roset followed the O'Briens in the spring of 1969. His Holy Spirit ministry, along with the musical talent of his family, made a great contribution toward the spiritual and numerical growth of the church. During his four and a half years, Rev. Roset was assisted for a time by Rev. Ken Bombay and later by Rev. Ken Ness and Bob Glasgow.

When Rev. I. Roset became the District Superin-

Gospel Centre Pentecostal Church

tendent, Rev. Ken Ness became the new senior pastor on January 1, 1975. The church grew so much that from the fall of 1974 to September 1977, larger facilities were rented for the Sunday morning and evening services. A new church was built on the corner of 153 Street and 95 Avenue. This is a very active church.

Among those, who attended Bible college and/or entered the ministry (*), are Janet Allen, Jeffrey Blum, Joyce Blum, David Booker, *Bette Anne Devanney, Tanny DePonto, Gloria Dille, *Ron Dowbush, John Emerson, *Bob Glasgow, *Joan Glasgow, Jack Harvey, Marilyn Johnson, *Edwin Joyes, Linda McAmmond, Ian McLellan, *Rhonda McLeod, Leslie Merrit, Gisela Molzahn, Leslie Nicholson, Sally Rogers, *Larry Tollefson, Elmer Watson, Mark Wilk, Hazel Wolf, *Nelson Wolfe, Gerald Zdrill, Marvin Wojda.

EDMONTON
HERITAGE CHRISTIAN ASSEMBLY

Ministering to people in south-west Edmonton has indeed been blessed of the Lord. Since its beginning in June 1981 the Lord has added families who were to find their place in the ministry of this pioneer church. The services are held in the Sweet Grass Elementary School. The Assembly was started with full District assistance and by September 1 they were totally self-sustaining financially.

The first Sunday in June 1981 fifty-eight people came to worship. On the first Anniversary service there were one hundred people present. Gospel Centre gave the Assembly an organ and the Beddington Assembly of Calgary gave the church hymn books. Minute Men contributed financially.

Several have been saved and eighteen people were baptized in water. The first Board members were appointed by Pastor Holomis. They were Glen Ellingson, Gordon Gibbs, Wes Lawrence, Howard Sinclair, Bob Stewart. About fifteen families began this pioneer work with Pastor Holomis.

Children's Church is conducted each Sunday morning and Junior Church in the evening. Christian Service Brigade was started in 1981.

Come visit this pioneer church when in Edmonton.

EDMONTON
HIGHWAY CHRISTIAN CENTRE
(Formerly Highway Chapel)

Mrs. Hazel Opheim and her son, Mervin, felt that they should start another church in Edmonton, so they spoke to Rev. R. W. Taitinger and the Board of the Edmonton Pentecostal Tabernacle (now Central Pentecostal Tabernacle). The Tabernacle pastor and board gave their approval and one thousand dollars. Then they received the District approval from Rev. S. R. Tilton plus a thousand dollars. Rev. Tilton told them to look for a spot on the south side near the Calgary highway. At 10436 63 Avenue, Edmonton, they found a little old white church, which had a steeple. This little Catholic church had been deserted for at least six months. Windows were broken, dead birds were inside and the church needed a lot of cleaning. In February 1963, they purchased the lot and church for ten thousand dollars — a real bargain even at that time. Merv worked very hard, early and late, to have it ready for services that same month. His mother and friends helped to clean and make it ready. Cecil Packer, who had recently been saved at Edmonton Pentecostal Tabernacle, came by and asked Merv if he needed any help. This man, who had a trunk full of power tools, was a skilled carpenter/cabinet maker. He helped make cabinets, pews and more. During this time, Rev. S. R. Tilton approved the name, Highway Chapel, which Merv and Mrs. Opheim had chosen. Central gave their blessing for five families to become the nucleus for this church. At the first service, the attendance was less than a dozen. Dedication took place that same month. Present at the dedication of the little old white church were Rev. and Mrs. Opheim; Merv Opheim (now Peterson); Rev. R. W. (Bob) Taitinger, speaker; Murray Dempster; Rev. S. R. Tilton, District Superintendent; J. Shirley Johnson, soloist, and many others to fill the little church. After the dedication, Rev. and Mrs. Eugene Opheim became the pastors. Shortly after this, Merv left to serve the Lord elsewhere.

The early families and individuals included Mr. and Mrs. Earl Gray; Cecil Packer; Mrs. Pearson; Mrs. Mildred Erickson; Brother and Sister Depner; Adeline Drisner and her parents; Brother and Sister Ed Kalke; Art and Lucille Sader and Milo Melvin.

In a years time, it was obvious that this assembly needed a better building. In due time, the old church building was demolished, a basement was poured

and the newly purchased German Baptist Church, which had been the first German Pentecostal Church in Edmonton, was set on the foundation. At the same time a foyer was added. Dedication of this building took place about 1968. Rev. Mervin Peterson pastored for his father for three months, when he was not well. Rev. Eugene Opheim, who was also a teacher at Northwest Bible College, had a few students live in the basement of Highway Chapel. These young men helped out at Highway Chapel and they helped establish a coffee house on 104 Street. There was a real revival at this coffee house, for quite a group were converted. Through this group the outreach at Klondike Days was started. Tony Salerno and Barry McGuire, from the United States, brought the Agape Force with them. They ministered very effectively at this outreach. The Coffee House at Klondike Days was right on the mid-way. At least one hundred were saved and many of them helped in the outreach. A number of these converts became part of the Agape Force and travelled across America. L. Harewood was youth pastor or leader. This outreach continues today with Central Tabernacle, Evangel and others involved. The Opheims left about July 1976.

Pastor and Mrs. Dave Lagore succeeded the Opheims. Highway Chapel's name was changed to Highway Christian Centre. During the Lagores ministry, the sanctuary was enlarged, a new foyer and office addition were added to what was the back of the church before. The sanctuary now has a balcony. The addition and changed sanctuary were dedicated to the Lord on May 10, 1981. Those present and taking part were Rev. Kenneth Bunting, Assistant District Superintendent; Rev. Ken Bombay, Guest Speaker; the Solovij Sisters, guest singers. Many others came to help make the day special.

Highway Christian Centre's motto is "Where People Enjoy Christianity." It appears that they do just that.

EDMONTON
KILLARNEY PENTECOSTAL CHURCH

Killarney Pentecostal Church was planned by the Lord. Reverend R. J. White approached Al Forsythe at Sylvan Lake Camp. He asked Al if he would consider starting a church in North Edmonton. The Lord had prepared Al's heart for this for Al had been looking to the Lord for His direction in his life. Unknown to either of them, the Lord had laid the need for a church in the northern part of Edmonton on the hearts of a few Pentecostal people in that part of Edmonton. Lillian Kuhn phoned Shirley Morsch to tell her that Al Forsythe was wanting to start a work in this northern part of the city. The Morsches made arrangements for Al and Bev Forsythe to meet the folks that were interested in starting this church. Present at the Edwin Morsch home at 12939-102 Street were Edwin and Shirley Morsch, Merle and Norma Bigam, Jean Taniguchi, Noli Abaya, Al and Bev Forsythe. At this meeting the board of trustees was elected — A. G. Forsythe, Edwin Morsch, Merle Bigam. Shirley Morsch became the first Sunday School superintendent. It was decided to have the services in Killarney Junior High School on Ninety-first Street and One hundred and thirty-second Avenue, across from the present church. On March 21, 1965, they had their first Sunday School and morning service. There were twenty-three in Sunday School that morning.

Mothers' Day Service 1966 in Killarney Junior High School.

At the first meeting in the school even more had joined the group. Among them, who came then and within the months that followed to the end of the year, were Blaine and Deanna Carruthers, Alf and Gertrude Schalm with Becky, Mr. and Mrs. Ken Crosby, Miss Sharon Wannamaker, Dr. and Mrs. Kenlin, Mrs. Beryl Adams, Mr. and Mrs. Haimila, Mr. and Mrs. Meachem, Mr. and Mrs. John Strilesky, Barbara Knudsen, Mr. and Mrs. Petry, Mrs. Marcenko, Mrs. Atkinson, Don Forsythe, Mrs. Saramaga, the Austads, plus the group that met at the Morsch home in the beginning. These names were on a Sunday School list as part of the adult class or as teachers. We were fortunate to have a number of Bible School graduates (Pastor Forsythe, Edwin and Shirley Morsch, Alf Schalm), undergraduate Ken Crosby, and a number of school teachers (Miss Taniguchi, Miss Abaya, Alf Schalm and Shirley Morsch) which helped a great deal in staffing our Sunday School. Other good teachers in the Sunday School at that time were Blaine and Deanna Carruthers, Dr. Kenlin and Miss Sharon Wannamaker.

Later Joe and Marion Young joined the assembly. They were a great help too. Joe became Assistant Sunday School Superintendent and later Superintendent. The first Sunday School Christmas Program

Mothers' Day 1966. Three babies were dedicated to the Lord. Left to right are Merle and Norma Bigam with Kevin; another couple with their son; Shirley and Edwin Morsch with Scott. Pastor Forsythe is giving Kevin to his mother.

was held December 19, 1965. They also had outings and gym nights for special activities, which were very enjoyable for both adult and child alike.

As Pastor Forsythe left the school after a morning service, God, by the eye of faith, caused him to see the finished church on a lot across the road — although they did not own it at that time. The church did buy that lot and had a sod-breaking ceremony May 15, 1966. About three months less than two years after the first meeting they moved into the basement and shortly after finished the sanctuary, seating two hundred. Dedication Day was April 30, 1967. This church was built with the pastor as the builder with volunteer labour from the church and other Pentecostal men from the city.

The congregation has never ceased to grow. About four years later they doubled the size of the church. Now they own three houses and lots next to the church and have plans for expansion. Most of all they appreciated the continued flow of divine presence and worship in the services and the spirit of love that prevailed in the congregation.

Over the years they were blessed with several good assistants — some of whom, were Reverend Rhondo Thomas, Reverend Gary Lindberg, Reverend Peter Cuke, Reverend Colin Wellard, Reverend Bob Norcross. The present associate is Reverend Ron Steinbrenner, the pastor's son-in-law.

The building programs were completed by the workers in the congregation. It was a means of fel-

Killarney Pentecostal Church

lowship and communication. God moved on their behalf many times. God has blessed and granted many healings.

Love is the Key at Killarney. John 17:21, paraphrased says, "When people see you love one another, they will believe I am the Christ." Love is also the Key to Evangelism.

Pastor and Mrs. A. G. Forsythe have pastored Killarney Assembly for over seventeen years.

Among those, who attended Bible College and/or entered the ministry(*), are D. Bruce Haddock, Sharolyn Lawrence, Terry Rankel, Harry Wannamaker, *David Wells.

They believe for continued growth and blessing in the days before them.

EDMONTON
PEOPLE'S PENTECOSTAL CHURCH

During class, one of the teachers at Northwest Bible College mentioned that a Baptist church was for sale. D. Sunderland and L. Hueppelsheuser prayed about it and felt led of the Lord to look into the possibility of purchasing it. Working in conjunction with Reverend J. C. Cooke and Reverend R. W. Taitinger, they proceeded to have it appraised for soundness by Mr. Al Carruthers. They then contacted the District Superintendent. The Urban Planning Commission was contacted and the possibility of opening a church was cleared with them. They put in a bid of twenty-five thousand dollars cash and this bid was accepted with possession date being May 20, 1967. This was a centennial project. The church was situated on the corner of Ninety-third Street and One Hundred Eight Avenue. It was built in 1912, a brick shell with a concrete foundation, seating three hundred seventy-five, including a balcony. Also there

was Sunday School space downstairs. The church was fully equipped and ready for immediate use. It had hand-carved rounded pews in good condition. It contained a pipe organ, a grand piano and three other pianos. The asking price was sixty-five thousand dollars, however, their purchase price was twenty-five thousand dollars. Bonds were issued with six percent interest paid on them, payable at the end of each year. The Board of Directors were: Reverend R. W. Taitinger, Reverend J. C. Cooke, Reverend L. Anderson, John Eastman, Gerry Walters, Eldon Johnson, David Cooke. Laurie Hueppelsheuser and Dennis Sunderland were co-pastors. The Dedication opening was on Sunday, May 21, 1967, with Reverend The Honorable P. A. Gaglardi, Minister of Highways in B.C., as guest speaker.

In September 1971 People's Day Care was started and was closed in September 1973.

In March 1972 group homes were started. Many young people, who came to know Jesus as their Saviour, had no place to call home or for some reason were unable to live there. Boys' and girls' houses were started. The main purpose was to provide a home with a Christian atmosphere where counsel, guidance and love were abundantly available.

In May 1972 the first Coffee-house was opened. Also in May 1972, Dave Townsend joined the staff of People's Church.

In June 1973 a full time office administrator, Paul Armfield, joined the staff.

In September 1973 the Covenant Community Training Centre (Kindergarten) was started. In September 1975 the Training Centre was enlarged to include grades one to twelve. Mr. Jim Ashton was Vice-pincipal.

In September 1976, Better Way, a twenty-four hour counselling service was started. Approximately eighty volunteers handled the phone. As many as four hundred fifty calls have been received in one month.

In July 1977 Community Catering was started but was closed. Also in July 1977 their first missionary couple, Dan and Mardie MacTavish were sent to Mexico.

In August 1977 the original People's Church was sold for ninety-five thousand dollars. In October 1977 the new church at 11205-101 Street, Edmonton, was dedicated.

In November 1978 twenty-six point seven acres were purchased at One Hundred Fifty-sixth Street and St. Albert Trail for future expansion. Also in November 1978 Jeff Jewett joined the staff as full time youth minister.

"Praise the Lord for He hath done great things."

EDMONTON
SPANISH PENTECOSTAL CHURCH

Pablo Kot came from Argentina. He was youth leader for Reverend Peter Kerychuk at the Ukrainian Temple for two years. During this time the Spanish people began attending the services.

In 1979 Pastor Pablo Kot began conducting Spanish services in two or three different homes. Then they moved to the Ukrainian Temple for a Saturday evening service and a Tuesday afternoon service.

They were looking and praying for a place, where they could have services on Sunday. In August 1981 God answered their prayers. They were able to rent a church hall at 6110 Fulton Road, Edmonton.

In April 1981 they held a water baptismal service, when eight people were baptized in water.

In October 1981 they became part of the Pentecostal Assemblies of Canada in Alberta. They had the official opening on October 31 and November 1, 1981, with Reverend I. Roset and Reverend J. Mac-Knight as special speakers. God has blessed the Spanish church. Many have been saved, filled with the Holy Spirit and healed.

On Sundays, they have Sunday School, morning service and evening service. They also conduct a Wednesday evening service. Families who come from South America are happy to find a place, where they can worship God in their own language.

EDSON
BETHEL PENTECOSTAL TABERNACLE

The first Pentecostal services in Edson were held in Reid's new storage house in the early 1920's with Pastor Stillton. In 1924, Mr. Reid needed the place to store the flour for his bakery, so the congregation moved to the Full Gospel Mission on Main Street where the Commadore Hotel is now located.

Then in 1928, the men started construction on the first church building on Fourth Avenue and Fifty-first Street. Mr. Reid and Mr. Holman did a great part of the work. In 1958, the church building was sold and moved to Peers and the present church basement was constructed under the leadership of Pastor Les Halliwell. Services were held in the basement until the log structure of the present church was completed. Work on the logs started in the summer of 1962, and was completed and dedicated in the summer of 1963.

A small parsonage which was across the street from the church was moved there in 1928. It housed the pastors until 1973, when it was sold for twelve thousand dollars.

Some of the founding families and faithful families throughout the years were: Mr. and Mrs. John

Pastor and Mrs. Clare Scratch

Reid; Mr. and Mrs. Holman; Mrs. Davidage; Mr. and Mrs. Davis; Mrs. Cooper; Mr. and Mrs. Simons; Mrs. Kassa; Mr. and Mrs. Street; Mrs. McLeod; Mrs. Tran; Mrs. Letwenuk; Mrs. Foster; Mrs. Trydal; Mrs. Newington; Mr. and Mrs. Bill MacDonald.

Pastors who ministered in Edson were: Pastor Stillton (1920-1925); Clare Scratch (1925-1927); Pastor Knight (1928-1931); Bob Moffat (1931-1932); Ruth Nystrom and Hazel Coulter (1932-1935); Morris Olson (1935-1940); Pastor Stronstad (1941-1945); Albert Schindel (1945-1948); Ernest Martz (1948-1950); Ed Miller (1950-1952); Les Halliwell (1952-1965); F. D. Carruthers (1965-1967); Jim McAlister (1968-1970); Peter Cuke (1971-1973); Dave Haimila (1974); Jack Hood (1975-1978); Spencer Bradbury (1979-1980); George Feller (1980-   ).

Mrs. Phyllis Trydal tells of her early days in 1928 when her father filled in preaching between pastors. She particularly remembers one Sunday when her father was to preach. They came out of their farm house and were going to get into their car when, to their surprise and also disgust, their baby goats had climbed up on the canvas roof of the car and fallen through. They rode to church that morning with a

The Women's Group of the Nineteen Thirties.

"hole-y" roof and it remained "hole-y" until her father sewed it together again.

Before the building of the present upper log structure, services were held in the basement for some six or seven years. Because of the layout of the building, a cubicle had to be built on top of the basement for the entrance. You had to climb seven or eight steps, then into the cubicle and down another flight. This cubicle, which certainly didn't add to the appearance of the basement structure, was a topic of conversation around town.

During the building of the present church, volunteer labour was very hard to come by, but a very faithful volunteer, Mr. William MacDonald was always on the job. When the pastor, at that time, Reverend L. B. Halliwell, would look out of the parsonage window at 6:30 A.M., he would see Mr.

Sunday School. Rev. Albert Schindel, pastor, is marked with an x.

MacDonald at the church, burning everything that wasn't tied down, to keep the area clean. He was soon nicknamed E. B. Eddy, after those famous matches.

Mrs. Corrie Halliwell reports: "During our evangelistic meetings in 1963 with Paul and Dorothy Olson from Minneapolis, we had some great meetings. We were still in the little old wood church, and we were packed out, having to put seats in the Sunday School rooms at the back to accommodate people. There was one marvelous answer to prayer and many decisions were made."

Log Church built in 1963.

Dedication of the Log church, the Bethel Pentecostal Church, in 1963. Rev. S. R. Tilton is at the pulpit. Rev. John Morsch is at the front right.

Other evangelists were Hilda and Minnie Mueller and Reverend Ken Bombay.

Those who attended Northwest Bible College in Edmonton were: Joyce Collin; Judy Collin; Gordon Foster; Bonnie Reid; Helen Shand; Pat Sloman; Robert Strachan.

45

EMPRESS
EMPRESS PENTECOSTAL
TABERNACLE

The events which led to the establishment of the Empress Pentecostal Tabernacle were meetings held in the Mayfield Community Hall, about ten miles north of Empress. George and Phil Hawtin, Jack Nash, and Pastor and Mrs. Holdsworth from Oyen held services there in 1935. Following this, some of those, who had been meeting there, wanted services in town. Hence, Jack Nash encouraged Mrs. Pearl Knutson, who had attended Star City Bible College, to come to Empress in 1937 to start the work. The first services were held in the Clarkson house, with Pearl Knutson until 1939. Some of the founding families and main families throughout the years were Mrs. Bentz, Mr. and Mrs. Robert Booker Sr., Mr. and Mrs. Ken Booker, Mr. and Mrs. Bob Booker Jr., Mr. and Mrs. Chris Flemmer, Mr. and Mrs. Lyle Gill, Mr. and Mrs. Emil Henning, Mr. and Mrs. John Habich, Mrs. John Klipperts, Mrs. Milton Leach, Mr. and Mrs. Peter Loose, Mr. and Mrs. John Martin, Mr. Don McCurdy, Mr. and Mrs. Oldridge, Mrs. Philips, Mr. and Mrs. Roy Rivers.

Sunday School sometime when Rhinds were pastoring.

Jack Nash took over the meetings from 1939 to 1941. In February 1941 the meetings moved from the Clarkson house to the Empress Express newspaper office, where they continued till the fall of 1949, at which time the basement of the present church was sufficiently completed for services.

A small parsonage next to the church was purchased for the price of two hundred dollars in De-

cember of 1943. Additions and improvements have made it a very comfortable three-bedroom home.

Pastor John Ehrhardt ministered from 1942 to 1945. In 1945 the first Daily Vacation Bible School was held. Mr. Moore and Mr. Churchill were in charge. In a campaign conducted by Reverend Winston I. Nunes in 1945 the young people of the assembly were stirred and blessed.

Miss Mabel Hyssop ministered from 1945 to 1948, Rev. John Morsch (part of 1948), and Reverend and Mrs. Jim Tyler pastored from 1949 to 1950.

In 1951, the main sanctuary was completed.

The following pastors ministered from 1951 to 1970: Pastor James Robertson (1951-1952), Pastor Floyd Schwindt (1952-1955), Pastor Angus McClain (1956-1958), Pastor Glenn Rhind (1958-1970).

Brother Don McCurdy tells of the Postmaster Dave Lush coming to church and getting saved in the early nineteen hundred and sixties. A couple of years later, he had a vision of heaven. Three days later, Brother Lush, who had been in good health, went to be with the Lord.

During the Rhind's ministry once during a church service, a bat flew into the church and landed in the hair of Sister Rhind, as she was playing the piano. She calmly got up and walked to the door, where she shook it out of her hair, and then resumed playing the piano.

The Tabernacle is on the right; the parsonage is next door to the Tabernacle.

Sister Velma Booker relates two stories about the Rhinds and their "animal friends." A window had been broken in the parsonage basement. When Sister Rhind when downstairs, she thought something was wrong with the hot water tank as it was making a rattling noise. Upon going to investigate, Brother Rhind discovered a coiled rattlesnake which had taken advantage of the open window. He quickly disposed of the intruder!

Pastor Doug Lindskoog ministered from November 1970 to May 1973; Pastor Brian Hall from May 1973 to December 1975, Pastor Ken Sumners from May 1976 to August 1977.

In 1977, work was begun on an addition to the church and completed in 1979. The Pastor's study, nursery, and bathrooms were a real asset to the church.

Pastor George Feller came to minister in January 1978 and left in 1980. Reverend and Mrs. Keith Bishop followed the Fellers.

Among those, who attended Bible College and/or entered the ministry (*), are Bernice Dodd (now Harding), Donna (Dony) Gill (now Habich), *Jo Lynn Gill (wife of Reverend Gary Lindberg), Paulette E. Gill (now Parker), Donna Loose, Don McCurdy.

FAIRVIEW
EVANGEL CENTRE PENTECOSTAL CHURCH

In the spring of 1956, Reverend and Mrs. Charles Howey arrived in Fairview to begin a Pentecostal witness in that town. Reverend Howey was engaged in construction work to help support his family. Reverend Nettleton and young people from Peace River Assembly came every other Saturday to help in street meetings. At first services were held in the Women's Institute Hall and later in two rented homes. About 1958, the Alberta District assisted them to obtain a large home, that could be used for church as well as living quarters. Among the first families to attend the services were the Banners, also, a building foreman and his wife from the Dunvegan Bridge. Fairview Assembly took part in a joint camp meeting with Full Gospel Churches in the Grimshaw area.

In 1959 the Howeys left Fairview because of ill health. They were succeeded by Mr. and Mrs. Glen Murphy. They also had services in Hines Creek and Worsley. In 1967 Mr. A. E. Tobin of Calgary took charge of the work. He remained for the next four years. He, too, had an outreach at Hines Creek and Worsley. Pastor and Mrs. Paul Slemming came after Pastor Tobin.

After Reverend and Mrs. Slemming left, local families continued house meetings and Sunday School. Among these families were Ted and Fern Gardecki, Harold and Lois Craig, Mr. and Mrs. C. MacLainePont.

The local families conducted services in the Rochan Building. In the fall of 1975, the Assembly called Reverend D. Lindskoog. During his ministry a church was built and dedicated in May 1979.

In April 1981, Reverend and Mrs. David Quigley came to lead this growing congregation.

One of the young people who attended Northwest Bible College was Mary Skrlac.

FORESTBURG
FORESTBURG PENTECOSTAL ASSEMBLY

The Pentecostal work in Forestburg began when Reverend and Mrs. Arthur Rosenau returned from the mission field in Kenya. Reverend Rosenau taught on a shop circuit with the Killam School Division in September 1957. The Rosenaus settled in Forestburg and travelled twenty-five miles to attend the Alliance Pentecostal Church where Reverend and Mrs. Steve Holomis were pastoring. The Rosenaus started a Bible study and prayer group in their home with three elderly gentlemen, Albert James, Julius Brickman and Merton Shillinglaw, attending.

After one year the Rosenaus moved to Edmonton where Arthur attended the University of Alberta for thirteen months obtaining his degree in education. They returned to Forestburg where Arthur became the Vice-Principal of the school under Principal Harry Ewasiuk in September 1959.

Bible studies continued in the Rosenau home and Reverend and Mrs. Don Hopkinson, pastors of the Killam church, came to assist in the meetings. Early in 1960 Sunday afternoon services were started in the Forestburg school. The meetings were well attended. A young couple out of Bible School, Mr. and Mrs. Larry Trodden, were called to help in the work. They stayed six months.

The Art Rosenau Family taken in 1967

Early in 1961 a piece of land was bought and the old United Church building which was being used as a storage facility for fertilizer was purchased for seven hundred dollars. With the help of Clifford

Larson of the Killam Assembly, the old church was moved on to its new site and completely renovated. The old building assumed its original purpose of feeding the souls of men.

At Sunnyside Camp that summer the Rosenaus persuaded Ken Ness, who had graduated in the spring, to come and pastor the new Pentecostal church at Forestburg. Ken and Velma were married in September and came to pastor in October. Work on the living quarters in the basement moved rapidly and by Christmas 1961 the young couple were installed in their cozy new quarters. All the work on the church and the parsonage was done after working hours and the men of the assembly still recall the good times they had together building pews and gluing down the linoleum. They laugh as they remember the twelve gallons of adhesive that were used to glue down the linoleum and how, when one strip did not line up properly, Reverend Ken Ness took off his shoes and socks and walked barefooted through the glue to the other end of the room to try and straighten it out. The men put on the crack filler in such generous gobs that the ladies of the church who sanded it off, vowed they would never help with crack filling again.

Some of the members of the fledgling assembly were the Shultzs, Roths, Siegfrieds, Vanderwoudes, Shoups, Dietrichs, Descheemakers, Wiedmers, Jones, Abe James, Julius Brickman, Merton Shillinglaw, Ken and Velma Ness and the Rosenaus.

The Rosenaus left Forestburg in August 1963 to teach in Wainwright and in 1968 they returned to Kenya. Reverend and Mrs. Ken Ness pastored until 1965.

Reverend and Mrs. Bill Lagore pastored from 1965 to 1969. During this time Reverend Lagore built a parsonage. Others who pastored were Dale Archibald; Reverend Virgil Lawrence came for one service on each Sunday, while he pastored Alliance; Reverend Jim Smart, who also ministered once on each Sunday, while pastoring Alliance; Reverend Arnold Dyck; then there was no pastor for several months. Reverend and Mrs. Gordon Powell were called to pastor. The Powells conducted childrens meetings and produced the Singing Christmas Tree. This performance filled the church to capacity and this program was also presented to the Senior Citizens Lodge. After the Powells resigned, Bob Bidwell and his wife became pastors in 1982.

With the closing of the Pentecostal Church in Alliance in 1973, the families from Alliance became part of the Forestburg assembly.

Among those, who attended Bible College, was Inga Wiedmer.

FORT McMURRAY
PENTECOSTAL ASSEMBLY OF FORT McMURRAY

In 1975, Pastor and Mrs. Reg. Kublik held meetings in their house trailer. As the group grew, they held them in the Birchwood Junior High School library.

From 1977 to 1979, Pastor Paul Thomas ministered. Sunday School was a little larger than the church services at this time. The Capitol Hill Assembly, in Calgary, sold this assembly a Sunday school bus for one dollar. They worked diligently to build up the work.

The next pastors were Rev. and Mrs. A. Werbiski, who came in June 1979. The population at this time was 26,000. Services continued in the Junior High School, using the stage and, within a few months, the gymnasium. Much of the growth was due to Pentecostal families moving in from Newfoundland (about half of the congregation) and most were oil sand workers. The population had grown to over 30,000. As a result of all this growth, Fort McMurray became a city on September 1, 1980. By this time, the services were held in the Thickwood Heights Elementary School. The Sunday school averaged 160 in eleven classes. Attendance has been up close to 200. A good number were saved, in one month two whole families were converted. 1980 graduates of Northwest Bible College, Don and Lorraine Richmond, came to assist in May of that year. They were involved mainly with the youth. The youth group had increased to fifty members and the regular services averaged about 180 to 200 in attendance. The congregation bought property in the Dickinfield area. They are building as they can afford it. In February or March of 1982, Rev. Werbiski reported that they were putting the shingles on the roof and they did not owe a penny. Ernie Hanson was the building chairman.

The Forestburg Congregation

The church here is active and is looking forward to continuing to serve the Lord.

Among those, who attended Bible college, were Susan Mercer, *Ernie Hanson, Richard Yaceyko.

Rev. Werbiski resigned in the spring of 1982. Finley Burt is the pastor at the time of writing.

FORT SASKATCHEWAN
FORT SASKATCHEWAN CHRISTIAN CENTRE

Several Bible students had endeavored to work in this area prior to 1977, but no Assembly was established. In November 1977, Rev. Ivar Roset, District Superintendent, and Rev. A. Lindoff, Presbyter, had mentioned to Rev. George Richmond the need to open a work in Fort Saskatchewan. In February 1978, Rev. George and Linda Richmond came to the Fort to pioneer this Pentecostal Assembly, which was an answer to prayer, as several families had been praying for this to happen.

Rev. George and Linda Richmond

The North West Bible College Students from Edmonton generously gave of their time distributing pamphlets in the community announcing the new work. There were approximately 26 in attendance for the first Sunday Evening Service on February 26, 1978, in the Pope John Catholic School. Since the school was not available in the summer months, in July and August, the services were held in the St. George's Anglican Church. In September 1978, they moved into the Old Golf and Country Clubhouse where Sunday School and Morning Worship began. As the congregation continued to grow it was necessary to relocate so in May 1979, they moved to the second floor of the New Professional Building, which is their present church home. In February 1980, the congregation purchased a parcel of land for future development of their church. July 1981 saw the church incorporated and named Fort Saskatchewan Christian Centre.

Some of the founding families were: Irvin and Grace Church, Ed and Rose Cymbaluk, Jim and Elaine Glasman, Mrs. Tillie Chwok, Judy and Shana Dumont, Ed and Nora Bailey, Lucy Schleuter, Carolyn and Guy Paradis. Others who came later were Gerry Zdrill, Dan O'Conner, Don Rempel and family, Martin and Katie Suelzle, Ernie Cowpersmith, Wendy Thate and Mrs. Jean McMahon.

Weekly Prayer and Bible Studies began in homes and later moved to the rented church facilities. A need for Prayer and Bible Study at Gibbons was made known. Robert and Sonja Hehl responded and are now in charge of that ministry. A Bible Study was held for a time in Lamont. Pastor Richmond was also very involved counselling prisoners from the Fort Saskatchewan Correctional Institute. Many contacts were made through families and individuals who phoned for assistance. Other contacts were made through the television program, 100 Huntley Street. Fellowship suppers were organized, and a number of people came to the Lord through this outreach.

Among the ministries of the church are the Christian Service Brigade, Pioneer Girls, Women's Ministries, an orchestra of guitars, accordians and drums.

On September 30, 1981, Pastor and Mrs. Richmond resigned to go to Altona, Manitoba. Rev. and Mrs. Gordon Powell came to pastor this Assembly in November 1981. Lester and Francis Lundall are assisting in the ministry.

Fort Saskatchewan Christian Centre continues to grow and contributes to the spiritual welfare of a growing community and surrounding area.

Among those, who attended Bible College and/or entered the ministry (*), are Millie Glockner, Chris Padlewski, *Don Richmond, Alfred White.

GIBBONS
GIBBONS PENTECOSTAL CHURCH

While attending the Fort Saskatchewan Christian Centre in 1980, Robert and Sonja Hehl took charge of the Fort Saskatchewan outreach prayer and Bible study in Gibbons. Because it was an outreach of the Centre, the Hehls worked in conjunction with Pastor Richmond. They continued this arrangement with the next pastor, Rev. Gordon Powell, until the group became a church on its own and affiliated with the Pentecostal Assemblies of Canada District of Alberta and the Northwest Territories (MacKenzie District) on May 31, 1982. The name of this Assembly is Gibbons Pentecostal Church.

GRANDE CACHE FULL GOSPEL ASSEMBLY

Grande Cache, a mining town, was one of the new towns established in 1966. It is situated in the foothills where there is a vast coal resource. In the nineteen hundred and seventies Reverend and Mrs. Ernie Siggelkow came to minister the Pentecostal message in this area. A group gathered together to worship the Lord, among whom were Mr. and Mrs. Barry McAmmond, Mr. and Mrs. Bernie McAmmond, Mr. and Mrs. Bernie Morris, Mr. and Mrs. Gunnar Samuelson. The Siggelkows remained for two years. The group continued to serve the Lord with the Baptist Church for the next eight years.

In February 1981, several people, who felt the need of a full Gospel message in Grande Cache, invited Reverend Roset, District Superintendent, for a meeting. As a result a Pentecostal Assembly was formed. Mr. Lloyd from England, who was visiting his son, ministered for two or three months.

In November 1981, Reverend and Mrs. Fred Hunter came as interim pastors. Services were held in the Sheldon Coates Elementary School with access to as many rooms as were needed. New people came to the services. Souls were saved. By then they had a membership of forty people. In a church service, approximately eighty people would be in attendance. This could have been well over one hundred, but due to shift work in the mines, everyone could not come on the same Sunday.

Women's Ministries were started. A Young People's group, under the leadership of Guy Shultz, was organized.

The Hunters remained until Easter 1982. Lester and Francis Lundall, of South Africa, came to pastor in April 1982.

May God continue to make Grande Cache Full Gospel Assembly a lighthouse in that mountainous area of Alberta.

GRANDE PRAIRIE EVANGEL ASSEMBLY OF GRANDE PRAIRIE

Evangel Assembly of Grande Prairie began as a burden in the hearts of Norman and Phyllis Labrentz for the street people of that city. The wave of the hippy craze peaked in the summer of 1972. Five families, who shared this concern, joined in prayer meetings and made the decision to step out in faith. They rented an old funeral home building and began a coffee-house ministry. The first regular church service took place on Sunday, November 12, 1972, with a two-fold purpose: (a) to meet the spiritual needs of the founding families and (b) to create a comfortable church atmosphere for the street and problem people.

It was a very humble beginning with around thirty present those first Sundays and a few dozen from the street who joined in the free coffee house. However, in a few weeks, the true concern for people brought acceptance. Attendance began to increase rapidly. Around the first of the new year, the threat of the sale of the building forced the Assembly decision to purchase it. In April of 1973, Evangel Assembly became the owners of the building. Walls and partitions were removed to enlarge the chapel area. Special evangelistic meetings swelled the attendance to capacity.

The coffee-house ministry continued to expand as well. The new converts went out, on to the streets, witnessing and bringing in others. Many of these early converts had no home, so they were invited to live in the building with the Labrentz family. There they were trained as workers.

The "ministry of concern" became known and workers began to minister to those involved with suicide attempts and drug problems. It was the local R.C.M.P., who began referring to this ministry as Teen Challenge. The name caught on, until the church was better known in the community as Teen Challenge. The coffee-house ministry adopted the name and it is known today as the Teen Challenge Coffeehouse.

As the years went by, it became very evident that the old building could not accommodate any more growth. In 1976 the congregation made an in-depth study of both Evangel Assembly's future, and the projected growth and needs of Grande Prairie. After much prayer, it was felt by all the congregation that the work was divinely placed in the downtown core of the city, with a mission to continue to reach out to the troubled segment of society. The church quickly purchased the two empty lots next door — lots which God held back from sale — for their expansion. Architects were engaged to draw up plans to meet city approval. July 1977 saw the beginning of the basement excavation.

There were a number of obstacles to overcome, such as arranging the finances, waiting for steel and a lack of skilled tradesmen. Grande Prairie suddenly found itself in a boom-town situation and experienced problems of supply. After many seasons of prayer followed by victories, the new church home of Evangel Assembly was dedicated on November 11, 1978. That dedication service saw the building filled with a crowd of about five hundred including many out-of-town friends. Present were Reverend Ivar Roset, the Alberta District Superintendent, and guest speaker, Rev. Marvin Forseth of New Westminster, B.C.. Reverend Forseth was born and raised in the Grande Prairie area.

In the two years following, the ministry staff was enlarged to include Assistant Pastor and Mrs. Bruce Moffat, and office secretary, Miss Inez Nystedt, as well as Pastor and Mrs. Labrentz. In the eight years of the assembly's existence, nearly three hundred new converts have been baptized in water. There have been seventy-five marriages and a great number of 'marriage enrichment' services. Many of the "hippies" got married after their conversion and those, who were married by a Justice of the Peace, asked for God's blessings upon their homes. Pastor Labrentz has been involved in marriage counselling and has seen the restoration of a number of separated and divorced situations. God heals not only broken bodies, but also broken homes.

Tent meetings contributed greatly to the spiritual maturing of the young converts. In the summer of 1974, a tent-truck unit was purchased. A fifteen-member team did house-to-house visitation, afternoon children's church and evening evangelistic services. They ministered that summer with tent meetings spending a week each in Fairview, Fox Creek, Cherry Point, and Grande Prairie. This was repeated the next three summers including other locations such as Peace River, Silver Valley, Valleyview, High Prairie, Dawson Creek, and Fort St. John. A faith venture saw the tent set up in 1975 in the Roman Catholic church yard at Falher — a community that was ninety-nine percent French Catholic. A charismatic prayer group was born in those meetings, and it continues to this day. The meetings were largely responsible for encouraging the Fairview Assembly and opening Savanna Lighthouse Assembly in Silver Valley area. This was in addition to strengthening local churches in other areas. The first workers of these new churches were young people of the tent team, who stayed behind to lead the converts in being established in the Lord. Pastor and Mrs. Labrentz continue to have a fruitful ministry in Grande Prairie.

Among those who attended Bible College and/or entered the ministry (*), were Sam Lima, *Bruce Moffat, Violet Nysted, Linda Robbins, Linda Wiebe, Wilfred Wiebe.

HIGH PRAIRIE
HIGH PRAIRIE CHRISTIAN CENTRE (formerly High Prairie Pentecostal Church)

In July of 1963, Pastor and Mrs. George Lagore moved to High Prairie. Because difficulty was encountered in finding both living accommodation and meeting facilities, it was decided to begin immediately to build a church. On July 25, 1963 the basement was dug and work commenced on the foundation. The main structure and the roof were completed in early September. The first service was held in the basement on September 8, 1963 with thirty people present. The back part of the basement was used for living accommodation. Stan Lagore spent the year 1963-1964 assisting Pastor George Lagore in the work. The Peace River Pentecostal Tabernacle assisted in opening this assembly.

The Pentecostal Church built in 1963.

Pastor George Lagore also was the principal of a school in High Prairie while he was pastoring the assembly.

The church was visited with two gracious moves of God. In 1964 and 1965, many new people came into the church fellowship and twenty people received the infilling of the Holy Spirit, most of them young people. In the nineteen hundred and seventies another move of God was evidenced which paralleled the Charismatic renewal. Many people were saved during this time.

Pastor Lagore resigned in the summer of 1981. Peter Hudel followed the Lagores. He pastored the church in 1981 and 1982.

HINTON
HINTON CHRISTIAN CENTRE
(formerly Hinton Pentecostal Tabernacle)

Don Schneider and Dwain Carruthers arrived in Hinton in May 1958. Don found work at the Imperial Lumber Company and Dwain worked on construction. They began Sunday school in their cabin at Cabin Court with about half a dozen children. In June, they began holding Sunday school in an old empty school in the Old Town. On their first Sunday there, they had about twenty-five children, mostly from the Cecelia Park area, but, of course, attendance went up and down like a yo-yo.

Preparing for the Water Baptismal Service.

In June, when Rev. S. R. Tilton came out, the decision was made to purchase the two lots, where the church now stands. They made plans at that time to bring the Portable Tabernacle from Evansburg. The Town of Hinton agreed to let them place it on the lots temporarily. So in July, they had it towed in by a Mr. Anderson, with many flat tires on the way. It was finally settled on the second lot of the property.

They began Sunday School and Services as soon as it was settled on the property. Mrs. Greanya Sr. was the first adult to come to services. Esther Tews came in September to teach school and was a co-worker, organist and Sunday School teacher. She was a great help and encouragement. Verda Anderson and her four or five children were the next family to come. The Denis Roy family came soon after and were strong supporters, in those early days, with finances and moral support. The Schneiders did not think they would have made it without them. Then,

of course, Mrs. Karl Borzel and family began to come near the same time. They did a lot of Sunday School visitation.

Dwain Carruthers went back to school at the end of September. Don carried on the work on his own, until the following summer, when Shirley and Don were married. She came to share the ministry with him.

The basement of the Church was dug and footings poured in the summer of 1959. A crew of men poured the walls of the basement. By this time, Tom and Carol Skinner were part of the congregation and were helping the Schneiders. Karl Borzel laid the footings and helped them pour them. In fact, he did a lot of the work. Joe Vanderveer, also, helped pour the footings. With volunteer labour, they built a basement church with a suite for the pastor. The upper structure (shell and roof) were put up. Only the lower auditorium was finished.

The Schneiders' son, Trevor, was born in Hinton on June 12, 1960, when Nurse Madeline Rhodes was on duty.

On their final Sunday in Hinton, their basement church was packed and they had a record of over eighty in Sunday School. The Vic Wollens, one of the first Sunday School families, were there as usual. The Schneiders left to become the pastors at Sylvan Lake, in November 1962.

In mid November 1962, Rev. and Mrs. Virgil Lawrence arrived as the new pastors. They, too, lived in the basement suite.

The Christian Centre Board and Pastor Tollefson

The Ken Dafoe family was added to other already faithful families, so were Lil Debrinski and family, Elsie Flewwelling and family, the George Nicholson family. The board members were Tom Skinner and Denis Roy.

Under Rev. Lawrence the upper sanctuary was finished and dedicated September 21, 1965.

The Lawrences' farewell Sunday was September 28, 1965.

Under the Lawrences, the Sunday School had grown to ninety-nine. Brown Reynolds held a Kids Crusade with as many as two hundred and twenty-five attending.

Lester Markham, a young Christian university student, came to Hinton to work for the summer. While there he came to this Pentecostal Tabernacle. He had never been to a Pentecostal Church before so he walked past the church a couple of times and on the third trip past, a gentleman invited him to come in for service, which he did. Sunday School was still in session. He was impressed with the gusto and sincerity of the children's singing. He said to himself, "These children have more enthusiasm for Jesus than I do." He was "hooked." Through the summer, he grew closer and closer to the Lord again, as God dealt with him through the Word and by His Spirit. On Lester's last Sunday there, Pastor Lawrence challenged the congregation to become active in the Lord's work. At the end of that service, the folks gathered around him to sing God be with You. After they had sung and said a few words, Lester announced, nervously, that he would not be going back to university because he believed God was calling him to Bible school. So it was that Lester Markham did attend Bible school, entered the ministry and became one of our missionaries to Thailand. By that time he was married to a very lovely lady and had a son and a daughter. At the present time, the Markhams are pastoring in Calgary (1982).

Rev. and Mrs. R. L. Donnelly filled in from the Spring of 1974, until the new pastors, Rev. and Mrs. Kenneth Smith arrived. This was about two or three months. The Donnellys seem to have really enjoyed being with the congregation in Hinton.

The population in Hinton is quite transient. This affected attendance at the church. The church also went through some hard times. However, under the Smiths, the Lord increased the congregation again. An addition was added to the church and pews were donated by the Red Deer Church. The Art Rosenaus moved to Hinton; they were a real blessing.

Mrs. Smith started a Wee College. Those, who helped after the first year were Glenda Mitchell, Annette Allen.

Among those, who were really appreciated by the Smiths, were Marge Greanya and Bob and Anne Wood.

Other Ministers, who served this church, were Rev. Mike Bernadsky, Rev. Meloshinsky, Rev. Bill Lewis, Rev. Dennis Arnold, Del Young, Rev. Bowman.

The present pastor is Pastor Larry Tollefson who came on March 15, 1978. They, Larry, his wife, Gladys, and his family did not arrive with a bag of tricks, but came to be led of the Holy Spirit in leading this congregation. The Tollefsons have been experiencing a very rewarding ministry at Hinton. Many people have accepted the Lord as their own personal Saviour, many have discovered the power for Christian living is realized through the Baptism of the Holy Spirit. To help these Christians assume more leadership in the church, the Lay Leadership Institute program was used to educate and equip the lay people there. In the last four years, Pastor Tollefson has baptized eighty-five people upon the confession of their faith in Christ. Spiritual gifts are in operation there. Brother George Corris has been appointed an Elder in the Christian Centre. They also have five deacons on the Board. They also have a new Deacons in Training Program in order to train their young men for this important position and ministry. Pioneer Girls has an enrollment of fifty-five girls and thirteen leaders. Wee College is starting again this fall (1982). Men's Fellowship is going strong under Brother Rooks. These men are planning a 1982 big game hunt in the fall. The Christian Fellowship Banquets, every second month, have been a tremendous blessing. Many have been saved, healed and/or Baptized in the Holy Ghost or Holy Spirit.

The Christian Centre's main emphasis is "Build Bible Ministries." Pastor Tollefson is so full of enthusiasm for the work of God here, so grateful to God for the annointing on so many in his congregation. It is obvious that this church is on the move for God.

Among those, from this assembly, who have attended Bible college and/or entered the ministry (*), were Ken Bozel, Jim Flewwelling, Lois Flewwelling, Ed Greanya, Ken Griffiths, *Lester Markham and Charlie Neuman.

HUGHENDEN
HUGHENDEN PENTECOSTAL CHURCH

Most of the early settlers, who came to the area about 1909, were of Scandinavian origin. Many of these folks brought their faith in Christ with them. House meetings began even before 1918. Folks travelled as far as twenty miles by horse and buggy or sleigh. As automobiles began to make their appearance fellowship was extended to reach other villages. People from Amisk, Wainwright, Veteran, Metiskow and other points gathered for several days in tent meetings and in barns made ready for that purpose.

In the early nineteen hundred and thirties, a Reverend C. Peterson had tent meetings in the Gooseberry Hills, where people gathered from all around the

Beginning excavation for basement of the church, 1936.

area to worship the Lord. Reverend Peterson was instrumental in bringing Dr. John G. Lake to Hughenden to hold meetings in the Community Hall. Many were saved and healed. Mr. and Mrs. Ernie Dixon, who owned the blacksmith shop were saved. Mr. and Mrs. Archie Laforge were saved. Archie ran the pool hall in Hughenden, but he closed his business when he gave his heart to the Lord. Dr. Lake gave a prophetic warning to the people of Hughenden that unless they turned to God, disaster would come to their village. Sometime after the revival with Dr. Lake, a terrible fire broke out in the village. The hardware man set fire to his store, then shot himself. The village feared that it would be a total disaster. Dixon's blacksmith shop was in direct line of the fire. Mrs. Dixon went out to the roadway, prayed to God to intervene. The wind changed and the building was saved.

Cottage Meeting at the Holmstom Home, 1931.

In 1934 Reverend Ernie Robinson, then pastor of the Killam Assembly, had a burden for Hughenden. He commuted from Killam to hold services in Hughenden. In the spring of 1935 they moved there to take charge of the band of christians in that area. That summer Reverend Ernie Robinson and Rever-

end Clifford Nelson of Edmonton conducted successful meetings in a tent set up just north of the village. Several families were saved during this outreach. These new believers and other established christians desired to continue meeting.

The United Church was rented for a few months. Then services were moved to the Lumber Yard. The owner, Mr. R. Ekstrom, who with his wife had been two of the new converts, made his office available for services. When the office became too small, he offered the use of his shop. This was much appreciated, but it entailed a great deal of work getting the shop ready Saturday night for Sunday services.

Reverend Ernie Robinson invited the Alberta District to hold a summer camp at Czar Lake. This was the first camp meeting held in an area not near a church. Reverend A. G. Ward was the speaker. The camp meeting was a success both spiritually and financially. The charge per person was three dollars and fifty cents a day for food and lodging. At the close of the camp, there was a surplus of eight hundred dollars. It was understood that the host church would absorb any deficit so the profit went to the Hughenden Assembly. This was used to build a church in Hughenden.

Brother and Sister Ernie Robinson, who pastored possibly from 1935 to 1937. This picture was taken about 1944.

That fall local men dug the basement of this church. They used horses and large scoops drawn by horses. The building was to have log siding and measure twenty-six feet by forty-eight feet. The basement was finished and the congregation worshipped there that winter. By spring the building was completed. In May 1937 it was dedicated with Mr. Walker, caretaker of the Buffalo National Park at Wainwright, as special speaker.

Reverend Robinson pastored Amisk as well. In 1937 the Robinsons were called to the Pentecostal church, now Glad Tidings Pentecostal Church, in Victoria, British Columbia.

The fall of the same year, Reverend and Mrs. Harvey McAlister came to pastor. Sunday services were held in the afternoon in Amisk and in the evening at Hughenden. In the winter months prayer meetings were held in people's homes in the Amisk area as well as in the Hughenden area.

The first Hughenden business meeting recorded was November 26, 1937. The board members were R. Ekstrom; O. Peterson; O. Holmstrom; Secretary-Treasurer, Mrs. E. Dixon. Many charter members (R. Ekstrom, Mr. and Mrs. O. Peterson, Mr. and Mrs. O. Holmstrom, Mr. and Mrs. Pete Johnson, Mrs. Lindskoog, Mr. and Mrs. Matt Lund, Mr. Art Strandberg, Grandma Knutson, Mr. and Mrs. Ernie Dixon) have passed on to higher service. Still living are Albert Niles, Ernie Peterson, Eno and Alice Peterson, Clifford and Emma Knutson, Mrs. Art Strandberg (who for many years cooked at the Sylvan Lake Camp), Mr. Harvey Johnson, Mrs. R. Ekstrom, Mabel Broughton, Ellen Broughton, Dorea Lindskoog, Herbert Holmstrom, Lawrence and Dagny Lindskoog and others, who were children at that time. Some of these no longer live in Hughenden but are serving the Lord elsewhere.

The first baby in the Hughenden parsonage was Grace McAlister. While the McAlisters were waiting for this event in Wetaskiwin, Hazel Coulter (now Opheim) ministered, with Marjorie McAlister assisting as pianist. The McAlisters resigned June 26, 1939.

In the early days of Sylvan Lake Camp many young people as well as old came from Hughenden and Amisk in the back of Ole Carbol's truck. After being filled with the Holy Spirit, they returned home with a deep desire to serve the Lord.

Reverend and Mrs. Gunnar Gulbransen became the next pastors. They remained until 1945.

Financial records for the year 1940 show that the clergy were not in it for the money. Total revenue for the year was two hundred four dollars and fifty-one cents, expenses one hundred ninety-four dollars and fifteen cents, net income ten dollars and thirty-six cents. However God supplied the needs. Farmers from one area would supply the Pastor with milk, vegetables, meat, etc. for one week, the next week another group would bring in supplies. God truly blessed.

Part of the congregation with Rev. Wendell Lewis on the lower right. His wife is directly behind him.

In 1945, Amisk began having their own pastors.

Reverend and Mrs. Wendell Lewis pastored the Hughenden church for the next four and a half years. They had two children, Jean and Bill. Brother Lewis was excellent in horsemanship. He helped with the harvesting to supplement his income.

Following Reverend Lewis' resignation on June 22, 1949, Pastor H. Rosenke filled in very capably

Marjorie McAlister, Rev. and Mrs. Harvey C. McAlister with daughter, Grace.

until November, when Pastor and Mrs. R. J. White came from Vernon, B.C.. Their family consisted of Samuel, Gordon and Madeline.

Some improvements were made to the church building. The basement walls were straightened and reinforced, a new cement floor was poured. Worn hymn books were replaced and a library was started. A boy's club was established. A cantata sung by some local citizens, not necessarily all from the church, was performed in a number of surrounding towns. Reverend White also helped in harvest and drove a school bus to supplement his finances. In 1951, while he took a trip to Ireland, Miss Anne Twerdochlib filled the pulpit.

Congregation on the left side of the sanctuary, about 1968.

Reverend and Mrs. W. F. Ball came to pastor in 1953. They served the church until 1956, when the Balls accepted a pastorate in Kelvington, Saskatchewan. Their daughter, Evelyn, pastored the church in 1957. Pastor and Mrs. Turnbull served the church from May 1958 to May 1960, when Reverend and Mrs. A. A. Lewis became pastors. Don Cantelon's visits were much appreciated. Ardena, Don's wife, is Reverend and Mrs. Lewis' daughter. In January 1965 Reverend and Mrs. H. Osterhouse came to take charge of the work. The congregation prospered under their ministry.

Next to assume leadership in 1969, were Pastor and Mrs. Asselstine. They had two children. Reverend Asselstine helped in harvesting. He also took part in the activities of the community. Mrs. Asselstine taught in the Public School. They resigned in 1975. They accepted a call to Peace River.

Reverend and Mrs. Del Pierce followed Asselstines. They have three little girls, who are loved

dearly by the people. The parsonage, a small house bought in 1938, has been enlarged and improved until today it is a modern home. The church also has been updated with carpeting, organ, kitchen facilities, and a lovely new foyer.

Congregation on the right side of the sanctuary, about 1968.

Among those, who attended Bible College and/ or entered the ministry (*), are Shirley Asselstine, *Janet Balkwell, *Keith Balkwell, Lynn Balkwell, Wendy Balkwell, Dale Broughton, *Ila Broughton, **Larry Broughton, *Darrel Johnson, Sandra (Sandy) Johnson, Robert (Bob) Lewis, *William (Bill) Lewis, *Allen Lindskoog, Brian Lindskoog, *Dorea Lindskoog (Mrs. Stuart Acheson), Albert Niles, *Douglas Lindskoog, Don Niles, *Ethel Niles, Georgina Niles, *Ernie Peterson.

INNISFAIL
PARKLAND COMMUNITY CHURCH

In 1960 some families from Innisfail had been attending the Red Deer Woodlea Tabernacle. Reverend Ernie Peterson, District Presbyter, and Reverend Bill Pipke, Pastor of Red Deer, asked these families if they desired a Pentecostal work in Innisfail. This was their wish.

Prayer meetings started in the Trekofski home. Brother Gerald Smith from Red Deer came out to minister. In February or March of 1960, Reverend Pipke, of Red Deer, held meetings in the Jackson Hall. Later meetings were held in the Legion Hall.

The first summer three ladies, Mrs. Smith, Mrs. Trekofski, Mrs. Petracek, canvassed the town for Sunday School. The Sunday School grew from six to forty.

The founding families were the Sid Smiths, Trekofskis, LaMarshes, Mrs. Petracek and family.

During the summer of 1960 Reverend and Mrs. L. Kokot came to pastor this work. That summer they began building their church. This was done by volunteer labour. By winter, they were able to use the basement for services.

After three years, the Kokots were followed by Keith and Rhelda Evans. Others, who ministered there, were Reverend and Mrs. Hector McDonald, Henry and Janet Borzel, Laura Holdsworth and Sister Erickson, Reverend and Mrs. Ted Tobin (1974-1978).

In May 1973 in Innisfail, when Reverend Borzel was pastor, a Central District evangelistic crusade was held with Evangelist, Reverend Alan Caple of British Columbia, as speaker. The attendance at these meetings was outstanding and results were gratifying.

During the ministry of Reverend and Mrs. Tobin, a seminar on the Baptism of the Holy Spirit was held by Reverend Thiesen. Mrs. Tingy received the Baptism of the Holy Spirit during these services.

The church was without a pastor and no services were held for about two years.

In November 1979, Reverend and Mrs. G. Jeske came to minister. For several months, Reverend Jeske was youth pastor at Red Deer Woodlea Tabernacle. His salary from Woodlea and Home Missions helped to provide their needs. Thirty people from Innisfail, who had been attending the Red Deer Tabernacle, formed the nucleus for the church at this time. The church was renovated including foyer, nursery and installed new washrooms. Attendance grew to about one hundred and twenty-five. Reverend Jeske resigned in June 1982.

Among those from this assembly, who attended Bible College, is Elaine Trekofski.

JASPER
ASSEMBLY OF GOD

The Jasper Assembly of God was founded in April 1971 with four families participating — Andrews, Craigs, Hills and Peters. The Assembly was affiliated with the Pentecostal Assemblies of Canada in June 1971.

In the beginning it was decided by the Assembly to have the Jasper Outreach. Students came from all across Canada for one specific purpose, that being to spread the Gospel of Christ to all people who were passing through that mountain resort town. They had the opportunity to work for some of the businesses in Jasper — stores, motels, service stations, hospital, in hotels as chambermaids, bellboys, pump jockeys, waitresses and dishwashers. When not working they were involved in the coffee house ministry on Thursday, Friday and Saturday evenings. During this time they talked to many young people from all walks of life. Although free coffee was available, their main purpose in coming to the coffee house was to rap about spiritual things. While some were in the coffee house, others were on the streets inviting people to come to the coffee house, as well as, handing out literature to all who received it.

A familiar sight in Jasper was a person standing out front of the "Way Out Coffee House," directing people up the stairs and giving literature to the people walking by. Others would be sitting on the lawn at the "Cabbage Patch" (a local park), rapping with the unsaved about Jesus. Others were back at the coffee house praying and calling upon the Lord in the little prayer room. This was a very important part of the ministry.

The first pastor was Reverend Dave Johnston, who was assisted by Reverend Ross. Early in 1972 Reverend Lloyd Richardson was called to pastor. Larry Breitkreutz came as youth director for the summer outreach. Reverend Richardson left the end of 1972. In 1973 Reverend Bill Lewis pastored the Assembly. Then Reverend Eugene and Lois Johnson pastored from May to September. Lou Harewood assisted with the outreach in 1973 and became the pastor until April 1975. Danny and Norma MacNaughton pastored from April 1975 to September 1977. Ron Wood assisted as youth director for outreach 1977. Other pastors were Pastor and Mrs. Fred Zinck (1981) and J. Kinnunen (1982).

Jasper Assembly does not have a church building of their own. There are only a few people to support the Assembly during the winter months.

One of the young people, George Elsey, attended Northwest Bible College.

KILLAM
KILLAM PENTECOSTAL
TABERNACLE

Killam is one of the older Alberta District churches. Contrary to the name "Killam" it is a life giving station. The roots of this church go back to 1922. In the strange providence of God, Miss Alma Johnson went to Calgary, where she stayed with a lady who had experienced the Baptism of the Holy Spirit. Alma was hungry for God. Before she returned to Killam, she too had received the infilling of the Holy Spirit. Alma prayed for her family. Soon they, too, had received this glorious baptism. The Johnson home became a place where people met to pray.

In August 1922 Alma and her brother-in-law, Mr. Andrew Sorenson, attended the Pentecostal Convention that was being held in Edmonton. The Evangelist was Mrs. May Eleanor Fry from the United

States with co-workers Roy Smuland and Hugh McAlister. Mr. Sorenson and Alma asked Mrs. Fry if she and her helpers would come to Killam to conduct a tent meeting. The invitation was accepted on condition that Killam would pay expenses for shipping and erecting the tent — one hundred dollars. Alma phoned her mother and the expenses were guaranteed.

Upon returning home Mr. Sorenson obtained permission from the town authorities to erect the tent in a suitable location. He then proceeded to secure lumber to build seats and a platform. The meetings in the tent were well attended. The Still family came at the beginning of the meetings and were regular attenders. Mrs. Whittington, who did not miss a service in the tent, was the first one to receive the Baptism of the Holy Spirit. The revival did not end when the tent came down. Miss Anna Johnson conducted meetings during the fall and winter months. A two-roomed house was rented for living quarters and prayer meetings. Reverend and Mrs. Hugh Cadwalder lived in this house and conducted the Sunday services and prayer meetings. Many received the Baptism of the Holy Spirit in that little two-roomed house. Young Clare Scratch was there for a time, later a Mr. Moses from the United States gave leadership to the assembly. For a while services were held in the Eula Hall, then in a hall upstairs on Main Street. While Mr. Moses was still with them the Merchants Bank, a nice brick building on a corner lot, came on the market. The congregation decided to buy the building. Mr. Still and Mr. Sorenson shouldered the financial responsibility. The former bank was soon renovated with a meeting hall at the front and living quarters at the back. Reverend E. E. Clements from Saskatchewan became pastor. Soon the sign, PENTECOSTAL MISSION, appeared on the front of their new church home. The church was set in order as an assembly by Reverend John McAlister.

The Frank Fox family had had a business in Killam, but due to illness the family moved to Edmonton. In 1925 Charles S. Price came to Edmonton for an Evangelistic Healing Campaign. During these meetings Mr. Frank Fox, his daughter Ethel, his son Lorne were all marvellously healed by the power of God. Ethel Fox received the Baptism of the Holy Ghost, also, a call to the ministry. The Killam church invited the Fox family to come and Ethel to take charge of the assembly. The church was never without a pianist as Ethel was a music teacher, also Lorne excelled as a pianist. The congregation loved the anointed ministry of Ethel Fox. Frank Fox was a real help in Ethel's ministry (Sunday School and Prayer Meetings), as well as building a pulpit, platform and most of the seats. New families were added to the

church continually. Among them was the Hunter family, whose three sons entered the ministry — two of them as pastors in Canada and one as a missionary in South Africa.

After the Fox family, Reverend A. Scratch came as pastor. A list of pastors over fifty years reads like Who's Who. Already mentioned are Alma Johnson, Mr. Moses, Cadwalders, Clements, the Fox family, Clare Scratch and Alfred Scratch, to continue — Misses Black and Wood, G. Atter, E. W. Robinson, W. McPherson, William O. Rourke, G. Baycroft, N. F. Langford, J. C. Cooke, Mr. Britten, D. Anderson, Ed Miller, D. Hopkinson (1959-1964), E. Siggelkow (1967-1969), C. Preston (1969-1974), G. Rankel (1974-1975), F. Hunter (1975-1978), and Lorne Fisher (1978-   ).

In November 1941 Pastor W. F. Rourke had a Mortgage Burning Ceremony. The liquidation of this mortgage — thirty-six hundred dollars — was made possible by the fact that the Bank of Montreal cancelled the major portion of the indebtedness leaving only five hundred dollars for the assembly. A letter of appreciation and thanks was forwarded to the Bank of Montreal for their contribution to the Lord's work. However, the sacrificial efforts of the members cannot be forgotten.

As the congregation outgrew the bank building on main street, new facilities were evidently needed. Under the ministry of Don Hopkinson, a new church was built and dedicated in the spring of 1961. They also built a parsonage.

Who can estimate the influence of a church in a community? Every pastor, every family, every individual has made a contribution.

"To God be the Glory, for the great things He hath done."

Among those, who attended Bible College and/or entered the ministry (*), are *Phyllis Aitcheson, Bietta Anderson, Robert Bruso, Charles Evans, Richard Erickson, *Marion Gammon (wife of Reverend James House) (Sedgewick), *Ernie Hansen, Randy Hansen, Jocelyn Hansen, *Bernard Holmstrom, Lillian (Larson) Holmstrom, Sharon Holmstrom, *Roy Hunter, **Bernard Hunter, *Fred Hunter, Elaine Huybe, *Doris Hunter, Irene Laughlin, *Mrs. Gladys Lagore, *Alice Olsenberg, Esther Sorenson, Clayton Still, Norman Spalding, Albert Spalding, Gordon Shaber, Ruth Sorenson, *Evelyn Still, *Edith Still (wife of Reverend Walter Frederick), Jerdis Taralson (Mrs. Ernie Hansen), David Taralson, *Talmage Taralson, Carolyn Taralson, Dale Taralson, Doris Taralson (Mrs. Ben Anderson), Shirley Upshall, Arlene Weeks, Valerie Weeks, Inga Weidmer.

LACOMBE
LACOMBE PENTECOSTAL
TABERNACLE

In July 1956, Evangelist Paul Olson, of Minneapolis, Minnesota, U.S.A., conducted a tent crusade in Lacombe. This resulted in a group of people, who became affiliated with the Pentecostal Assemblies of Canada. Previous to the tent meeting, Mrs. Gladys Prest held some services. After the crusade, Mr. and Mrs. Tom Raisbeck served as pastors for a time. Later Mr. Len Matz also gave leadership to the Assembly and students from Northwest Bible College came to assist. During this time a house was purchased for a parsonage, church services were held in the I.O.O.F. hall and later in the Legion hall.

Lacombe Pentecostal Tabernacle

Among the early and founding families in the church were Goodbrands, Scotts, Erkses, Peter Kurneys, Whites, Karolls, Stoners, Heistads, Petrys, Wollners, Gustafsons, Mrs. Parsons, Miss Vickerson, Mr. Rud, Fern Brewer, Mrs. Staples (now Mrs. Reuben Ganski) and family. Most of these people have either moved away or gone to be with the Lord.

In 1957 Rev. and Mrs. Jack Keys came as pastors. The church now felt the need of a building of their own. To gain finances to purchase land, they endeavored to sell the parsonage for the cost price of $3,000.00, but to no avail, until Rev. Keys painted the house. It was sold for $3,800.00. A basement was dug and finished. While the main sanctuary was being constructed, the Keys family lived on one side of the basement. Services were conducted on the other side. The church building was started in 1958.

It took one and one-half years to build by volunteer labour and buying material as the finances allowed.

Rev. Keys and family remained until 1960 when they were appointed as missionaries to the West Indies. Rev. and Mrs. Harvey C. McAlister pastored the church during 1960-61. Rev. and Mrs. Egan Roller served the church from 1961 to 1964. In 1964 Rev. and Mrs. Mel Jenkins came and remained until 1968. During their time a three-bedroom parsonage was built on the lot next to the church.

Rev. and Mrs. Frank White pastored from 1968 to 1970. As several families had moved away from Lacombe, the Assembly felt they were not able to support a pastor financially. They thought that perhaps they would have to close the church. Rev. and Mrs. Harvey C. McAlister, who were living in Red Deer, offered to come as pastors. They served the church until 1974 when in September of that year Pastor McAlister passed away. The church was without a minister until 1976. During 1974 Rev. Cameron of Sylvan Lake commuted for services during the absence of the pastor.

Picnic at the Agricultural Farm.

From January 1976 to December 1977, Mr. and Mrs. Sid Ruffo of Edmonton commuted for Sunday Services. Rev. Rudy Schappert was called as pastor and served until the fall of 1980. Then Pastor and Mrs. Dean Steel came to minister in the Lacombe church. The Assembly is showing signs of growth in every department — souls have been saved, new families have moved into the area and are finding fellowship in the church. There is a need for a bigger facility so the church has started a building fund.

Many lives have been influenced over the years by the various ministries in the church including the Sunday School, Young Peoples, Women's Ministries, girls and boys clubs. Pastors have conducted services in the Senior Citizen's Lodge and the Nursing Home.

Among those from this assembly, who attended

Bible College and/or entered the ministry (*), are *Rod Harrington, *David McAlister and Alden Stephenson.

LEDUC
CALVARY PENTECOSTAL TABERNACLE

Very appropriately the information on the first Pentecostal church established in Leduc, came from the couple who pioneered the work and led the congregation through the time of building. While many looked on in discouragement and suggested the work be given up, they continued to work and pray together trusting God to see them through. A special thank-you to Reverend John C. Cooke and his wife, Ida, for the work they did here and for the fine account of the growth of the assembly.

Mrs. J. C. Cooke, Two Ladies (Charter Members), Rev. J. C. Cooke.

When the Cookes (1957-1967) were approached in the spring of 1957 to begin a work here, they told Reverend Stewart Tilton, the superintendent at that time, they would accept the challenge. Many times they felt the need of a permanent work here, and so with the promise of the rent for the Elks Hall being paid by the District they began. Financially they were on their own to begin this new work.

For their first service they brought out a group of Eskimo people that could neither understand nor speak English. Also two German ladies, Mrs. Anna Plett and Mrs. Julia Tews, who spoke very little English but had the zealous spirit needed, came. The pastor turned that service into one of prayer and they sought the Lord for His blessing and guidance. That afternoon they went visiting a couple who had moved to the area and whom they had known previously as

neighbors in Edmonton. It was their privilege to lead Ralph and Eileen Steer to the Lord at that time and they attended the evening service. Services continued and in September a Sunday School was begun with fifteen members in attendance. The Lord answered prayer for a pianist when Adolf and Ruby Shaffrick began to attend. In the progress of the work God provided a new mahogany Heinzman piano and a Hammond organ. As they labored God blessed and added faithful workers to the assembly.

Among those sent to be faithful in attending and working were: Mr. and Mrs. Ralph Steer, Mr. and Mrs. John Brown, the Bienerts, the Domeresks, Mr. and Mrs. Henry Siemens, Mr. and Mrs. Dennis Muth, Mr. and Mrs. Adolf Shaffrick, Mr. and Mrs. Herb Tews, Mr. and Mrs. Leonard Muth, Mr. and Mrs. Plunkie, Mr. and Mrs. Jobs, Mr. and Mrs. Edwin Schade, Steems, Kalkes, Glesmans, Triebers, Terriaults, Rumaks, Wesoloskys, Roths, Teskes and the Price family.

In the spring of 1959 a lot was purchased for five hundred dollars and the basement was dug. Ralph Steer drew up the blueprints. Reverend Al Forsythe put in the electrical system, donating his labor. The majority of the work was done on a volunteer basis. Mr. Schier was a carpenter by trade and his move to Leduc was also in the Lord's timing. Services continued in the Elks hall while the church was under construction. November 1959 showed progress by walls and roof of the new building in evidence. Brick laying and stuccoing began in 1962 and Superintendent Tilton was invited for the laying of the corner stone ceremony. That event marked five years of continuous services. The first promotional Sunday school service was held in the hall confirming permanent growth in that area. The work was completed and dedication of the church was in May 1963. Reverend R. Taitinger, pastor of Central Pentecostal Tabernacle in Edmonton, was the guest speaker for the service. Brother Ernie Shedden led the Central Tabernacle Choir in special numbers. Sister Eunice Meyer was the visiting evangelist and she preached to a capacity crowd. In the dedication service the two original members, who were at the beginning often the only people in attendance, Mrs. Anna Plett and Mrs. Julia Tews, were honored in a special way by the presentation of a dozen roses. Refreshments were served by the ladies of the church that day to a crowd of seven hundred guests.

During this time of growing and building, the lots on either side of the church site had been purchased and eventually used for Sunday School facilities and parking lot. A parsonage had been bought as well. By the fall of 1963 the Sunday School reached one hundred and seventy in attendance.

When the Cookes resigned, Reverend and Mrs. Ernie Peterson were called to pastor. They served from 1967 to 1970. Reverend and Mrs. Doug Gaetz pastored from 1970 to 1972 with Colin Wellard assisting. Reverend and Mrs. Ronald Ellis pastored from 1972 to 1979, assisted by his son and his wife.

When Reverend Dave Webster and his wife, Sandy, came to minister, a building program was again considered and a new structure was dedicated on October 18, 1981. Over one thousand people attended the dedication service. Dr. Murray Dempster of California was the guest speaker. The mayor of Leduc, Mr. Oscar Klak, brought greetings on behalf of the town council. Reverend Kenneth Bunting, Assistant District Superintendent, led in the act of dedication and the presbyter, Reverend Mel Jenkins, offered the dedicatory prayer.

The church, which cost over one million dollars to construct, is built in the shape of a cross. The length is two hundred and thirty feet and the arms one hundred and forty feet wide with a total floor area of thirty thousand square feet. It includes a gymnasium and educational facilities which are used by the Leduc Christian Academy, a Christian Day School.

Reverend Webster resigned in June 1982. Reverend Jack Keys cared for the assembly until the end of August 1982. Cal Keys assisted from 1980 to 1982.

Among those, who attended Bible College and/or entered the ministry (*), are Gary Bienert, Paul Ellis, Leslie Nicholson, Dianne Rumak, Karen Rumak, Yvonne Schafrick, Karen Steem.

LETHBRIDGE
GLAD TIDINGS PENTECOSTAL FELLOWSHIP

This congregation was formed in January 1979 in North Lethbridge. There were about one hundred and eighty, who were in this first congregation as founding members. Their first pastors were Mel Israelson and Ron Steinbrenner. Their first meeting place was the Italian Centre in North Lethbridge, then in a school gym and, at the time of publication, they met in Westminster Hall. Since Pastors Israelson and Steinbrenner left, John Morland has been interim pastor.

LETHBRIDGE
LETHBRIDGE PENTECOSTAL ASSEMBLY

The Lethbridge Pentecostal Assembly has a long history in Lethbridge. Coalhurst reported that a Mr. and Mrs. Simonette from this early assembly took the Pentecostal message to Coalhurst before 1917. This outreach so early speaks well of this early group of believers. This group was brought together

through the efforts and interest of one of its earliest workers, Rev. Charles M. Neve (1913-1919). In 1919 Rev. W. E. McAlister came as pastor. This young man married Miss Ruth Manley of this Assembly. From the Canadian Pentecostal Testimony of December 1920, a report on this assembly was given by Rev. John McAlister as pastor in charge of this Assembly. He stated that the Presbyterian Church had been purchased and was being remodelled and expected to move in right away. He also reported that there had been a campaign in June of 1920 that was conducted by Evangelist Aimee Semple McPherson. These meetings were so wonderfully blessed of God with many being won for the Lord, some wonderful answers to prayer including healing were received and believers encouraged. Rev. McAlister reported that there had been a continual steady progress in the work since those McPherson meetings. They were experiencing a marvelous move of the Holy Spirit in their midst and looked forward to better times. Rev. John McAlister left in 1923.

Aimee Semple McPherson

Among the founding and early families were William and Ethel Dutton, Joseph and Miriam Crowther, Mabel and Cory Baer, Mr. and Mrs. Crozier, Mrs. Staines, William Grysdale, John Norgardt, Mr. and Mrs. Simonette, Carles and Barbara Harding with Edina, Fred and Mavis, Ruth Manley.

Rev. J. Saunders was pastor from 1923 to 1926. Then Rev. Clare Scratch came to pastor. Edina Harding was his first candidate for water baptism. Rev. Scratch pastored from 1926 to 1929. Rev. C. Nelson arrived with his wife and family the first Sunday in

June 1929. In September 1929, he started their first radio program over CJOC. The program was known as The Sunshine Evangel Hour. In 1931, Brother and Sister Nelson left and Rev. G. R. Upton came. Brother Upton ministered well until he left in 1936.

Rev. George Bombay had a very fruitful ministry from 1936 to 1939. He had marvelous results from his radio ministry, which reached from Cranbrook, B.C. to Swift Current, Saskatchewan. In his three years of this radio ministry, over 300 were saved. One Sunday morning in late January 1937, there was a desperate need in a family about 45 miles north-east of Lethbridge. They were snow-bound and had no telephone. A blizzard had blocked the roads and they stayed blocked for three weeks. On that Sunday morning, the mother tuned in Rev. Bombay's program. He made a special prayer that morning, so did she, who prayed right along with him. God answered her prayers right away. What a blessing! Rev. Bombay would have meetings in certain areas, where his broadcast was heard and folks in those areas let him know that they heard and were interested or needed help or counselling. Among those places were the Crowsnest Pass area — Coleman, Pincher Creek and Blairmore. Beside these house meetings, he baptized believers. If he was not able to go, he would send someone else out to hold the services. e.g. Edina Harding was sent out to Vulcan and Kirkcaldy in

April 1938. She stayed in Mrs. Vaughn's home in Vulcan and commuted to Kirkcaldy, for a few months. She arranged her time so that she could have services in both places.

Rev. and Mrs. J. C. Cooke served from 1939 to 1946. They were both excellent speakers. Mrs. Cooke was appointed Women's Missionary Council District Director, the first one. Other ministers, who ministered were Rev. A. A. Lewis (1946-49), Rev. G. W. Allen (1949-57), Rev. J. H. Hazlett (1957-65), Rev. Gamble (1965-72), Rev. M. L. Israelson (1973-78), Rev. Marvin Dynna (1978-82).

The second church building, built on the site of the first church, was built in stages — the lower part was commenced under Rev. G. A. Bombay and completed under Rev. J. C. Cooke. The educational unit was added while R. H. Hazlett was pastor. The third building, a lovely new church, was dedicated on September 6, 1981. This church was built under the ministry of Rev. Dynna.

Among those, who attended Bible college and/or entered the ministry (*), were/are *Mrs. Ole (Dorothy) Austring, *Ole Austring, *Eileen Boguski (married to Rev. David Lagore), *Myrna Boguski, *Grace Crowther (wife of Rev. Alec Ness), *William Dutton, *Ethel Dutton, *William (Bill) Dutton Jr., Arne Dyck, *Sam Frederickson, Velma Fritzler, Sandra Gillet, *Edina Harding, Valentine Kaerna,

Lethbridge Radio Broadcast Group. Back Row: Charlie Heslep, Mr. Hardy, Rev. George Upton, Mr. Heslep, George Heslep, Ray Archer. Front Row: Sam Fredrickson, May Hardy, Mrs. Upton, , Melrose, Ray's wife, and Edina Harding (pianist).

Marlene Klassen, *Judy Kropinak, *Adelgunde (Adele) Manntai, *Ruth Manley (wife of Rev. Walter McAlister), Daniel Manntai, *Doris Manntai, *Irene Manntai, Margaret Manntai, *Hugh McAlister, Dorothy Meyer, Lynda Meyer, *Alec Ness, *William Raccah, Judy Raccah, *Darlene Rodgers (wife of Rev. Doug Lindskoog), *Clare Scratch, *Joyce Sinclair, Edna Stannard, Marie Villebrun, Verlie Vipond, *Al Werbiski.

LLOYDMINSTER
LIVING FAITH PENTECOSTAL TABERNACLE

During the early spring of 1974, a beautiful church built to accommodate over 400 people was dedicated to the furtherance of the gospel in Lloydminster. It seemed almost unbelievable to the few old timers that attended. In the late 1920's they worshipped in private homes, a tiny place over an old bakery, in a small band hall, even in an unused and uncompleted funeral parlor. In those days the grace of hospitality was practised. Often many extra places were set for friends and strangers. No one was ever turned away. The parents of Mrs. W. F. (Sarah) Ball were among this early group.

In the early spring of 1927, two young men from the newly organized Pentecostal Bible College in Winnipeg, Gordon Atter and Wesley O'Brien, opened a work in the Onion Lake District north of Lloydminster. They introduced the Robinson family to Pentecost. Family worship was a regular feature of their home and heaven was touched as they prayed. Gordon Atter spoke of the move of the Holy Spirit and, with Wesley O'Brien at the organ, they began to sing choruses and the Lord's presence was very real.

Pastor and Mrs. Alfred Scratch, Clare's parents, were pastoring at Cutknife, Saskatchewan, at that time. In the spring of 1928, with the encouragement of Bro. Walter McAlister, District Superintendent, and the help of Mervold Jackson of Spruce Lake, Saskatchewan, a small gospel tent was erected on the edge of an oat field, which is now 147th Street and 54th Avenue. A small group of people attended these services. Miss Nellie Hendrickson, who later became missionary to Kenya, and Miss Ivy Sparks were the workers in charge. Victories were won in the Lord's Name. God had begun to do a good work.

Among those, who gave leadership in those days, were Miss Hilda Volens and Pastor and Mrs. Tom Kennedy. Rev. Wilbert Greenwood (1931-   ) was another early pastor, who lived on $5.00 a month. He lived in one room, then in a tent until February 1932. It had a wooden floor and sides about three feet up. He had to chop wood each day and usually had to sleep with his clothes on to keep warm. The Robin-

sons brought over many hot meals. After the tenting experience he moved into a little house with a young couple. The three of them lived on $6.00 a month; lots of cracked wheat, not much milk or sugar.

After these early pioneers, the work became intermittent and almost dormant for more than a decade. It is to our Slavic brethren, Samuel Peregrym in particular, that the credit must be given for getting the work established. Samuel Peregrym lived in Beaverdam, Alberta, with his family of seven boys and three girls. The land was not very productive. Since neighbors had bought land near Lloydminster, in the fall of 1947, Mr. Peregrym decided to go and see what he could find. While Mr. Peregrym and his son, Peter, were walking the streets, they noticed a poster on a billboard advertising special services in the Baptist Church. They attended the service and met Mr. Cox, who directed them to the Tom John's Real Estate. The next day they met Paul Berezuik, who was instrumental in selling them a half section of land. The next year the Peregryms moved to Lloydminster area.

Mr. Peregrym started meetings in the home of Nick Kutney. The services were in Ukrainian, often interpreted into English. Fred Shorland, an Apostolic brother, and his wife moved to Lloydminster and helped greatly in the work. Soon there was a small congregation. Mr. Peregrym invited Brother Bill Melnychuk, Superintendent of the Western Slavic Conference, and other ministering brethren and it was decided to build a church. A number of English brethren learned that there were plans of building a church and asked if it would be possible for them to join this effort. Brother Peregrym was delighted to have them join and it was decided that services would be conducted in both languages. In 1952 a parcel of land on the north side of Lloydminster was acquired from Ray Nelson, who was in the lumber yard business.

The third Sunday of March 1954 people from the surrounding assemblies, Bonnyville, Glendon, St. Paul, Vilna, High Valley, Andrew, Edmonton and the local congregation attended the dedication exercises. The church was packed to capacity. When the need to defray the cost of materials was presented, enough money was received in cash and pledges to meet the immediate need.

Brother Peregrym continued as pastor for a time. In the spring of 1955 he resigned, feeling it would be best for the assembly to have a pastor who could speak both languages.

Reverend Peter Kerychuk pastored the congregation from the spring of 1955 to the fall of 1958. During his time of ministry, a manse was built for the pastor. The congregation had increased to about one hundred. Because of the economic recession in

Lloydminster, many were laid off and had to move to where work could be found. The attendance was reduced to about fifty. Brother Kerychuk conducted the services in both the Ukrainian and English languages.

Brother W. F. Ball pastored from 1958 to 1963. During Brother Ball's ministry there several were young couples in the church. There were many baby dedications.

Brother Wall with his wife and two boys, accepted the call to come and shepherd this congregation. Brother Wall loved children and it was not long before all the children started calling him Uncle Mike. When these children were all old enough to go to school, he would have them come to the front of the church and sing for the congregation. He called them "his choir" and the children loved the attention that they received. Brother Wall spent eight years as pastor and resigned in the fall of 1971 and moved to Drumheller. By this time the congregation had grown to a full church and building a new one was discussed.

Brother George Richmond came to pastor in January 1972. They had two teenage girls and one boy. Brother Richmond pursued the idea of building a new church. Land was purchased on the south side of Lloydminster. In October 1973 the contractor began the work of erecting the new church building and in April 1974 the building was completed except for the stucco on the outside and landscaping. The new facilities were dedicated on April 7, 1974. After moving into the new building, the old church was sold. Brother Richmond resigned in January 1977.

Brother Ken Smith accepted the call to pastor Lloydminster. He came with his wife and four boys. Brother Smith began a telephone Dial-A-Meditation program, a two minute devotional. Also Wee College was started, where four-year-old boys and girls learned crafts, Bible stories, to draw, print, sing, etc.. The name of the church was changed to Living Faith Pentecostal Tabernacle. Brother Smith resigned October 31, 1980.

Brother C. A. McClain, with his wife, Hilda, came to pastor in 1981. Their son, S. McClain, and his wife are assisting there.

Among those, who attended Bible College and/or entered the ministry (*) are Ernie Cowpersmith, Wynn Dietrich, Lynette Jonson, *Michael Kutney, Dwain Peregrym, Richard Simpson, Randy J. Stauffer.

MAYERTHORPE
MAYERTHORPE PENTECOSTAL ASSEMBLY

In the fall of 1960, Mrs. Gladys Prest and Ruth Maser came to Mayerthorpe to begin a home missionary work under the Pentecostal banner. Each Sunday night, services were held in the Legion Hall with a good number of faithful folk in attendance.

In the spring of 1961, a lot was purchased. Then an Anglican hall was bought and moved on to this lot. This building had also been the Padstow Community Hall.

About this time, Mrs. Prest and Miss Maser moved to Whitecourt. Since most of the congregation came from Whitecourt, Mayerthorpe was left with a small group — Granny Mills, Edith Fryer, Minna Mills, Mr. and Mrs. Bill Bray, Mr. and Mrs. Ernie Hartwig and family, Robert and Alice Ryks with Ken and Melvin, Bert and Lydia Hughes.

Mayerthorpe Pentecostal Assembly

In May 1961 Pastor Keith and Rhelda Evans, with their boys, came to minister. To help with finances, Pastor Evans worked as a mechanic in Crochet Motors and in the Shell Service at Sangudo.

A basement, living quarters and a porch were added to the church. Pastor Virgil Lawrence, of Stony Plain, came as often as possible to help Pastor Evans with the building. The walls and ceiling were rough boards, but well insulated with wood shavings, which kept flying down continually like giant snow flakes. For a time, revenue, from a kindergarten held in the church, helped defray expenses.

Good times of fellowship were had with Youth for Christ speakers, missionaries and in other activities. The church also was involved with services in the Senior Citizens Lodge.

In 1964 Keith and Rhelda Evans resigned. Student Pastor Dave and Eileen Lagore, with son Robert, came to pastor the church. Student Pastor David Haimila assisted Pastor Lagore. While completing their second and third years of Bible College, Dave Lagore and David Haimila drove out from

Edmonton early every Sunday morning to minister. The congregation rejoiced as new families were added. Improvements — a new pulpit, a little white table, lino-tile on the floor, gyproc on the ceiling and venetian blinds — were made.

After Bible School graduation, David Haimila took up residence in the back of the church. He also worked at MacLeods to supplement his salary. He served as pastor until 1967.

Torrance Bobb served the church until Doug Lindskoog was called. After the Lindskoogs, Arnold and Helga Dyck pastored.

The church was without a pastor for about one and a half years. In December 1975, Reverend and Mrs. Brian With, from Cranbrook, accepted the call as pastors. He had been in the Fellowship Baptist ministry for twenty years. He then received the Baptism of the Holy Spirit, which brought him into the Pentecostal Fellowship.

The congregation had families from various denominations. About half of the congregation left to form a Baptist Fellowship in Mayerthorpe. The remaining folk continued to believe God for His blessing under the ministry of Pastor and Mrs. With.

In August 1977 the Ryks family (8 members) moved to Whitecourt. This left a couple of benches empty. The Assembly continued to trust God for new families.

In January 1978 Pastor and Mrs. With left. Brian and Valerie Rutten and small son, Doug, were called to Mayerthorpe. As the assembly continued to wait on God, new folk were added to the church. They needed a pianist. One Wednesday night, they agreed in prayer for this need. The next Sunday a new couple, Lourne and Karen Anderson, came to Church — God had answered prayer. Their pianist had arrived.

Their building was old. Plans were made for a new one. On May 3, 1980, a building banquet was held at the Mayerthorpe Legion Hall with Pastor Doug Stiller of Spruce Grove as special speaker. About sixty attended. After hearing this challenging message, the people were encouraged to arise and build for the glory of God. A sod-turning ceremony was held in May 1980.

In April 1981 the building was completed and dedicated. Volunteer labour and generous giving made this possible.

The congregation is growing, God is blessing in the community. The church continues to believe God for souls to be added to His Kingdom.

Among those, who attended Bible college, are Miss Patsy Hayes, Kenneth Ryks, and Barbara Sim.

MEDICINE HAT
FIRST ASSEMBLY OF GOD

As early as sometime in the nineteen twenties Walter McAlister and Cyril Brooks had some meetings. However, it was not until the summer of 1946 that Rev. and Mrs. J. C. O'Brien travelled to have services in Claresholm for six weeks. On the way to Claresholm, there was a short train stop at Medicine Hat. Rev. O'Brien left the train long enough to ask if there was a Pentecostal church there. He also was told there were lots of churches. Something began to stir in his heart regarding Medicine Hat at that time. Though while they were at Claresholm, they were asked if they would become the new pastors at Claresholm, Rev. O'Brien felt that it was not where God wanted them to be at that time. His health was so much improved there — his asthma was not bothering him. All in all they returned to Ontario. In very short order, he became very ill with another severe attack of Asthma. He knew he had to leave Ontario. He, after talking to his wife, told the church that his health made it impossible for him to carry on and that he would be going to Medicine Hat to begin a new church, where his asthma did not trouble him. His wife finished out the month of September 1946. Rev. O'Brien arrived in Medicine Hat in early September 1946. He had just enough money to pay for one night's lodging but nothing more. He brought a large suitcase of Christmas cards. The next morning he went out to sell some Christmas cards. He sold some soon after he went out so he was able to buy some breakfast. Accommodation was very, very scarce in 1946. He walked everywhere since, he did not have a car. He would look for houses he thought that might have a vacant room. One day he thought he had found one. The lady, who answered the door, lived in this home with her mother. They had been house cleaning that is why the curtains were down in one of the rooms. This is why Rev. O'Brien thought there would be a room for rent. He did not look very well. The lady talked to her mother as to whether they would rent their attic room to him; they did decide in his favor. He kept looking for a place large enough for the family. After much asking and praying, someone told him about three sleeping rooms. He walked over to see the folks who were looking after renting the rooms. This couple were none other than Jack McMullen and his wife; many will remember Jack for his daily Gospel broadcasting. They contacted their landlord to see if they could rent the three rooms to the O'Briens as well as install a gas stove. The landlord agreed and Rev. O'Brien phoned his wife to let her know that he had a place for them and when to leave so that he could meet them. On the way, she stopped in Toronto, where friends gave her money handshakes of one, two, five or ten dollars. The same thing happened in Winnipeg when she stopped there. When she arrived in Medicine Hat she had the exact amount that she needed for the freight bill for their belongings. The bill was seventy-six dollars and some cents. They were very grateful. They felt that God had used those dear folk to provide for their need. The accommodation was comfortable, even though they just had two single beds — one for Brother and Sister O'Brien and the other for their young boys, Clifton and Calvin. Christmas that year was one of the best they ever had. Gifts were really wonderful including two turkeys, one beef roast, one duck, one dump truck, and much more.

Back to the beginning, the O'Briens held their first service in the Moose Hall, October 22, 1946. The Sunday afternoon meetings were held in halls. At that first meeting there were seventy-five people. Rev. O'Brien asked if anyone wanted to have a midweek service in their home to let them know. Right in the service, Mr. Turcotte volunteered to have one in their home. Others volunteered later.

Among the early families were George and Stan Johnson's dad; Mr. McCaddam; Mr. and Mrs. A. J. Splane with their children including Clara, who was a lovely soloist; Mr. Bonesky, Mr. and Mrs. Jim Taylor; Mr. and Mrs. Jim Stoneley; Phyllis Johnson (sister to Grace); Grace Johnson (wife of Reverend John Erhardt and sister to George and Stan); the Turcottes, Mr. and Mrs. Glen Mitchell.

The first New Year's Eve service was held in the home of the Taylors. On January 27, 1947, services and Sunday School were held in the Orange Hall. Reverend D. N. Buntain was present for the first Sunday School with twenty-four present. He gave an object lesson by buttoning his vest so that it was not buttoned properly. His lesson was if you start right, you end right. He was the guest speaker for the day. The midweek services were held in the Orange Hall, also. When Reverend O'Brien enquired about starting a radio broadcast, he was asked if it would be like the one Reverend J. C. Cooke was airing in Lethbridge. When Reverend O'Brien said it would be, the station manager said he could have the time. This happened about fall 1947. Mr. and Mrs. Splane sang on the broadcast, Mr. Splane played his saxophone, Clara Splane sang, Richard Bonesky helped too. The name of the program was The Friendly Gospel Broadcast.

The services at the hall averaged about fifty to seventy-five. The O'Briens had no definite income, except for the cards Mrs. O'Brien sold so the Alberta District paid the rental fee for the Orange Hall.

A Sunday School bus was rented, Brother Turcotte was the conductor. Brother Turcotte canvassed. Sunday school children increased to ninety-one with the bus. The Sunday school continued to grow.

In September 1947, Rev. J. C. Cooke of Killam had a week of evangelistic meetings. In 1947, a building at 517 A North Railway Street was purchased by Mr. Glen Mitchell. The church paid him back in monthly installments. The building was made ready for services, even put in more church-like windows. At the dedication of this church, platform guests were Rev. A. A. Lewis, a Jewish Rabbi and the Mayor of Medicine Hat along with Rev. and Mrs. O'Brien.

In the spring of 1948, Rev. John Morsch came to be assistant pastor. John Morsch was loaned to Empress to be interim pastor between Miss Hyssop and Rev. James Tyler. In the fall, he left to join the staff of Canadian Northwest Bible Institute (Northwest Bible College).

In July 1953, there was an evangelistic campaign with the Upton Evangelistic Trio. Rev. and Mrs. J. C. O'Brien left in July 1953, after establishing a strong Pentecostal Assembly.

Rev. and Mrs. M. S. Yuke came to pastor the Assembly on July 28, 1953. On November 22, 1953, Rev. S. R. Tilton laid the corner stone for a new church building. On June 6, 1954, church services were held in the basement of the new church. Services were held there until the completion of the upper sanctuary. On September 26, 1954, was the dedication day of the newly completed church. The guest speakers included Rev. J. C. O'Brien (morning speaker), Rev. P. S. Jones (afternoon speaker), and Evangelist Laurie Price (evening speaker). Rev. S. R. Tilton led the dedication of the church, which took place in the afternoon. In 1954, Miss Edina Harding came to assist Rev. and Mrs. Yuke in the ministry. (In 1955 she married Roy Sponholz. She has been busy serving the Lord here and in the surrounding areas and still is. She was widowed in 1972.) The work continued to grow throughout the ministry of the Yukes and Miss Harding. Further property was purchased. Rev. and Mrs. Yuke held their farewell services on October 15, 1961.

Rev. and Mrs. J. H. Law began their ministry there on Sunday October 22, 1961. A new parsonage was erected in 1962. Further property was acquired for a new church. Construction began in April 1967, the first services were held on January 14, 1968 and this First Assembly of God was dedicated May 5, 1968. Rev. and Mrs. Law resigned in March 1969.

Rev. and Mrs. A. L. Lindoff began their ministry there in July 1969. During their time, they inspired the assembly to aim to retire the debt on the building and much of the debt was paid. The Lindoffs left in July 1974.

Rev. and Mrs. Don Schneider came in August 1974. During their time, the thirtieth anniversary services were held from October 22 to 24, 1976. Among those present were Rev. and Mrs. I. Roset, Mrs. J. C. O'Brien, Rev. and Mrs. M. S. Yuke, Rev. and Mrs. A. L. Lindoff. The Board Members were Walter Gries, Chairman; John Ziegenhagel, Secretary; Jim Taylor, Treasurer; Lawrence Wittke; Charles MacKenzie; Barry Callfas. The Youth Pastor was Ted Brooks. For some years, the youth pastors pastored the Hatton Assembly. The Schneiders left at the end of December 1978. Pastor and Mrs. Keith Running came next. They have been busy leading this Assembly. There is a strong missionary vision, which is reflected in their giving to the cause of missions. They have done much to help the senior citizens. A new educational wing has been added to their church building. This church is still going ahead for God.

Among those, who attended Bible college and/or entered the ministry (*), are Ellis Bader, James Bader, Ardith Bonesky, Mary Buchholz, Lynda Callfas, Adeline (Addi) Davidson, *Gloria Davidson (wife of Rev. Darrel Hoeppner), Darrel Fauser, Dianne Fausser, *Norman Gill, Janice Graves, John Greiner (from Redcliffe), Margita Gries, Marlies Gries, Sid Heringer, *Jerry Johnson, Dianne Klaudt, Clayton Law, *Terry Law, Dwight Lees, Roxanne Lees, *Kathy Mast, Irene Miller, *Claire Rattai, Sylvia Rattai, Carol Sept, Ann Tessman, Eugene Wittke, Doreen Woods.

NEWBROOK
NEWBROOK PENTECOSTAL CHURCH

Mr. and Mrs. Buerger had moved from Bruderheim to Newbrook, which had just been opened for homesteading. They were starting to homestead from scratch — a piece of canvas stretched between two trees for a home, a hole for water, made by a post-hole auger, and very little else.

Due to the Wall Street Crash of 1929 and the prairie drought of the early thirties, many more people came here to homestead.

Roads were non-existant and what trails there were were without bridges and often through muskeg. However, there was a railroad. It was unlawful to use the railroad as a highway in the absence of roads but the homesteaders did, even though there were railroad patrols. Travel through muskeg could be very dangerous, for in many places it seemed there was no bottom.

Much pioneer work was done by Rev. J. Schatkowski, who visited all homesteaders and was

First Baptismal Service near Newbrook.

welcomed by all. Visitors were few on the homesteads and Brother Schatkowske carried pockets full of peppermints and Sunday School cards. Children loved him for his interest in them and, of course, the peppermints, which were a real treat. Adults welcomed him too, for he was a "walking Bible." He seemed to know the Bible by heart and could discuss any question. Often to reach the homestead, he would have to take off his shoes and socks, then roll up his pant legs to wade through water or mud.

See the Ellscott Church History section.

The first service of what developed as the German Pentecostal Church was held in the E. Muth

1950 Church in Newbrook.

home the summer of 1928. The home was unfinished at the time. The walls were up and the rafters laid, but no roof as yet. The services were led by Grandpa Muth.

Among those who came, were mostly German families who were the nucleus of the church — the M. Muths, E. Drisners (who recently had escaped from Siberia and reached a brother in Bruderheim from whom Mr. Drisner borrowed ten dollars for a homestead and walked to Newbrook), Mr. G. Millar, L. Kriegers, F. Schultz, E. Stebner, Julius Maser, E. Hartwell (a school boy at the time), F. Golzes, G. Rempel, Schoenlebers, Middlestadts, Eckerts, and E. Langes.

A. A. Eckert, who had homesteaded in the district, moved into what is now Newbrook. He built a store. There was a large upstairs room above the store where the first Sunday School Christmas Program (1933) was held. Services were held here from fall 1932 until the log church was built in 1935. The congregation had been set in order by Rev. L. Posien on June 11, 1933, with twenty-five charter members. Visits from Rev. Posien were greatly appreciated but were few and far between.

There was very little money in the country in those days but there was wood and water and the people had a mind to work. Homes were built of logs and plastered with mud mixed with straw, inside and out.

Twenty-Fifth Anniversary Service with Rev. R. J. White at the pulpit.

Brother E. Janke was the first student pastor and served for two summers. Mr. A. Schultz succeeded him and served for two more summers, until 1944. Both were students from the Pentecostal Bible College in Winnipeg. Miss Busenius and Miss Maser arrived in December 1945 and Miss Maser continued until 1949.

April 6, 1950, the congregation bought the church, parsonage and one acre of land from the Lutheran Evangelical Conference. The German Pentecostal congregation already owned one acre of the two acre cemetery and the Lutheran Conference asked them to take over the other acre. The cemetery is open to all, but legally and formally belongs to the Newbrook Pentecostal Church. Sunday evening services were now held by the young people led by E. Hartwick and Harvey and Ira Johnson.

The first full time pastor was Reverend and Mrs. A. W. Sorge, they pastored until 1954. Miss A. Guretzke then served until some time before Reverend R. J. White and family came from Claresholm, Alberta, in the fall of 1956. Pastor White was from the English Conference.

During the forties many people had moved away but others came in and strengthened the church family — Revegas, Slobodas, Meyns, and Johnsons. Reverend White's ministry continued from October 1956 to October 1966. Many conveniences were lacking in both church and parsonage, but there was one great asset — a large group of delightful young people whose congregational singing was like a great choir. It seemed all were very musical and much

Johnson-White Wedding, 1960. Mel Johnson and Madeline White, daughter of Rev. and Mrs. R. J. White, married and entered the ministry.

singing of choruses was done on the school buses as they made their rounds. An active cradle roll department augmented the Sunday School, baptismal services were held at one of the lakes, an annex was built to the church, parsonage was stuccoed. Improvements came gradually from the old wood burning barrel heater to an oil furnace, firewood cutting and wood and water carrying gave way to progress. A bell was installed to call to worship.

There were many times over the years when the church was without a pastor but visiting ministers and laymen carried on. Reverend Sam Wolfe was the next pastor, who was succeeded by Ted Richardson. At present the pastor Miss Minnie Mueller (1975-   ) has given good leadership. Further improvements to the parsonage and church have been made.

How can we, or who can, estimate the influence of a small church in a community. The end is not yet, praise the Lord. May the bell keep ringing until Jesus comes.

Among those, who attended Bible college and/or entered the ministry (*), are Mareen Crosswell, *Adeline Drisner (now Mrs. Walter Emde), *Reuben Drisner, *Mel Johnson, *Madeline White (wife of Rev. Mel Johnson).

OKOTOKS
OKOTOKS PENTECOSTAL ASSEMBLY

On September 1, 1981, Reverend and Mrs. Jim Tyler opened a new Pentecostal work here. For a few months the services were held in the United Church on Sunday at nine in the morning. Since then Sunday School, morning and evening services have been conducted in a school. During the week they meet for Bible study in their cell groups.

This new Assembly has an attendance of forty-five to fifty people. Reverend and Mrs. Doug Schneider came to minister in July and August 1982 for the Tylers.

OLDS
OLDS PENTECOSTAL ASSEMBLY

The Olds Pentecostal Assembly beginnings were actually quite a distance east of Olds in the Mayton District. The Mayton Pentecostal Tabernacle began with evangelistic meetings held by Mr. Calvin Peterson in a country Baptist Church. It caused no small stir when Mr. David Hemke, Mr. Daniel Gill, Mr. Edward Maetche, Mrs. David Hemke and more received the Baptism of the Holy Spirit. See the Mayton District history for more information.

In 1959, because a number of families moved away, some to Olds, and a number had passed away, the decision was made to close the church and relocate in Olds. This was done under the initiative of Rev. E. Peterson, District Presbyter, and Rev. S. R. Tilton, District Superintendent. Late in 1959, the people of Pentecostal faith here bought the Olds Baptist Church. This church then became the Olds Pentecostal Assembly. The first services that were held in the church were held on Thanksgiving Sunday, October 11, 1959. The guest speakers were Rev. S. R. Tilton and Rev. W. McAlister, General Superintendent of the Pentecostal Assemblies of Canada. This church building was used from 1959 to 1977. By 1977 it was apparent that they needed a larger and better building. That year the old church was demolished, a basement was made and the Idylwylde Tabernacle from Edmonton was moved on to this basement. The purchase and move of that Tabernacle to Olds was done under the direction of Miss Linda Schnedar, the pastor at that time.

The following are the pastors, who served in Olds, Rev. D. Carruthers, first pastor in Olds (1959-61); Rev. M. Jenkins (1961-65); Rev. E. Weibe (1965-66); Rev. K. Ness (1966-67); Mr. Earl Tegart, layman (1967-68); Miss Minnie Mueller (1968-72); Rev. Dave Harris (1972-74); Rev. Don Eshleman (1974-77); Miss Linda Schnedar (1977-78); Rev. Lynn Rosaasen (1978-   ).

This church is looking forward to even more growth.

Among those, who attended Bible college, are Lynn Roberts, Valerie Johanson, Marilyn Taylor.

OYEN
GLAD TIDINGS TABERNACLE

In the early nineteen hundred and thirties Mr. and Mrs. Peter Mervin (Todd) Cantelon came to do secular work in the Sibbald and Alsask area. They held house meetings in these places as well. They also had services at Benton. They conducted street meetings in Oyen. Souls were saved. The first regular meetings were held in the old S. A. Miller Store. In 1935, when Lawrence Holdsworth was pastor, services were conducted in the Co-Op. Later, when Doris Hunter and Violet Pike were in charge of the work, meetings were held in various homes. Mr. Kenneth Bunting also ministered here for a time until Reverend and Mrs. J. R. Allen came to pastor in 1939. They remained until 1941 when Mr. Andrew Wek came to minister.

Many of these ministers had meetings in Sibbald and Benton as well. They would travel about sixty miles on a Sunday. When it rained the roads would have deep ruts and many mud holes.

Faithful lay members, Dan McDonald and C. V. Johnson, hosted many of the early pastors and gave tirelessly of their energy and means to assist in the work. Other early families were Johnstons, Finstads, whose daughter married Reverend Fred Hunter, Gilbertsons and Walkers.

With his bride, Jean, Robert Peel came in 1941 to pastor the Oyen church. The services were held in an old restaurant building. They had a large Sunday School which made the need for a larger building very evident. The Peels introduced a plan known as the "Lord's Acre." Farmers donated the proceeds from one acre of their harvest. The first three hundred dollars for a church was received from this plan. The Peels also continued to minister in Alsask and Sibbald as well as in Oyen.

In 1945 Pastor and Mrs. S. R. Tilton came to Oyen. This was their first pastorate. A school house was bought and moved to town. Fifty song books and a piano were purchased. Now they had their own permanent house of worship. Another old building was obtained and located on the property next to the church. This was their parsonage.

In 1949 Grace Brown accepted the leadership of the work. She was assisted by Dorothy Carson. They carried on a large children's work during the week. This was known as Church School. For many years, Grace Brown served as Dean of Women in the Central Bible College of the Pentecostal Assemblies.

Other pastors who served were Reverend and Mrs. James Robinson, Reverend and Mrs. Swann, Reverend and Mrs. Les Halliwell and Reverend and Mrs. F. Schwindt. During Pastor Schwindt's ministry, a full-sized basement was made under the church.

In 1959 Pastor and Mrs. Boymer came to minister. Many improvements were made to the church — a new gas furnace, new song books, new platform, pulpit, drapes and carpeting. A study and Sunday School rooms were added to the basement. In 1962 trees were planted around the church lot. In the fall of 1962 they began building a parsonage. With help from men of the Empress congregation, the house was completed so that the pastor and his family were able to move in December 26, 1963. In 1967 a parsonage mortgage burning ceremony was held.

In 1973, Glad Tidings Tabernacle Sunday School received a citation for the highest Sunday School Missionary Crusade per capita giving in their category with twenty-two dollars per member in Class A schools with up to fifty average attendance.

Pastor David Michie came to minister in Oyen. In the 1981 Conference, Pastor Michie reported evidences of growth in the Assembly. Three new families were added; souls were saved; believers filled with the Holy Spirit.

PEACE RIVER
PEACE RIVER PENTECOSTAL TABERNACLE

Rev. S. R. Tilton, District Superintendent, was impressed in his travels throughout Alberta that Peace River needed a Pentecostal witness. Rev. Harry Nettleton, who was pastoring in Montgomery, Calgary, wanted to go north to minister. He accepted the challenge to pioneer a work in Peace River in September 1955.

Sunday School was held in the Nettleton home. A lot was purchased by the Alberta District in "Moccasin Flats" along the river road. Here in a garage, services were held. A Womens Missionary Council was organized, a cradle roll was added to the Sunday School. Mrs. Louise Desjarlais and Mrs. Linda Sims were among the first ladies to help in these ministries. Art Taylor, a graduate of Northwest Bible College, found employment in Peace River. He gave invaluable help to the work of the church.

The garage became too small so a building program was started. With a loan from the Minister's Fellowship Fund, also help from Doug Marsden and partner from Montgomery, the construction of a building thirty feet by sixty feet began. This included living quarters for the pastor. The footings were dug by hand. Rain or shine the work on the structure continued until completed. On Thanksgiving Sunday 1956, the church was dedicated. There was no special speaker but the Chester Banner and Fred Tunke families were present that day.

Baptismal service in the mighty Peace River at a camp, spearheaded by H. Nettleton.

Later in the fall, Joyce Sinclair and Beryl Berg, graduates of Northwest Bible College, found work in Peace River. They were a tremendous help with the Sunday School, playing the piano and providing special music. The next spring Ken Bombay and

Rusty Berg, along with other students from the Northwest Bible College held an Easter Rally. The Lord blessed in the salvation of souls. As a result one girl, Elizabeth Wilson, went to Bible College. After some time a full-sized basement was completed under the church.

Rev. and Mrs. Nettleton laboured in Peace River for twelve years. Street meetings were held. Camp meetings in the valley along the Peace and at Lady Lake were conducted for several years. The Assembly assisted in beginning works in Keg River, Fairview and High Prairie.

Rev. and Mrs. David Lagore pastored the church for the next four years. Rev. George Corris followed the Lagores and served the church until 1975, when Pastor and Mrs. Elisha Asselstine came to minister.

On September 1, 1975, the assembly moved into the former Baptist Church. After much work (such as painting, carpeting) and purchasing new pews, the church was rededicated on April 11, 1976. On that occasion a joint-baptismal service was held with the Faiview Assembly.

The fall of 1978 saw a fresh move of God within the hearts of the people. Souls were saved, filled with the Holy Spirit, and some were healed. The Peace River congregation is looking forward to greater things from the Lord as they continue in the Faith.

Among those, who attended Bible College, are Elaine Asselstine, Evan Asselstine, Mary Ann Corris, Kenneth Jobson, Julienne Roy, Dawn Simpson, Elizabeth Wilson.

PINCHER CREEK
PINCHER CREEK PENTECOSTAL ASSEMBLY

Pincher Creek, a beautiful town of four thousand people, is nestled in the southwestern corner of Alberta, one hour's drive from the American border and one hour from British Columbia. Approaching the town from the east, you travel across true prairie, flat and treeless, but gradually and very gently, the prairies turn to rolling hills, and finally the foothills give way to the world famous Rocky Mountains. With the prairies on one side and the mountains on the other, the area boasts of being a fishing and hunting paradise. While its main industries are ranching and several gas plants, another major industry, naturally, is tourism. With Waterton National Park, the Crowsnest Pass and beautiful ski facilities readily available, Pincher Creek has its share of visitors.

As early as 1939, Pentecostal services were held in the Drywood District by Mr. and Mrs. Gerald Smith. In 1960 Mr. Ernest Geitz began to hold meetings in his home in the country. In these weekly services the Pentecostal message was preached. In 1962 Pastor Labrentz and family came to Pincher Creek. On May 27 of that year they held their first meeting in the Oddfellows Hall with over thirty people present. June 10 to 24 saw tent meetings with Reverend Earl Vance and Mr. Ron McQuat. Many curious came. Among them were various preachers including the local Roman Catholic priest and Anglican priest. The Anglican preist was provoked by what he saw. He started to search and later received his personal Pentecost. The following year saw good fellowship with the Anglican priest preaching in the Pentecostal Church and Reverend Labrentz at the Anglican Church. Another group to visit the tent meetings were the Hutterites, who also helped out with donations of groceries. Upon an invitation to have dinner at the colony, the Labrentzes, the tent crew and Miss Eunice Meyer responded. At the close of the meal, Reverend Labrentz said, "We want to express our thanks for the fine meal by singing our love." The group then sang several songs and gave their testimonies — something usually not permitted on a colony.

On August 8, 1962, the first official business meeting was held. A motion was passed that the congregation undertake to build a church. Present at that meeting were Reverend and Mrs. N. Labrentz, Joe Boisveno, Mrs. E. Boisveno, Dean Gillett, Lois Raisbeck, Warner Schmidthe, John Ratzke, Mr. and Mrs. E. Geitz and Mr. and Mrs. Hans Inniger.

The first year had some special experiences. A mother of four, whose husband had run away from home, had a most unique problem. Another lady, recently saved, shared her testimony with this mother. Her pastor, Reverend Labrentz, helped solve the problem. That lady came to church the next Sunday and got saved. During the following week, she was on her knees at home seeking the Lord for direction for her fatherless family. Suddenly a Presence came into the home. The room filled with a bright light and footsteps approached where she was kneeling. A hand lightly touched her shoulder. She dared not look up but did open her eyes looking down. There were the sandled feet with the nailprints. The Master of the Universe spoke softly, "My daughter, put your trust completely in Me and I will heal your home." Praise the Lord, He did work it out. A few years later in another city, both husband and wife and their children were baptized in water. They had already been filled with the Holy Spirit.

By the summer of 1964, work was well under way on the completion of the church basement. Plans were made to finish the entire structure. On July 10, 1966, the Labrentz family said goodbye to Southern Alberta. That same year Pastor and Mrs. Ritchie Haward came to Pincher Creek. During their ministry, the church building was completed and dedicated by District Superintendent, Reverend S. R. Tilton. Reverend R. Taitinger was the special speaker.

Pastors, who followed, were Henry Borzel, now a missionary in the Orient; Vic Munshaw; David McAlister; Brian With; Dan Keys. Because of the growth in the Assembly, possibilities of expanding the facilities have been considered.

Now in 1982, Pastor and Mrs. Tony Nash have come to minister. They are excited about the opportunities before them.

Among those who attended Bible College were Beverly Friebel and Ruby Hopkins.

PROVOST
PROVOST PENTECOSTAL ASSEMBLY

The town of Provost lies east on Highway Thirteen near the Saskatchewan border. It is on the edge of the open prairie and is an excellent farming area. During the drought and the dust of the early thirties, there were years without a crop. Banks and mortgage companies foreclosed. A considerable number of farmers took what livestock they had, loaded what they could on hayracks and went away looking for somewhere to start again. Some of these were Christians, who lived to serve God in other places.

In 1955 a young man, with a shining happy face, arrived in Provost to start a Pentecostal church. His name was Harvey Schmautz, a recent graduate from Northwest Bible College, Edmonton. With help from Pastor Rhind and some people from Metiskow, Sunday afternoon services were held in the I.O.O.F. hall.

The Glen Murphy Family

These were the years, when Pentecostal expansion was taking place under the leadership of District Superintendent S. R. Tilton. Provost was one of the forty new churches opened during a ten year period. With help from Reverend Reuben Drisner and volunteers from Metiskow, construction of a church building began in 1958. Excavation took place. Cement was poured. Walls were built. The lower auditorium was ready for dedication in February 1960. At this time Mr. J. Finnman, chairman of the building committee, presented the keys of the basement church to Pastor Harvey Schmautz. District Presbyter, Reverend M. L. Olson, was present at this service.

Later in 1960 Reverend and Mrs. Schmautz left Provost to enter the evangelistic field. They were followed by the Mueller sisters, Hilda and Minnie. The Sunday School grew. An outreach was launched in the Ribstone District.

The Provost upper sanctuary was completed and formal dedication took place June 9, 1963. There were over one hundred twenty-five people in attendance. Hilda Mueller led the song service, Mayor G. Holmes spoke of what value the church was to the community and District Superintendent, S. R. Tilton, conducted the act of dedication. Mr. J. Finnman, Principal of the Provost Public School, paid fitting commendations to those who helped with the building including neighboring Pentecostal Pastors and people.

Brother and Sister Ed Wiebe followed the Muellers in 1963 and pastored until January 1965. Reverend Eli Fricker came as interim pastor and under his ministry, the Young People's work prospered. Reverend and Mrs. William Bridal took over pastoral responsibility in 1965 and led the congregation until July 1967. Very successful Daily Vacation Bible Schools were held during these years.

The Glen Murphy family were the next to minister. They were a musical family, who took part in Musical Festivals and community Christmas carol services. Mrs. Murphy conducted a Tuesday morning prayer service for women. Reverend Murphy owned and operated a shoe repair shop and also did odd jobs to support his family.

Reverend Arthur Townsend, well known writer, supplied until 1976 when Barry and Cathy O'Coin came as pastors. Pastor O'Coin served on a number of community committees. Mrs. O'Coin held morning coffee meetings. Vacation Schools were held with crowded attendance.

Pastor Steve and Rosalee Gavronsky followed the O'Coins in November 1979. Pastor John Emerson came to minister in Provost.

With the exceptions of the O'Coins and the

Frickers, all of Provost's pastors were graduates of Northwest Bible College.

The Women's Missionary Group of Provost has over the years been active and has given substantial gifts to home and foreign missionaries.

God has blessed in Provost and He will continue to do so in the future.

Among those who attended Bible College are Alice Converse, Loralee Dallyn, Kathleen Stewart, Ruby Tennant, *Lilly Tennant (wife of Rev. Peter Hubert).

RED DEER
WOODLEA PENTECOSTAL
TABERNACLE
(formerly called the Upper Room, Pentecostal Mission, Gospel Mission and Pentecostal Tabernacle)
© Copyright owned by J. Shirley Morsch 1982.

Red Deer was a town of over two thousand, when the first Pentecostal family, George and Esther Taylor with Nora and Violet, arrived in mid 1911. George and Esther Taylor received the Baptism of the Holy Spirit about 1909, under the ministry of Rev. A. H. Argue, while they lived in Cartwright, Manitoba. George, who had been a Methodist laypreacher in England, was one to witness for the Lord. In Red Deer, he usually gathered his family together for singing, scripture reading, an explanation of the Word of God and prayer. If they had guests, they were welcome to join the family at this time. Often, Samuel Taylor, a friend, would play for the hymn sing.

Esther and George Taylor, the first Pentecostal people in Red Deer.

George Taylor talked to a number of people in Red Deer about the Baptism of the Holy Spirit. This helped to form a base for Pentecostal services later on. Esther Taylor, too, dearly loved the Lord. In 1920, fourteen-year-old Nora Taylor received a marvelous answer to prayer, which was a tremendous blessing to her.

In June 1920 in Lethbridge, Alberta, Aimee Semple McPherson held a campaign with marvelous results. Following those meetings, Rev. and Mrs. Hugh Cadwalder of Texas and Brother Watson Argue of Winnipeg came to the Sam Collis farm four miles west of Blackfalds to hold tent meetings in that district.

Brother Cadwalder told them about George Taylor of Red Deer, who had sent money to Lethbridge to help pay the expenses of the Aimee Semple McPherson meetings there. He said he wanted to meet Mr. Taylor. They came to Red Deer but George Taylor was not at home. He, an interior decorator, was painting in Nordegg, but they did meet Mrs. Taylor that day, which was two weeks before the birth of her son, Arnold, on September 7, 1920.

Roy Collis remembers that, when his parents, Mr. and Mrs. Sam Collis, his sister, Hilda, and he would call at the Taylors, they had a little meeting. Sam Taylor would be there, too.

In October 1920, a fine young man from the Edmonton Assembly, Philip Snider, became the first Pentecostal Pastor in Red Deer. Philip really loved God and was highly regarded by the Taylors. Both Philip and his assistant, John Gilpin, lived with the George Taylor family. Mrs. Mae Snider, Philip's widow, reported that Philip loved the Taylors. He said they were so kind to him and gave him just the right kind of encouragement for a young preacher.

Upper Room Sunday School children and teachers

Services were held in the old dining room of the Alexander Hotel (later known as the Park Hotel and then the Western Inn).

When one young man heard about the Pentecostal meetings, he told his mother that the Holy Rollers were in town. She decided to come to a service to check them out. After attending a service, with Bible in hand, she knelt to pray in her own home. She told the Lord that she did not want to be led astray. She asked Him to show her whether what she had heard and saw were of Him or not. She opened her Bible to Acts chapter two. The words in verse sixteen, "This is that," seemed to stand out. She was convinced that what they spoke of and experienced in those Pentecostal meetings was truly scriptural, so she and her husband became faithful members of this group of believers. Both she and her future daughter-in-law were filled with the Spirit in due time.

One Sunday, while service was in progress in the old dining room of the Alexander Hotel, a man came in. He heard the music and decided to come in. This decision changed his life, for he accepted Christ as his own personal Saviour. He had come to Red Deer to find work as there was no work for him in Edmonton, where he lived. He found a job in Red Deer then lost it due to conditions beyond his control. He was so discouraged that he was contemplating suicide as he walked by the Alexander Hotel but the gospel music caught his attention. He was gloriously saved, went back to Edmonton, where he became a real blessing in the Pentecostal Assembly there.

After John Gilpin left, Freeman Hamilton assisted Philip Snider for a while in 1921. He, his wife and family also lived with the Taylors. Philip Snider was called to Edmonton to assist the pastor, Rev. Cadwalder, who was very ill, so he left in March 1921. The Hamiltons stayed on for a while.

Among those, who attended services at that time, were George and Esther Taylor with Nora, Violet, Joseph, Alma, Annie and Arnold; Mr. and Mrs. Sam Collis with Roy and Hilda; Samuel Taylor; Grandma Neilson; Mrs. Torgrud with Florence and Ray; George and Janet Maben; the Knutsons and Edith Hill.

The North Red Deer Municipal Hall, at the corner of 58 Street and 53 Avenue, was rented for services in 1922. During that time, a Pastor Willis, who was an Apostolic preacher, ministered for a while. Miss Georgina Waddell began attending the services in 1922 or 23.

Rev. Hugh McAlister held cottage meetings for a time in 1923. Roy Collis recalls him preaching in the Maben home on the north hill. Hugh McAlister lived in the Maben home.

At a cottage meeting, a sister said that the room

Pastors Eva Dale and Phyllis Aitcheson

was full of angels. Those present were very conscious of the presence of the Lord. That same night another sister received the Baptism of the Holy Spirit. Though she did not know a word of German, she sang a hymn in the German language by the power of the Holy Spirit. A German brother, who was there, said it was a hymn that his mother had sung to her family, when he was young. He had been skeptical about the Baptism of the Holy Spirit until this happened. It proved to him that this experience was real.

When a person accepted Christ as his own personal Saviour, he or she became part of the family of God, so were referred to as brother or sister. It was and still is a very special family.

Early in 1925, the Orange Hall on 53 Street was used for services. Pastor Denzil Miller was there then. Cottage meetings were held for some years again. In June 1926, Georgina Waddell married Robert Maben. In 1927 Helen and Harold Sage began attending. In 1925 Nora Taylor married Joseph Johnson. In May 1929, Rev. John McAlister visited the assembly and held a service. In 1930 Rev. John Wood ministered for a short time. He married Hilda Collis. About 1932 or 33, Clare Scratch ministered for about two or three months in evangelistic services. Nora Johnson, her husband and children were back for the winter of 1932-33. Nora enjoyed being able to attend services again.

About 1933, two young men, Clare Richardson and Willis McPherson, came to minister. At this time, the old St. Luke's Parish Hall on Gaetz Avenue was rented for services. George Hyslop, who worked in a bank, was a fine asset to this assembly. In December 1934, a hall above an implement or machine shop, was rented. Later the Kovac's Shoe Clinic took over this shop on 49 Street. That hall was referred to as the Upper Room. There was a room up there, just off the hall, that was used as a residence for the pastor or pastors. Willis McPherson left and other young people came to help in the meetings, including Harvey McAlister, who stayed for a time. Clare's sister, Alice, came to help. She played the organ. To bring in some financial help, she worked at the Provincial Training School. During these days in the Upper Room, an offering box was attached to the wall near the hall entrance. As folks came in, they would leave their tithes, offerings, and invitations to dinner (for the pastor) in the box. The tithes and offerings would pay for the rent, food and pastor's needs. Clare Richarson would check the box. Often the rent money appeared in the box the night before the rent was due. A Brother MacKenzie assisted for a while. Then Victor Graham came. He assisted Clare until he left, then Victor stayed on. He preached, led the services and conducted street meetings. Victor lived at the Dunn residence and later at the Willet home. During this time, a young man, Bob Peel, often came. Bob later became a well-known missionary to Africa. Victor Graham married Florence Torgrud. Sister Engel said that she could sense the presence of the Lord when she came to service.

Around 1937, Joe Valesko came to pastor. He was often heard saying in prayer, "Lord, there's no flies in Your ointment." Those, who knew him, would appreciate that. Don McNutt followed Joe. Then Albert Brant, brother of Ethel Tarbuck, came to pastor. Under his direction, the Upper Room, which was also called the Pentecostal Mission, was changed to the Gospel Mission. Servicemen, stationed in the Red Deer Army Base and the Penhold Air Base, began to attend.

A Soldiers and Airmens Christian Association was formed to meet the spiritual and fellowship needs of the servicemen. The Upper Room group helped in this ministry. Rev. Albert Brant became the director of this Association, so Mrs. Bert (Eva) Dale became the pastor of the Upper Room in January 1943. In the spring of 1943, under the leadership of Mrs. Eva Dale, the Red Deer Independent Assembly (the Gospel Mission) voted unanimously for affiliation with the Pentecostal Assemblies of Canada. At this meeting, the decision to invite Miss Phyllis

Upper Room Young People. Back Row, Left to Right: soldier, Shirley Johnson, Wes Duncan, Anna Neilson. Front Row: Elsie Johnson, Bessie Hallgren, Jessie Gross.

Aitcheson to become Mrs. Dale's assistant was made. Mrs. Dale had a large Bible Club in North Red Deer with over a hundred children in attendance.

Both Mrs. Dale and Miss Aitcheson endeared themselves to all. When Sister Dale heard someone say, "I'm awful!" She would say, "Yes, awfully nice." They did much to encourage both young and old, alike.

Eileen Edwards and Rev. and Mrs. Clare Scratch enlarged the vision of the congregation. Souls were saved and young people dedicated their lives to

Dedication Day of the Red Deer Pentecostal Tabernacle. Back Row: Rev. Harvey C. McAlister, Rev. A. A. Lewis. Front Row: Mrs. H. C. (Agnes) McAlister, Alice Leland, Alma Vance.

Christ. In July 1944, Phyllis Aitcheson left to prepare herself for missionary work in India. That door was closed so, after marrying Rev. William Hincks, went to Zambia, Africa.

Among the songs sung in the Upper Room, were My Sins Are Blotted I Know, Make Me a Blessing, Into My Heart, The Old Rugged Cross, Come We That Love the Lord, Showers of Blessings, Springs of Living Water and When We All Get to Heaven.

The Christ Ambassadors (a young people's group from teenagers to thirty-five year olds) was formed. The adults attended their meetings and socials and were very supportive. If the adults were asked to take part, they were glad to help. All the young people took part in the C.A. services — ushering, singing, leading the service, scripture reading, preaching and whatever. They did what they could. It was great training and experience. Elsie Johnson was the first president. Shirley Johnson was secretary. A number of these first C.A.'s attended Bible college — Jessie Gross, Bessie Hallgren, Anna Neilson, Elsie Johnson and Shirley Johnson. The C.A.'s sent Sunday School papers to the West Indies and a quilt to Phyllis Aitcheson. Sister Dale resigned in March 1945.

One of the marriages performed in the Upper Room, perhaps the only one performed there, was the marriage of Miss Jessie Gross to Rev. Ernest Hawtin, pastor of Carrot River Assembly in Saskatchewan, on September 9, 1946. Rev. Britton performed the ceremony.

Don and Phyllis McNutt served this assembly from May to August 1945. Every time Don McNutt would say, "Surely, someone has a testimony tonight," a certain Shirley would stand and give a testimony. In the fall of 1945, Edina Harding came to be the pastor. Her ministry and music were a real blessing.

Sister Harding loved the moving of the Holy Spirit, too. Under her ministry, Yvonne Ekstrom, who was about nine years old, received the Baptism of the Holy Spirit. Yvonne remembers receiving real liberty in the Spirit about two years later, when Mrs. Ida Cooke prayed with her at Sunnyside Camp.

Sister Harding lived in a little house in North Red Deer. She taught Elsie and Shirley Johnson how to play their violins. Shirley often led the song service for Sister Harding. Sister Harding was and still is an excellent pianist.

Toward the end of 1946, Evangelist and Mrs. C. L. Ward conducted three and a half weeks of special meetings. On the evenings that Brother Ward painted an oil picture, quite a few had to stand for all the benches were filled. About this time Laura Holdsworth came to assist Sister Harding. Many blessed times were had in the Upper Room. Sister Harding left in 1947.

Among those, who attended services in the Upper Room, were George and Esther Taylor with Annie and Arnold (until George and Esther moved to Victoria, Annie to Vancouver and Arnold went into the Army); George and Janet Maben; Georgina Maben with Ernie, Marg and Lorene; Mrs. Dunn with Josie; Jim and Ethel Tarbuck with Doris and Bobby (They began attending when Clare Richardson was pastor.); Nora Johnson with Shirley, Elsie, Eldon (Bud), Doreen and Sharon (whenever they lived in Red Deer); the Molson children; the Willet children; Harold and Helen Sage; Mr. and Mrs. George Gross with Jessie; the Hallgren Family including Bessie; Mrs. Jacobson; Elmer Jacobson; Mr. and Mrs. Jake Littau with Edna; Mr. and Mrs. Rudolf Ekstrom with Yvonne; Marie, a friend of Annie Taylor, and Anna Neilson. Among the servicemen, who attended were Wes Duncan, Wes Bloye with his wife and family, Jack McMullen (who played his Hawaiian guitar beautifully) and Gordon Donaldson (who married Anna Neilson). All these mentioned servicemen were in the Army. There were others, too.

Wedding of Elsie Johnson to Robertson Howatt at the Red Deer Pentecostal Tabernacle.

Sister Tarbuck played a guitar. Helen Sage had Bible Club and made a ministry of inviting children to Sunday School. In a smaller congregation, each person's ministry was really needed.

During the ministry of Alice Leland and Alma Vance, the Penhold Presbyterian Church was purchased and moved on to a basement at 4832 51 Street in Red Deer. An apartment was built in the basement for the pastor's residence. This church was dedicated as the Pentecostal Tabernacle by Rev. A. A. Lewis on September 26, 1948. Rev. Harvey C. McAlister and his wife, Agnes, were present. Rev. McAlister was guest speaker in the evening service.

The assembly continued to grow in number and in faith. Among those, who received the Baptism of the Holy Spirit while services were held in this Tabernacle, were Nora Johnson, Lorene Maben, Doreen Johnson, Sharon Johnson, Jim Tarbuck and Helen Sage.

Among those, who ministered in this Tabernacle, were Rev. S. R. Tilton, who was well-known for his Holy Spirit ministry and for building up the assembly in faith and numbers; Rev. J. Pearce (1952-56); Rev. W. Pipke (1956-   ); Rev. Don Cantelon (-1964), who also conducted the popular telecast, Melodic Moments; and Rev. Ross Pennoyer (1964-71).

Rev. and Mrs. Daniel Anderson and family came from Denmark and lived in Red Deer for a time. They, too, attended the Tabernacle on 51 Street. Then they entered the ministry in Alberta and later as missionaries in South Africa.

During Ross Pennoyer's ministry, Woodlea Pentecostal Tabernacle was built on the east bank of Waskasoo Creek at 5350 46 Avenue — a very pretty setting. It was dedicated February 12, 1967 by Rev. S. R. Tilton, District Superintendent. Rev. R. W. Taitinger was the guest speaker.

In March 1972, Miss Beryl Shannon left for missionary preparation in Switzerland and Quebec. Then in September 1973, she went to Zaire, Africa, as a children's worker and bookkeeper. She has been home on furlough twice.

Under Rev. Albert Werbiski's ministry (1971-1978), Woodlea grew so much that an addition, which also increased the sanctuary seating from two hundred and five to three hundred and sixty-eight, was built and dedicated November 6, 1977 by Rev. I. Roset, District Superintendent. Rev. R. W. Taitinger, General Superintendent, was the guest speaker. An item of interest is that Gilbert Snider, second son of Rev. Philip Snider, was on the Deacon Board and the building committee at that time. Mrs. Gilbert (Dorothy) Snider also served as church secretary for some time. Rev. Werbiski's assistants for varying lengths of time were Wayne Walters, Gerry Jeske, Lyle Johnson, Greg Wyton and Dave Miller. Rev. R. Norcross pastored from 1978 to 1982. For a time two morning services were held. His assistants for varying lengths of time were Rev. D. Wells, Larry Lindoff, Frank Jacobs and David Pedde.

Rev. Egan Roller, his wife and daughter arrived. Rev. Roller's first service was the Sunday of the Labor Day weekend 1982. At these services there was an air of expectancy. The congregation was looking forward to the future.

Among those from the George Taylor family, who are presently (1982) attending Woodlea Taber-

Wedding of Doreen Johnson to Everett McCauley. Guests seated are Pastor's wife, Mrs. J. Pearce; Gwen Donaghy; Yvonne Ekstrom and   (left to right).

nacle, are Nora Johnson (nee Taylor), daughter; granddaughter, Doreen McCauley (nee Johnson) and her husband, Everett McCauley; great granddaughters, Wendy McCauley and Bonnie McCauley.

Among those, who served the church for some time, were Helen Sage, treasurer for a long time; then Betty Arthur became treasurer and Gerald Smith, who was secretary for quite a few years.

Woodlea Pentecostal Tabernacle

Among those, who attended Bible college and/or entered the ministry (*), are *Gerda Anderson (wife of Rev. William Brown), Daneen Burk, Dennis Burk, Calvin Carruthers, Edith Christiansen, Russell deBruijn, Sharon Elaschuk, *Jessie Gross (wife of Rev. E. Hawtin), Emily Guilbault, Bessie Hallgren (now Mrs. Hankins), Gary Harding, *Gerald Jeske, #*Elsie B. Johnson (now Mrs. R. L. Howatt), #*J. Shirley Johnson (now Mrs. Edwin Morsch), *Wanda Kanten, *Carol Kanten, *Colleen Kanten (married Rev. Reg Carbol), Doreen Krien, Marilyn Kwantis, Joyce Liddell, Gladys Maetche, #Carol McCauley (now Mrs. Ronald Barbour), Glenda McPeek,

*Anna Neilson (now Mrs. Gordon Donaldson), Clayton Peterson, Dale Plante, Irvine Rangen, *Beryl-Jane Shannon, Elsie Smith, Jessie Smith, #*Joseph Taylor, *Doris Tarbuck (Mrs. Don Greiner), *Florence Torgrud (wife of Rev. Victor Graham), Maxine Wood, Ron Wood. (# marks the descendants of George and Esther Taylor.)

ROCKY MOUNTAIN HOUSE
ROCKY MOUNTAIN HOUSE
PENTECOSTAL ASSEMBLY

Having felt the call of God to Rocky Mountain House, Reverend Lyle Carbert came to this booming gas and oil town on December 2, 1971. He left his wife and three children with his parents in Red Lake, Ontario, until he could find accommodation for them. Contact with one family led to others and on December 5, 1971, at seven o'clock he held his first service in a home on the corner of fifty-fourth Street and fifty-first Avenue with one man in attendance.

The following Sunday, December 12, 1971, services were held in the Legion Hall. A group of about twenty-five worshipped here for six months. The founding families were Alex and Esther Boguski, Jim and Betty Bond, Sam and Grace Brown, Steve Kapty, Grandpa Tom Lewis, Frank and Gloria Durocher and others, who attended off and on. The congregation then decided to rent the closed-down Full Gospel Church on forty-sixth Street. So on Easter Sunday of 1972, the first Sunday School and Morning Service were held. An evening service was also held at seven o'clock. Mid-week prayer meetings were held in different homes. The congregation met in this church for the next eighteen months. During this time, other attending families were Ed and June Bevan, Rudy and Doreen Klaassen, Art and Eilien Lebsack, and Diane Reddekopp and children, to name a few.

In the meantime, the pastor and men were tearing down an old house and denailing all re-usable lumber to build a twenty by thirty foot garage, which was to double as a place for Crusaders to meet. During this time the Crusaders had grown to around fifteen and were meeting in the pastor's living room. The children were asked not to invite more children because the space was limited. While this building was going up, the people decided to make the garage into a small chapel. This they did and on December 21, 1973, the congregation held a Christmas Fellowship Supper in the Good News Chapel at 4715-47 Avenue. This was truly a time of rejoicing and blessing.

Within six months, the small congregation of thirty or so had doubled and continued to grow with an average of one soul per week being saved over the next two years.

The growing congregation made plans and took action into getting a new church built. There were many volunteers, including a group from Sunnyside Pentecostal Camp, who helped build this church. Donations of money were received from Saskatchewan, Montana, Las Vegas, and many centres in Alberta and other parts of Canada. What a day of excitement and praise to God when on July 20, 1975, Brother Roset, Alberta District Superintendent, came for the official sod-breaking ceremony. On October 7, 1975, the machines moved in to dig the basement and then the people worked, prayed and shared together for the next two years as block upon block, piece by piece, the beautiful serviceable church was erected.

Because of constant growth, the congregation moved into the basement of the new church on August 29, 1976. Construction continued on the upper level. This, too, was a glorious day as now there was room for expansion and new people.

With united effort and oneness of body, soul and spirit the three hundred thousand dollar church was put in readiness for the Dedication Service on October 15, 1977. Today at 4715-47 Avenue stands a testimony to the faithfulness of God.

During the summer of 1972, the first Drive-In-Church was held in the Rocky Mountain House I.G.A. parking lot. Every summer since that time Drive-In-Church has been held at the same location.

God continues to move saving souls and filling lives with the Holy Spirit, healing sick bodies, and mending broken homes.

Among those, who attended Bible College and/or entered the ministry(*), are *Bonny Ayrchuk (wife of Reverend Harvey Leshner), Bette Jean Boguski, Ben Durocher, Beverly Lebsack, Dick Medin, Chris Small, Melody Small, Leonard VanDyck, Dana VanDyck.

ST. ALBERT
ELIM PENTECOSTAL CHAPEL

Mr. and Mrs. John Albrecht lived ten miles west of St. Albert near Villeneuve. Because of their faithfulness to testify of their faith in God, the Pentecostal message was accepted in St. Albert. Some, even though they were not of the Pentecostal faith, suggested that Pentecostal meetings would be good for their town. About 1956 or 1957, thanks to Jean Ferron, the Club Mocombo was obtained rent free for two years but they paid the janitor for his work. The services were held on Sunday afternoons.

At the first service, the Mayor of St. Albert spoke to the congregation. He said he was glad to have the Pentecostals in St. Albert. Reverend Bob Taitinger ministered in that service. Central Pentecostal Tabernacle cared for these services until Reverend Paul Kerychuk became the full time pastor. Reverend Kerychuk and several families left to establish the Beverly Pentecostal Tabernacle English group.

In the winter of 1961-1962, Mr. and Mrs. Harry Onishenko and family came to pastor. The meetings continued in the Club Mocombo for a short time then the meetings were held in the Sir George Simpson School.

Among the families attending were Alfred Schalm family, Bob Job, Stan Carlson family, Linda and Dawn Hagen, Jack Berg family, Marie Berg family.

Property was purchased, a basement was poured. An Anglican Church in north Edmonton was bought and moved on to the foundation. A spacious foyer and Pastor's study were added with much work being done by members of the congregation.

Bob and Gisela Ekstrom assisted Onishenkos (1969-1971). Onishenkos concluded their ministry in St. Albert in early 1971. The Ekstroms were interim pastors until Reverend and Mrs. K. W. Agrey came to minister.

On June 11, 1972, the church, Elim Pentecostal Chapel, was dedicated to the Lord's service. Reverend P. A. Gaglardi was guest speaker and Reverend Charles Yates, District Superintendent, led the dedication.

Among those, who pastored after the Agreys, were Dan Knol and the Latimers. Student Pastor Tony Yakielashek ably cared for the assembly while Pastor Latimer was so very ill.

Among those, who attended Bible College, are John Berg, Dallas MacIntyre, Darrell McIntyre, Ronald Rattai.

ST. PAUL
BETHEL PENTECOSTAL CHURCH

Prior to 1940 John Harbarenko and L. Krawchuk held street meetings in St. Paul. During the late summer of 1940 Reverend Winston Nunes, held evangelistic meetings with the District tent. St. Paul was a strong Roman Catholic centre. However with the able and generous support of the Ukrainian folk in the community, a real work was done and within ten weeks a forty year old two-storey building, at the site of the present church, was purchased and completely paid for and a foothold secured in St. Paul. People pledged support for a pastor and invited Reverend Walter Frederick, then pastoring at Mayton, to take over the work. Reverend Frederick came in November 1940.

The building was a wooden structure that had never been painted. Half of the first floor was an auditorium for church services. Living quarters were overhead. The other half of the building was a furniture and secondhand store with a storage area on the second floor. The living area entrance was at the rear corner of the building. It was necessary to climb a long flight of stairs, then walk down a dark hallway to the door. All the floors in the building sloped toward the big brick chimney in the center. The ceilings were of beaver board. Rain had leaked through and warped the panels which hung down in a twisted fashion. The weather was very cold. The living quarters' heat came from a wood burning heater in the living room. The wood was green and black smelly creosote dripped from the stovepipes. Potatoes would freeze in the kitchen at night. When they thawed out during the day, you could squeeze water out of them like a sponge. At times there would be loud noises, like a giant hitting the roof with a club, as the building contracted from the cold. In the front bedroom lay a long coil of rope tied to the head of the bed. This was the emergency fire escape. Thank the Lord it never had to be used.

In the spring of 1941, the old building was torn down and the present church was constructed out of the old lumber. The Fredericks lived in the center apartment of a large house on the east side of town. Mrs. Frederick cooked meals for the carpenters. Food was brought in mainly from the people of the Glendon church. All the work was done by volunteers. Brother Frederick did the stucco work. As soon as the doors and windows were in, the Fredericks moved into the new living quarters. When the finishing work was done and the new building was ready for services, friends gathered from neighbouring areas for the dedication. In November 1941 at a three-day Convention in St. Paul, Superintendent George R. Upton dedicated the new church building to the glory of God. It was the first convention of its kind in the north-east section of Alberta and the workers, mostly Ukrainian, responded well.

In St. Paul, Pastor Frederick conducted Sunday services while Mrs. Frederick looked after the Sunday School. Brother Frederick travelled about two-thirds of the time, visiting churches in Glendon, Bonnyville, Iron River, Therien, Elk Point, Vilna and other settlements.

Brother H. Graves, of Edmonton, became interested in this home mission field and gave twenty-five dollars in order that pictures could be taken of the various churches and congregations. Slides were made up and were shown at the Moose Lake camp meeting in July 1943.

In 1943 Walter Frederick was elected District Superintendent of the Pentecostal Assemblies of

Canada in Alberta. In August 1944 the Fredericks left St. Paul.

Pastor Charlie Warkentine (1945) followed the Fredericks; then came George E. Clark, who started a church register. Next came John Tymchuk. Under his ministry a fair number of young people gave their hearts to Jesus. One of them was Steve Holomis, who later pastored the St. Paul church. Jack Hunka put in five profitable years. There was a large young people's group and a number of souls were saved. H. M. Graves followed Jack Hunka.

Gladys Prest ministered here after Brother Graves. She was very good with young people. She was a firm believer in water baptism. A number who had been saved years earlier were baptized while she was pastor.

Steve Holomis spent four years (1959-1963) in St. Paul. Under his leadership the assembly reached its highest numerical growth. They won the 1961 Sunday School attendance award at the District Conference that year. Steve ministered in Ukrainian and English. Improvements were made in the church and parsonage. Water and bathroom facilities were installed. With gains in June 1961 of one hundred twenty-three percent and in September of sixty-two percent, the church was filled to capacity. A number were saved during this time and Pastor Steve wanted to build. Property was purchased and plans were made to sell the old property, but the plans never did materialize. Steve resigned March 25, 1963.

Rudy Mantik was asked to pastor the assembly. He was just out of Bible School and showed an eagerness to work hard with the Sunday School and young people. His wife played the piano and saxophone.

Helmut Eisert came to pastor in February 1966. The church was going through a difficult time and was on Home Mission support for six months. Brother Eisert resigned on January 23, 1967. He did a great deal of electrical work at Moose Lake Camp.

Brother George Corris pastored for four years 1968 to 1972. The property originally bought for a new church was sold and money was raised to build a new three bedroom parsonage. Forced air heating with thermostatic control was installed in the church in 1971.

Gerald Anderson stayed as pastor for six years 1972 to 1978. During his tenure, a radio program called River of Life was aired. It has since been discontinued.

Phil Eshleman followed (1978-1980), then Keith Balkwell (1980-1981) and the present pastor is Hector McDonald (1982-   ).

One interesting thing to note about this church is that through the years it has reverted back and forth between the English and the Slavic Conferences of the Pentecostal Assemblies of Canada. At present it is with the English Conference.

Among those, who attended Bible College and/or entered the ministry (*), are *Steve Holomis, Colleen Hull, Linda Hull, Bill Kenneth Junior, Helen Polachuk, Kevin Dale Semeniuk.

SHERWOOD PARK
SHERWOOD PARK PENTECOSTAL ASSEMBLY

In 1974 Reverend Mel Jenkins, from Kamloops, B.C., was the Youth speaker at Sunnyside Pentecostal Camp. Reverend C. Yates, District Superintendent, shared with Reverend Jenkins the plan for opening a Pentecostal work in Sherwood Park. The Alberta District of the Pentecostal Assemblies was negotiating the purchase of an eight-year-old Alliance Church. Reverend Yates asked Reverend Jenkins if he would be interested in going to pastor this new work. Reverend Jenkins had already been sensing the Holy Spirit leading him into a change for his ministry. He soon felt convinced that Sherwood Park was where God wanted him.

Sod-Turning Ceremony, Rev. I. Roset and Mr. Sam McCaughey, a senior charter member, turning sod; Rev. K. Bunting.

By September 8, 1974, Sunday School and a morning worship service were started in the Band Room of the Cloverbar Junior High School. Another service was conducted in the afternoon in the building that was to be their church home. Reverend Jenkins attended the opening service. He returned in October to begin his ministry in Sherwood Park. God blessed in those first meetings. Souls were saved.

On January 1, 1975, the church building and 2.26 acres of land were purchased from the Alliance church for one hundred seventy thousand dollars.

On February 11, 1975, the church was officially

organized by Reverend I. Roset, District Superintendent. The Assembly adopted the Local Constitution of the Pentecostal Assemblies of Canada.

February 23, 1975, was a glorious Dedication day with Reverend R. W. Taitinger, General Superintendent, as special speaker.

The first annual meeting showed reports of God's goodness. This was held on March 19, 1975. Those elected on the Board of Deacons were John Barker, Win Bowen, Don Bunting, Frank Drader and Gordon Knott. Charter members of the church were Mr. and Mrs. D. Bunting, Mr. and Mrs. J. Barker, Mr. and Mrs. F. Drader, Mr. and Mrs. S. McCaughey, Mr. and Mrs. L. Smith, Mr. and Mrs. R. Monk, Mr. and Mrs. G. Nash, Mr. and Mrs. P. Holomis, Mr. P. Kadatz, Mr. and Mrs. W. Bowen, Mr. and Mrs. G. Knott, Mr. and Mrs. A. Venters, Mr. and Mrs. K. Busenius, Mrs. O. White, Mr. and Mrs. J. McEwen, Mr. and Mrs. G. Ainslie and Mr. and Mrs. K. Jenkins.

At the Sod-Turning Ceremony, left to right in row one: *John McEwen; *Frank Drader; *Gordon Knott; *Howard Vader; Gordon Fletcher, Christian Education Director; Rev. Mel Jenkins, Founding and present pastor; *Don Bunting, Building Committee Chairman; *Rudie Harder; *Syd Spiker; Walter Dressler and Paul Holomis. Building Committee Members are underlined. Past or 1982 Board Members are starred.

The Assembly continued to make progress in the Sunday School, with over one hundred attending the morning worship service. Youth services, Women's Ministries and Men's Fellowship were functioning as well.

In May, Evangel Assembly in Edmonton joined Sherwood Park Assembly in their first baptismal service. Seven candidates were baptized. As church attendance and Sunday School grew a temporary mobile unit was placed on the property. Later space in a nearby Recreation Center was rented. Soon the need for expansion was obvious. In 1979, a twenty-acre plot on the north edge of Sherwood Park was purchased, of which half was subsequently sold.

A sod-turning service for the new sanctuary was held on June 15, 1980. Construction began later in the summer. On May 10, 1981 a cavalcade, escorted by three Royal Canadian Mounted Police, made its way from the old church to the new. A great crowd gathered outside the sanctuary for a ribbon-cutting ceremony. After a brief tour of the facility, each teacher took their class to the classroom. Three hundred thirty-five people were present at that first service in their new church. It has a total seating capacity of six hundred fifty. Its total size is eighteen thousand square feet. The building costs were one million one hundred twenty-five thousand dollars.

Sherwood Park Pentecostal Assembly

On June 7, 1981, the new Sherwood Park Pentecostal Assembly was dedicated by Reverend I. Roset. Dr. David Lim was the special speaker at this service. Pastor Mel Jenkins welcomed the people. Pastor G. Fletcher gave the Scripture reading. Others taking part in this service were Reverend K. Bunting, Assistant District Superintendent; Don McIntyre, architect; Henry Woo, M.L.A. for Sherwood Park; J. D. Morrow, Reeve for the County of Strathcona; Rev. J. Hazlett; Sharon Harder and Renae Jenkins, soloists; Glen Ellingson, who presented Don Bunting with the keys.

There has been a strong evangelical emphasis in this Assembly from its beginning. The very first winter, they distributed three thousand handbills advertising the film, "Road to Armageddon." Souls were saved. In March 1975, six thousand more handbills announcing the ministry of the British Columbia A.I.M. team were distributed. These young Ambassadors In Missions were heard by hundreds of junior and senior high school students plus many others in evening concerts. The first evangelist to conduct services in the Assembly was Miss Eunice Meyer. In September 1975, the First Anniversary Crusade was held with Reverend Ken Bombay as evangelist.

Throughout the short history of this Assembly,

The Mel Jenkins Family

God has worked wondrously in the lives of many people. Various ministries for men, women, youth and children have been initiated. Spiritual and social needs in this constituency have been met by the inspired ministries of Sherwood Park Pentecostal Assembly.

Among those who attended Bible College are Dan Eagle, Edna Heidelberg, Randy Sylvester.

SILVER VALLEY
SAVANNA LIGHTHOUSE ASSEMBLY

Before any organized work began in Silver Valley, there were several Pentecostal or charismatic families in the area who were influenced by various ministries. God was preparing the hearts of the people to do a work. In March 1976, a family of seven and several members of another family all accepted Christ at Max Solbrekken's meetings in Dawson Creek, B.C.. Shortly after that, a tragic accident took the life of a relative, Benny Dick, who was living in the community. Rev. Norman Labrentz, of Grande Prairie Evangel Assembly, conducted the funeral, at which two people accepted Jesus as their Saviour. With this contact, teams were sent out from Grande Prairie to minister at various times. In one meeting ten young people were filled with the Holy Spirit.

Another highlight was a baptismal service in a dugout, at which time ten followed the Lord in baptism.

In June 1979, Pastor Brian and Connie Moffat took up residence in Silver Valley. They supported themselves by janitorial duties at the local school. Shortly thereafter an Assembly was formed and affiliation granted by the Pentecostal Assemblies of Canada. The first board consisted of Mr. Keith Wilson, Mr. Dwayne Frostad and Mr. Robert Keirs. Mr. Leroy Rehaume served a two year term. Now in 1982 the board consists of Mr. R. Keirs, Mr. M. Sexty and Miss Bertha Dyck.

The founding families were the Keith Wilsons, the Dwayne Frostads, the Robert Keirs, the Leroy Rehaumes, the Sid Payettes, the Dick Foxes, the John Dycks Sr., the Stewart Weighills. Later the Re Larivieres, who moved into the area, added their support to the church. The George Budd family brought a much needed music ministry. Recently the Larry Gebhart family were saved and became regular attenders. Since the formation of the church, there have been a number saved and filled with the Holy Ghost.

A church has now been erected and is nearing completion. God miraculously undertook for the financial and building needs. Ten acres of land were obtained for one thousand dollars. The previous owner of this land has since been saved and filled with the Holy Spirit. Allan and Terry Purvis and family moved into the area for six months to oversee the construction of building. Work teams came from the Pentecostal Churches in Peace River, Grande Prairie and Fairview, as well as a group from the Caroline Bible School. During a discussion regarding purchasing and installing a furnace unit, Mark Bastelle from Grande Prairie walked in and overheard the deliberations. He offered to install the furnace at virtually no cost for labor. The building was completed mainly with volunteer labor. The official opening of the church was March 28, 1982.

The Pastor now has a trailer on the church land and is supported by Home Missions. The Assembly is looking forward to a bright future as they believe God for an outpouring of the Holy Spirit in their community.

SLAVE LAKE
CHRISTIAN CENTRE

The Stan Lagores arrived in Slave Lake in August 1970. The work was started by having boys and girls clubs in the apartment they rented. From this core of boys and girls a Sunday School was started. It was held in the Legion Hall every Sunday afternoon at 2:30 P.M.. As many as one hundred fifty-nine came to the Children's meetings but the average attendance for Sunday School was twenty-five to thirty.

During 1971, a morning service in conjunction with the Sunday School was started. The services were held in the Centennial Hall. In September 1971, the first Pentecostal family moved into Slave Lake. Their friendliness, teaching and musical abilities were a real blessing and inspiration to the church.

During 1972, the church basement of the former Baptist congregation was purchased. On October 31, 1972, work on the building began by resupporting the basement floor joists. Brother George Lagore assisted in this first endeavour. Shortly after, the cement, to lay the cement blocks upon, was poured. The first blocks were laid the first week of December 1972, but due to problems of cold weather and the shortage of a brick layer, the block-laying was not completed until the middle of March 1973. The Lord performed many miracles during this time. The rafters were put up during Easter week. On Victoria Day 1973, the roof was completed.

In the spring of 1973, Brother Bill Sim's daughter decided to get married. Her father wanted her to be married in the church, so they had two months to get it ready. The cement floor had to be poured and the front tower needed to be built. After many long hours of labour the building was now ready for the June 30 wedding. The first service was held in the building on June 24, 1973, one week prior to the wedding. From then on, the inside work of the building was gradually completed.

The church was dedicated in memory of Reverend David C. Haimilia, who went to be with the Lord, August 29, 1974. Dave spent many long hours labouring on the church. He mixed by hand most of the cement for the bricks. He helped pour the basement floor and paint the outside of the building. Without his help, encouragement, friendship and perserverance, the building would never have been ready for use in 1973. The guest speaker for the dedication was Reverend Mohan Maharaj and Reverend C. Yates led the Act of Dedication.

Donations were received from several people. The Alberta Womens Ministries contributed fifteen hundred dollars for furnishings in the church. Harry Bauer, of Sun Appliance in Edmonton, donated a piano. The Alberta District donated a small organ. Helmet Eisert gave the light fixtures for the Parsonage and Church.

The Lagores resigned in 1976. Pastor Spencer Bradbury came to pastor. Many improvements were made in the interior of the church and parsonage. Pastor Bradbury served the church until late summer of 1978. The church was without a pastor for some time. In mid winter Pastor and Mrs. Lutz Koeppen took up the challenge to serve the assembly.

One of their young people, Henry Borzel attended Bible College and married Janet Balkwell. The Borzels entered the ministry and are presently missionaries in Hong Kong.

SPRUCE GROVE
SPRUCE GROVE COMMUNITY
CHURCH

Six Pentecostal families having moved to the growing community of Spruce Grove were concerned about their own spiritual needs and the spiritual needs of their community. At the same time Pastor Douglas Stiller resigned a pastorate in Vancouver and sensed a stirring in his heart to pioneer a new church. The Holy Spirit brought them together. In January of 1976 the Spruce Grove Community Church was officially organized. Prayer and sacrificial giving were characteristic of this new congregation.

The founding families were Dave and Suzanne Larson, Willard and Ruth Kile, Larry and Lynn Kryger, Corny and Maryann Funk, Peter and Lily Hubert, Ken and Edith Pratt, Ken and Jeanne Harrington.

Initially Sunday School was held in private homes while evening services were held at St. Matthew's Lutheran Church. In February 1976, facilities were made available in the Spruce Grove Composite High School. Because of the outstanding growth being experienced, additional space that was needed was made available.

Pastor Stiller's calling card

Spruce Grove's first Sunday School bus ministry was initiated in the summer of 1976 to broaden the outreach ministry of the Spruce Grove Community Church.

A desire to minister to the needs of the youth of the church and community prompted the addition of Mr. Brian Glubish to the pastoral staff in January

1978. Others who have served on the pastoral staff were Lloyd Kupka (January to June 1981) and student pastors for one year terms — Albert Clarence (1979-1980), Roc Weigl (1980-1981) and Cameron Milliken (1981-1982).

A church home for this growing congregation was a must. God miraculously made available six acres on Century Road. It took three visits to gain an agreement from the farmer to sell. The price was five thousand dollars an acre. Because the property was outside the limits of Spruce Grove, the Edmonton Planning Board and the Greater Edmonton Planning Board turned down the request for this subdivision application. However, the Alberta Government Provincial Planning Board reversed these decisions and approval was granted in the summer of 1978. Construction of Phase One of the new church began in October of that year. This Phase was dedicated by Reverend I. Roset, District Superintendent, on June 17, 1979. Reverend M. P. Horban was the guest speaker.

Phase One includes chapel, offices, classrooms, washrooms, kitchen and an area that doubles as class areas and a fellowship area. Water is trucked into cisterns that hold three thousand gallons.

By April of 1980, the assembly had outgrown their facilities. A ten thousand square foot new wing and more water capacity was added and in use by November 1981.

The church has grown from six families to over four hundred people in about six years. They have two Sunday morning services to accommodate this fine congregation.

Among the folk, who attended Bible College and/or entered the ministry (*), are *Del Duncalfe, Laverne Johnston, Lana Kozak, Loretta Kozak, Dwayne Turlock, Darlene Pasechnick, Wendy Schwartz, Melody Weigl, Roc-Allen Weigl, Wanda Willoughby, Tony Yakielashek.

STETTLER
STETTLER PENTECOSTAL ASSEMBLY

In the summer of 1950, Reverend Harvey McAlister and family decided to establish a Pentecostal church in Stettler, Alberta. There were at that time two full gospel families living in Stettler, who attended the Nazarene church — Dick and Edith Brewer, Ed and Dorothy Hart.

Reverend McAlister contacted these families. It was agreed to have an evangelistic thrust in the form of tent meetings with Eddie and Ruth Washington. The meetings created quite a stir. Some families were saved, among whom was the Ted Petersen family,

whose younger son, Doug, later became a pastor in the United States and is in missionary work in Belize.

After the tent meetings, they worshipped in an old hall, east of main street. Then they purchased an unused school building (formerly the Catholic Church) across the street from the main Stettler school complex. This is still their place of worship. The District Superintendent at that time was Reverend D. N. Buntain and the District Presbyter was Reverend S. R. Tilton of Red Deer. Through their efforts, loans were obtained to buy the building and renovate it.

Stettler Pentecostal Assembly

Through the years there were many ups and downs, both in attendance and finances, but the Lord blessed and the work grew. People were saved, healed and many received the Baptism of the Holy Spirit. Brother McAlister faithfully served as pastor for six years. During that time he received no wages from the church but labored sometimes at two jobs to support his family and to a large extent the work of the church.

Other ministers who followed the McAlisters were Reverend and Mrs. Sandy Johnson; Reverend and Mrs. Harvey Schmautz; Reverend and Mrs. Max Hornby; Reverend and Mrs. Paul Dyck, who had previously been part of the assembly; Reverend and Mrs. Ray Lindgren; Reverend and Mrs. Darrel Hoeppner; Reverend and Mrs. James Smart; Reverend and Mrs. Leonard Rosenfeldt, who are at this time serving the Assembly.

The church has experienced growth in every aspect. On November 9, 1979, seventeen people followed the Lord in water baptism. Three acres of land have been purchased for a new church site. Plans have been drawn up for a sanctuary, which will begin as soon as finances permit.

Some of the early faithful, not to be forgotten members are Bonnie Falkenberg and her family, Mr. and Mrs. Willard Marchant and daughter, Ruby. Mr. Marchant also served as a board member for many years. Among other board members have been Roy Lee, Ted Petersen, Ed Hart, Ed Whiteside, Paul Dyck, Cliff Everett and Bob Hollings.

Families have come and gone. Some who live far from Stettler will always remember the contribution the Stettler Pentecostal Assembly has made to the Kingdom of God.

Among those, who attended Bible College and/or entered the ministry (*), are *Robert (Bob) Haring, *Diane Hart (married to Reverend Danny Moe), Lawrence Hart, Helen Johnstone, Effie Mabel Murray, **Douglas Peterson, *Cheryl Snyder, *Paul Dyck.

SWAN HILLS
SWAN HILLS PENTECOSTAL ASSEMBLY
The Saga of the Swan Hills Church

In 1898 the magic word was GOLD. One of the overland routes to the Klondike was the Swan Hills route. The one hundred and twenty miles from Fort Assiniboine to Lesser Slave Lake presented every conceivable difficulty. Some made it to the Klondike but many didn't. The price men pay for search of gold is well recorded.

In 1950 another magic word was OIL. Another rush was on the forbidding hills beckoning with promise of black gold. This, too, is a tale of courage, hardship and suffering but with much more wealth taken out than that of the Klondike gold rush.

In the summer of 1959 another search was on for something more precious than gold or oil, the lives and souls of MEN. Without headlines, fanfare or financial support, three young theology students made the trip to Swan Hills in an old truck. They camped in the bush. A Vacation Bible School was started with one boy but closed with thirty children two weeks later. This was the first religious effort as far as is known. Melvin Johnson, one of these men from the Church of God Bible College of Camrose, felt called to return and minister there. That summer, he married Madeline White, daughter of Rev. and Mrs. R. J. White, then pastor of the Newbrook Pentecostal Church.

There was still no road in from Fort Assiniboine except the Forestry trail, which the oilmen were using. There were no bridges. Cats pulled vehicles through the worst places. There were no schools, no churches, two private homes, a few public buildings, a Royal Bank on skids and many trailers. After a quick honeymoon, the Johnsons pooled their resources, bought a housetrailer on condition it would be delivered to Swan Hills. It was parked on a lot next to the place where the church would be built. The old Swan Hills site was condemned and this new site was being hewn out of raw bush land. Soon there were roads and sidewalks, a welcome relief from the famous Swan Hills mud. A modern four-room school and homes were built almost overnight. Plans for a church were made.

Mel did most of the building of the church with occasional help. Oil crews helped with raising the arch-rib rafters, excavating and so on. Local people contributed to the finances as well as some help from the Church organization. There was no music teacher, so Madeline taught music; no janitor or bus driver so Mel undertook both jobs as well as occasional catskinning. Here in this church, the first wedding and the first funeral were held. When the newspaper man was interviewing the town planner, he asked the planner, "Where is the Cemetery?" The planner replied, "We have none. No one has ever died here yet." Ironically he, the town planner, was the first to die and Mel conducted the funeral. Forest fires and oil well fires added to the excitement and hazards of those days. The Johnsons stayed eight years and were followed by a number of Church of God ministers.

Pentecostal families co-operated with the church from its beginning. Preachers, missionaries and youth workers of the Pentecostal faith ministered when the church was without a pastor. Among those were R. J. White, Manley Hodges, J. Muggleton, and others. Paul Dyck was the first Pentecostal man called to pastor in 1977 and stayed until 1979, when Pastor L. Rutten (1979-1981) came to minister. Presently Pastor and Mrs. Harvey Leshner (1982-   ) serve the congregation. The church is being rented from the Church of God. The population of Swan Hills is continually in flux. The Community Church is still the only church building in Swan Hills.

SYLVAN LAKE
SYLVAN LAKE GOSPEL CHAPEL
(formerly Pentecostal Tabernacle)

Jean Gardner reports that the Sunday school started about 1935 in Mrs. Wright's cottage, Rondebosch, which was still located across the street from the Gospel Chapel in 1982. It is thought that the first services began in 1938. The first pastor was the

Bentley pastor, Hugh Fraser, who commuted from Bentley each Sunday. He and his wife would bring Bentley young people with them. Among these was John Morsch. The services were held in the Wright cottage. Later services were held in the Women's Institute Hall. In 1939, Hugh Fraser left Bentley and therefore left Sylvan Lake.

Congregation — Adults.

Miss Mabel Hyssop, first full-time pastor of Sylvan Lake Gospel Chapel.

The first full-time pastor was Miss Mabel Hyssop, who arrived in late summer 1939. For the first year, she stayed at the Gardner farm, then she rented a small house downtown. One time in Sunday school, Miss Hyssop offered little Bud Johnson a nickel or a New Testament. You could buy something with a nickel then. Bud chose the New Testament. Inside the cover, a dime was taped. That was quite a reward for choosing part of God's Word.

After about two years of using the W. I. Hall, the congregation desired to have a church building. Miss Hyssop found a building at Lower Camp. In early 1942, this building was purchased from Mrs. O'Neil and put on a lot about two blocks west of Main Street, near the West Crescent of Sylvan Lake. The movers were kind families from Bentley, the Spychers and Edwin Morsch Sr., assisted by Amié Vandurene, Gordon Gardner and other people of the congregation. This church was called the Pentecostal Tabernacle. It had a seating capacity of ninety. There was a small room at the back for the pastor's residence. Jean Gardener wrote regarding Miss Hyssop, "After the building was on the foundation, the men worked taking out partitions and remodelling. Miss

Hyssop worked just like the men. It was quite usual to go down and find her, with wrecking bar or hammer, ripping away whatever needed to go." She certainly did her best. Miss Hyssop left in March 1943.

Miss Hyssop was succeeded by an exceptionally fine young man, Andrew Wek. His term was very short due to illness. He left to be with his parents and, shortly after, God called him home.

Miss Gladys Halverson was the next pastor. She was assisted by Miss Eunice Meyer for a short time. She was followed by Misses Emma Hemke and Esther Mallow. Miss Mallow left when Miss Hempke married Rev. Ernie Peterson, who became the next pastor in October 1946. While the newly weds were away, Freda Spycher, Jack Whitesell and Mr. Grant Sanders filled in for them.

Before Rev. Peterson arrived, a kitchen and a bedroom were added to the preacher's quarters. The Petersons were a beautiful couple and are still special to many of the congregation. Under Rev. Peterson, the first official board of the church was appointed. Members of that first board were George Petterson, Hans Quam, Al Stone and W. Gardner (secretary). About this time, an eighteen-to-twenty-voice choir was organized. About fifty young people were added to the church one winter so in 1947 the church building was enlarged to accommodate them. While Petersons were there, there were two very successful campaigns. One was with Eunice Meyer, resulting in many being saved and/or filled with the Holy Spirit. The other was with Reg and Doug Carbol and Mel Delgatty with similar results. In 1949, eleven were baptized in water.

Another dearly loved family, Reverend and Mrs. James Tyler and son, Kenny, came in December 1950. Their notable visitation ministry was carried out on foot until some months later they bought a car.

Former remuneration to pastors consisted of free-will offerings. When the Tylers came, the first weekly salary was paid to them — twenty dollars per week. A successful Vacation Bible School was conducted by June Miller and Laverne Hinkle of Edmonton. Shortly after, the Tylers left for Hay River.

In the fall of 1952, Reverend Laverne Poirier from Quebec came to be pastor. Later he married a Winnipeg lady. The Wright cottage was used for the parsonage.

In 1953, a new graduate of Northwest Bible College, Sandy Johnson, with his wife, Lillian, and sons, Danny and Wayne, arrived as the next pastor. Under Rev. Johnson's leadership in 1955, the church constitution was drawn up and accepted. The church's name was also changed to Gospel Chapel. The Johnsons were very interested in the children of the chapel and Sylvan Lake area. The Sunday school grew so much that more space was really needed. In March 1957, the Johnsons were followed by Reverend and Mrs. Arvin Sorge.

Rev. and Mrs. E. W. Peterson with their first daughter.

In October and November 1958, Edmonton's Idylwylde Sunday School and the Gospel Chapel Sunday School entered into an enlargement contest. The Gospel Chapel won. During this contest, the facilities were so taxed that the Chapel congregation decided to immediately begin the work of adding the needed space. A concrete basement under the sanctuary was completed in July 1959. Then, on a pay-as-you-go basis, they built a new front on the church, which included a foyer, nursery, pastor's study and basement entrance. Six-foot-five Rev. Sorge was a Jack-of-all-trades, who kept the building project going until it was completed.

Mrs. Sorge showed outstanding musical ability. Her talents, whether on the piano or accordian or vocal, touched the hearts of many. The Sorges were well-known for their hospitality. Sister Sorge was a fantastic cook.

In November 1962, the next pastor, Rev. Don Schneider, his wife, Shirley, and little Trevor arrived.

1966 was another time of building. The old Sunday school hall was renovated for the pastor's suite and the sanctuary was ready for worship. On November 13, 1966, Rev. S. R. Tilton dedicated this new sanctuary, which was absolutely debt free. In spite of this building program, they experienced new heights in Missions giving. The Schneider ministry proved to be a great blessing to all.

Rev. and Mrs. Hector McDonald (1969-77) served the Chapel congregation longer than any other pastor. Brother McDonald's pleasant personality made him everybody's friend. In December 1975, Rev. Ken Bombay's campaign was very well attended. People were converted, physical needs healed and the Holy Spirit moved in a remarkable way. Reverend Bombay was and is an annointed speaker.

Visiting ministers served the congregation until Reverend and Mrs. Nick Wynychuk arrived March 15, 1978 and served until 1981. One summer, Reverend Wynychuk baptized fourteen people. On October 5, 1980, a special Sunday School Two Hundredth Birthday Celebration was held featuring various local participants, J. Shirley Morsch of Edmonton as special speaker and a beautifully decorated two hundredth birthday cake, which was made by a lady in the Chapel. They all had a piece of cake following the service. It was a lovely celebration.

Four acres of land, just south of town, were donated to the chapel as a place for a new church sometime in the future.

Reverend and Mrs. Sandy Johnson have been serving this congregation since the Wynychuks left the Chapel. Johnsons are well known here, since they were pastors here some years back.

Among the early families were Mr. and Mrs. Will Gardner with Gordon and later his wife, Jean, and family; Lars ("Howdy, howdy") Petterson and his wife with George, Alma and Leonard, who was, also, a lay preacher; the Hallgrens with Bessie, Gordon and other children; the Johnson children — Shirley, Elsie, Eldon (Bud) and Doreen; Mrs. Martz; Mrs. Light; the Nick Halvorsons; Mrs. Louise Kraft with Helen and Betty; Mrs. H. Loiselle (first white person born (1878) in the Sylvan Lake area); the Stones from Benalto; Ernie and Marguerite Spycher with Bruce, Glen, Susan, Jimmy, Wendy; Mrs. Anna Kanten; Adie Kanten and later his wife and family; Mrs. Hulda Kanten with Colleen, Wanda and Carol; Mrs. Helen Flick with Yvonne, Audrey (wife of a minister, Howard Bishop), Pat (now Ammeter); Mr. and Mrs. Hans Quam and family; Mr. and Mrs. George Petterson with Ernest and Myrna (wife of Bob Dipert); Mr. and Mrs. William Marks with Bill; Mr. and Mrs. Cecil Barker with Joyce and Muriel.

Later other active families were the Ammeters, the Algers, Mrs. Merron Carruthers, Mrs. Ethel Anderson and family, the Arends, the Plantes, the Camerons, Mrs. Marie Hottom, Mrs. Tjitke Bos and family.

George Petterson was a board member for over thirty years. Colleen, Wanda and Carol Kanten were the Gospel Singers on the CKRD Mark Electric Presents the Gospel Singers program. The Hallgrens and the Henry Kanten Families moved to Red Deer and became involved in the Pentecostal church there.

Among those, who attended Bible college and/or entered the ministry (*), are Don Burdeck, *Audrey Flick (wife of a minister, Howard Bishop), Robert Holtom, *Coreen Kanten (wife of a minister, David Frey), *Howard Lund, Alma Martz, Yvonne Milne, Alma Petterson, Donald Pitkanen, Sharon Weatherly.

THORSBY
IMMANUEL PENTECOSTAL
ASSEMBLY

Although some of the charter members of the Thorsby Pentecostal Church had moved into the district as early as 1922, it was not until 1937 that the church was organized. As is sometimes the case in pioneer areas, house meetings were held and fostered by concerned people to become a congregation in due time. A move from house meetings to a school became necessary to accommodate the people. The Dniester School was used. This group was composed of many denominations. By 1929 a church was built and called the Weed Creek Union Sunday School. Ministers from various denominations came to conduct services.

The Pentecostal faith was still quite new but by this time there was a desire by many for the Baptism in the Holy Spirit. Herb Vath and Reverend W. S. Frederick were used to introduce this ministry to Thorsby. Alma Frederick also ministered suc-

Home of Herbert and Lydia Vath, where church services were held most of the time before the church was built.

cessfully there for quite some time. Among others who ministered were Harvey McAlister, Martin McCallum, Melvin Stronstead, Willis McPherson.

In the summer of 1937, Walter S. Frederick conducted a tent meeting on the Anton Dedio farm. This brought together people from various nationalities — Polish, Ukrainian, German and English. New families were added to the Pentecostal group. House meetings were held in the homes of the Herb Vaths, George Zingles and Rhinhold Pauls. On one Sunday each month they could conduct a service in the Union Sunday School. Ministers who contributed their services were — William Miller, R. Pohl of Leduc, Reverend Schatkowski, Reverend W. Melnychuk, Reverend W. Kowalski and others. The congregation worshipped by each ethnic group singing in their preferred language. The sermon may have been in English, German or Ukrainian with interpretation. The congregation grew and soon it was necessary to have a church building. An administrative executive was set up. This group of people were incorporated under the Religious Societies Act of Alberta as the Thorsby Pentecostal Assembly. The building, completed in 1939, was situated one-half mile east of the Union Sunday School. Reverend Walter S. Frederick and the Wiesenthal congregation, with their twenty-piece brass band, participated in the dedication. William Miller became the first pastor. He was followed by Ewald Guze, Herbert Weurch, P. R. Kabanuk. The congregation became one of the largest rural churches in the Alberta District. During Reverend Kabanuk's ministry, the assembly built a church in Calmar.

In 1952, the congregation experienced some change. Several families left the church to worship elsewhere. However under the pastoring of Reverend Steiner, Adam Schultz and student ministers the church prospered.

Reverend R. Dowbush pastored the church from 1964 to 1967. There was an increase in attendance

Dedication of the Thorsby Pentecostal Tabernacle (the country church) in 1939. This church was closed October 2, 1972.

during this time, which necessitated an expansion of church facilities. Rather than add to the old building, it was decided to move into the town of Thorsby, where water, sewer and electricity were available. Property was purchased and a church was erected in Thorsby. Reverend Steve Holomis built this church.

Some of the families still felt that services should continue in the old country church. Pastors who ministered here were Reverend A. Lamb, Reverend G. Setterlund and Reverend W. Trapp. In 1972, the country church transferred its assets and congregation to the church in town.

Ministers, who followed Reverend R. Dowbush, were L. Kokot (1967-1970), G. Rhind (1970-1974), A. Coleman (1974-1979), H. Lund (1979-   ). On October 4, 1981, Pastor H. Lund was ordained in a special service with District Superintendent, Reverend I. Roset, and Assistant Superintendent, Reverend K. Bunting, officiating.

God is blessing in Thorsby. Several candidates have been baptized in water. In 1981 there was an increase in numbers and finances. In 1982, although twenty adherents had moved away, the attendance in the services remained almost the same.

Among those, who attended Bible College and/or entered the ministry (*), are Allan Dublanko, *Judy Dublanko, *Lawrence Dublanko, Hylda Neuman, Paul Neuman, Charlene Postnikoff, Edward Shram, *Mary Shram, Ruth Shram, Douglas Vath, Esther Vath, *Lewis Vath.

Helen Guze (nee Dedio) and her husband, Ewald Guze, who was the first pastor.

TURNER VALLEY PENTECOSTAL CHURCH

As early as 1917, perhaps even before, prayer meetings and Sunday School had been known to be held in various locations in the valley. In August 1933 Jack Field was invited to Turner Valley to conduct an evangelistic campaign. For three weeks, these meetings were held in the Legion Hall. Souls were saved. After this special endeavor Pastor Field continued to hold Sunday services and Sunday School in the Legion Hall. On October 23, 1933, Pastor Field married Eileen Murray of Bentley, Alberta.

In November 1933, the Assembly was organized by Reverend Clare Scratch, District Superintendent. The first board members were Floyd McCreary, Frank Flower, Ernest Johnson, John Vetters. Some of the early families were Johnsons, Flowers, McCrearys, Vetters, Mrs. Lila Wells, Mrs. Lyons. Others who attended later were Cutlers, Hammonds, Louths, Doyles, Mrs. Mitchell, Miss Rhinehart, Mrs. Bertnese and families.

1956-57 Missionette Group

In January 1934, twelve people were baptized in water in the Standard church in Black Diamond.

Pastor and Mrs. Field left in September 1935, when Reverend and Mrs. John Wood came to take charge of the Assembly. They were followed by Mr. and Mrs. Basil Leonard who arrived on December 6, 1938. A new church building was taking shape with pastor's quarters attached. Natural gas lights and heat were supplied free of charge. At an Anniversary Service, Reverend George Upton ministered. The Calgary Pentecostal orchestra was present. During that year twenty-four had followed the Lord in water baptism.

In September 1940, Reverend and Mrs. M. Olson and family came to minister in Turner Valley. Previous to this, a church and parsonage had been built, but they were only "shells." During the Olson's ministry, the church, including Sunday School rooms, and the parsonage were completed. Electricity was installed in both.

They, also, started Sunday School and church services in Black Diamond. Here, Brother Olson converted a truck garage into a church. While Brother Olson was doing this, a little boy asked him what he was doing. Brother Olson replied that he was building a church. Thinking that Brother Olson was joking, the boy said, "Tell me another one." The day the church opened, this boy came to discover that the garage had been made into a church.

In another place in the Valley, Royalties, Mrs. Laura Holdsworth opened Sunday School and church services in 1940. Mr. Stronstad also ministered here for a time. About 1941 or 1942 Reverend Olson was asked to take charge of this work.

Sunday became a very busy day for the Olsons. Mrs. Olson would minister in Turner Valley in the morning while Reverend Olson went to Royalties for church and Sunday School. In the afternoon the Olsons would go to Black Diamond for Sunday School and church service, then back again to Turner Valley for an evening service. During the week they would minister in services in these places as well as visitation. Reverend Olson had a fruitful hospital ministry. George Godkin, who through an explosion had been severely burned, was one who was led to Christ in the hospital. Later he became a distributor of Christian literature and gifts.

Rev. and Mrs. Bill Lagore with Doniel.

90

For seven weeks in 1947 the three points in the Valley enjoyed the rich ministry of Reverend Jack Brooks of Chilliwack, B.C..

The Olsons left Turner Valley in September 1949.

Ministers who followed were Reverend and Mrs. Wendel Lewis, Reverend Johnson, Arnold Taylor, Reverend and Mrs. Bill Lagore, Reverend and Mrs. George Corris, Laurie Hale, Reverend and Mrs. Len Schmautz, Miss Alice Olsonberg, Reverend and Mrs. Spencer Bradbury, Victor Cooper, Miss Ivy Stickle, Reverend and Mrs. Don McNutt and R. Bruce.

The Turner Valley area has a transient population due to oil business. However, over the years there has always been a group to serve the Lord.

Among those, who attended Bible College and/or entered the ministry(*), are Myles Clifford, *George Johnson, *Bernice Olson, Ruth Taylor, Lloyd Taylor (from Manitoba), Viola Taylor.

VALLEYVIEW
EVANGEL TEMPLE

About thirty-five miles from Valleyview, a small group of people were meeting for services. Three families drove from Valleyview every Sunday to attend the services. Reverend C. Ray Lindgren, who was pastor here, felt impressed to start house meetings in Valleyview, which he did.

In the fall of 1966, when the group showed much enthusiasm, the Memorial Hall was rented for Sunday morning and evening services.

Two lots were purchased in June 1967. Plans were made to build an educational wing and a sanctuary. The education wing was to be built first, then, as the work grew and funds would allow, the sanctuary would be constructed. By Christmas 1967, the people were worshipping the Lord in the educational wing.

Reverend C. Ray Lindgren was pastor until 1971. Then Reverend Doug Johnston served the church for eight months. Reverend and Mrs. Dave Haimila followed as pastors for the next two years, then Pastor and Mrs. Bernard Holmstrom came to minister.

The Holmstroms, also, pastored the church for two years. During this time, the church experienced growth. The new sanctuary was built and finished, except for the basement. Also faithful in the church ministry was Adelgunde Manntai from Northwest Bible College in Edmonton. She assisted in Church and Sunday School work. She wanted to gain ministerial experience with a view to future missionary work. At the District Conference 1974, Pastor Bernie Holmstrom had asked Adele to help in Valleyview. She did not receive a salary nor was her appointment an official position because the church was not large enough to afford an assistant pastor, even though she did the work of an assistant pastor. Adele, who was willing to help, found secular work and assisted in the church. Her activities included some preaching, teaching in Sunday School plus assisting Conrad Lehman in an afternoon Sunday School for Indian children. For years, Conrad had conducted this Sunday School in an Indian house. When they outgrew the house, they picked up the Indian children and brought them to the church. The Indian children who lived in town came on their own. Adele worked here until the end of July 1975 when she left to be married to Dennis Walker. Her work was appreciated.

Reverend and Mrs. R. Manntai from Lethbridge followed as pastors. Not only were they efficient in pastoring, but also they put many finishing touches on the new sanctuary, educational wing, basement, sidewalks and lawn.

Later Mrs. Helen Chezick did a wonderful work caring for the church as pastor, raising a family and keeping house. After Mrs. Chezik resigned, Ernie Slopianka, a local man and son of one of the founding folk was the supply pastor and pastor. Since the summer of 1981, supply ministers have been brought in to fill the pulpit.

Among those, who attended Bible College, are Dean Adolphson, Albert Caouette, Paul Caouette.

VEGREVILLE PENTECOSTAL
CHURCH

In the late forties and fifties, there were services conducted there. When Rev. D. N. Buntain was Superintendent, property was bought and later sold, except for the mineral rights, which the Pentecostal Assemblies of Alberta still own. Before this time of services, Rev. Harvey McAlister held house meetings. It is not known who the other ministers were.

In 1979 Mr. A. Bartlett held some house meetings. Then on July 1 of that year, Pastor and Mrs. Albertus Clarence began their ministry there in the Queen Elizabeth Elementary School with two couples (Robin and Carol Cuikshank and Ben and Carmen Mykula). At first only one family, beside the Pastor and his wife, were Spirit filled. Pastor Clarence was anxious that people accept Christ as their Saviour and then be filled with the Spirit of God. In April 1980, Evangelist Dudley Fairbairn came for a weekend of services. The first two nights averaged fifty-two people and the final night, the film, A Thief in the Night, was shown with Rev. Fairbairn speaking. During these meetings there were sixteen conversions, nine were filled with the Holy Spirit and some were healed. This assembly is gaining recognition as a Spirit filled church. In January 1982, Pastor Clarence was ordained in the presence of his congregation. Rev. and Mrs. Kenneth Bunting and Rev. Ken Roset were there for the joyous occasion. Rev. Bunting is the Assistant District Superintendent and Rev. Ken Roset is the Sectional Presbyter.

The congregation has grown to forty or fifty. The Lord has a great deal in store for this congregation.

VERMILION
GLAD TIDINGS PENTECOSTAL ASSEMBLY

The history of the Vermilion work started like so many of our Pentecostal works. In the early weeks of 1981, a small group of people started meeting in the home of Allen and Carol Bartlett. In the spring of 1981 a small church was rented and Reverend Ken Smith called to pastor this assembly.

April 22, 1981, with ten members present, it was decided that the name would be Glad Tidings Pentecostal Assembly. Mr. and Mrs. H. Sorenson, Mrs. Donna Spinks and Miss Gladys Boyce were among the original ones who attended regularly.

The meetings had been held in the Gospel Hall which belonged to the Brethren people. The rent was forty-five dollars a month. It was brought to their attention that the building was up for sale. The Gospel Hall people were willing to sell the building for thirty thousand dollars, an unheard of price for the nineteen hundred and eighties. The lot alone was almost worth that price. Payments were started at five hundred dollars a month and no interest. These payments were set up to continue from the fall of 1981 to September 1982. Then the Pentecostal Assemblies of Canada arranged a loan for the balance from Head Office.

Now they were able to set up a new service schedule and start a Sunday School. Many of the folk were new or young Christians. God continues to add people.

The building needed some repairs. There had been weeks of discussion regarding removing the wall behind the pulpit. One evening Pastor and Mrs. Smith decided to see how solid the wall was. In half an hour the wall was down and renovations started. It was discovered that at one time there had been a complete platform area behind the wall. They built a new wall behind this platform. Much work was done. On the wall behind the platform was a chimney. One big puzzle remained. What should be done with the chimney? One of the men of the Assembly said, "When I look at that old chimney, all I can vision is a large cross." There was their answer. The chimney was cased in, plastered and painted. A wooden cross was hung on the front of it and blue lights were installed behind the wooden cross. What had once been an eyesore was now a thing of beauty.

The Glad Tidings Pentecostal Assembly extends a warm welcome to members and visitors alike.

VULCAN
VULCAN PENTECOSTAL TABERNACLE

For several years, a few Pentecostal people in the Vulcan area desired a Pentecostal church. During the May 1957 Annual Alberta District Conference of the Pentecostal Assemblies of Canada, a challenge was given to graduate students to go into communities, obtain employment and help establish churches. The town of Vulcan was one of the communities for this project, to which Reverend George Lagore, a school teacher, responded.

During the summer at the home of Mr. and Mrs. O. H. (Bud) Schneider in Champion, Reverend S. R. Tilton, Alberta District Superintendent, and Reverend J. W. Watts, District Presbyter, met with Reverend and Mrs. George Lagore, Mr. and Mrs. Bert Somerville and the Schneiders to make plans for beginning the work in Vulcan. The first board members were Reverend and Mrs. Lagore and Bert Somerville. They served until the spring of 1959.

On September 8, 1957, the first meeting was held in the I.O.O.F. Hall with seven present. A Sunday School was organized with five children and eight adults in regular attendance. These services continued in the hall for a year and a half.

Vulcan Pentecostal Tabernacle.

During the first year, Pastor Lagore taught school in Armada, commuting from Vulcan, making about a sixty-mile round trip each school day. It was then decided that the rental money should go into a building fund and that they should build a church. A lot was bought from the town of Vulcan. They began excavating during the first week of October 1958. During their second year as pastors, the Lagores lived in a teacherage at Armada and commuted to Vulcan for services and building of the church. Pastor Lagore and local people worked many long hours constructing their place of worship. Much appreciated assistance was given by the Calgary and Lethbridge congregations. In the fall of 1959 Pastor Lagore joined the teaching staff in Vulcan. Then the Lagores moved into the church basement suite. Services were held in the church basement chapel, though it was not quite completed.

In 1959 the new board consisted of O. H. (Bud) Schneider, Fred Reath and Bert Somerville, secretary-treasurer. Bert acted as secretary-treasurer until 1970. Mrs. Bert Somerville kept the Sunday School records until April 1962.

The Lagores (Row Two) and folks at an early service in Vulcan.

The Sunday School and congregation grew so fast that it was necessary to use the main sanctuary before it was complete. The first service was held upstairs on December 6, 1961, when Vulcan hosted a rally with Reverend L. Hale as guest speaker. The first wedding in the church was that of Emily Henry and Arthur Connelly on December 23, 1961.

The official dedication was held June 16, 1963, with the church packed for the occasion. Reverend S. R. Tilton dedicated the church and Reverend C. Yates was the guest speaker. Mayor of Vulcan, William Munro, spoke highly of the church's influ-

ence. Mr. J. Schmale brought greetings from the Eighth Avenue Tabernacle in Calgary. Miss Eunice Meyer led the song service. Reverend and Mrs. Lagore had done a fine work on the church and had made a great spiritual impact on the town.

Reverend and Mrs. L. Hale followed the Lagores in August 1963 and remained until 1965. Pastor Hale conducted a Radio Broadcast over the Drumheller Radio Station. In August 1965, Pastor and Mrs. Jess Lynn, recent graduates from Northwest Bible College, came to Vulcan. During their ministry the Missionettes group was organized. The Lynns continued the radio broadcast, "Echoes of Praise," which they taped at the Lethbridge Tabernacle and aired over the Drumheller Radio Station. During his time here, Pastor Lynn was ordained in 1967. In November of that year the Lynns left to become missionaries in Liberia.

The following pastored the Tabernacle from December 1967 to the present time: Layman Erle Tegart, December 1967-June 1968; Sidney Mitchell, an X-Ray Technician and interim pastor, January 1971-June 1971; Pastor and Mrs. Bernard Holmstrom, June 1971-fall 1973; Pastor and Mrs. Richard Manntai from Lethbridge, fall 1973-1974; Pastor and Mrs. Douglas Knoll, who commuted from Calgary, 1974-1975.

Many times during the years, there were several supply pastors, Mr. Maurice Glover and Reverend Ernie Peterson of Calgary, Earl Sargent of Claresholm.

During Pastor Roberta F. Irvine's ministry, November 1976-August 1979, an Alberta A.I.M. team, including Dave and Kathy Miller, held very successful concerts in the high school and in a very packed Pentecostal Tabernacle. Reverend I. Roset, District Superintendent, came to conduct a baptismal service. As he and the candidate stepped into the tank, it overflowed. Miss Irvine led the congregation in choruses, while the tank was drained of the excess water, so the baptismal service could continue.

Mr. and Mrs. Henry Conrad, pastored both Coalhurst and Vulcan, 1979-1980; Pastor Schmuland commuted from Coaldale, 1981-1982.

Those who served on the Tabernacle board for varying lengths of time were Reverend and Mrs. Lagore, Bert Somerville, O. H. Schneider, Mrs. Lois Schneider, Fred Reath, Allen Taylor, Mrs. Jean Connolly, Mrs. Bonny Dann, Sidney Mitchell, A. Buhlin, Mrs. Jean Davey, Mrs. Violet Reath.

During the summer of 1981, the Tabernacle received a new look — new drapes and a paint job on the main auditorium, new paint for back and front entries and a new rug for the main entrance.

The Lord has continued to bless throughout the

years. There has always been an active Women's Ministries group. Teacher training courses and Vacation Bible Schools were conducted for many years. Souls have been saved and filled with the Holy Spirit. The Pentecostal people of Vulcan continue to believe God for His blessing in the future.

In February 1982, Cal Keys became pastor.

Among those, who entered Bible college, are Faith Reath and Laverne Reath.

WAINWRIGHT
WAINWRIGHT PENTECOSTAL ASSEMBLY

At the July 1940 District Conference held at Sunnyside Camp, Mr. Wilson, who had been saved in Edmonton, requested the District Executive to make an effort to open a Pentecostal work in Wainwright. The Wilson family owned a farm about five miles from Wainwright.

The District Executive felt that a single young man would be the one to send to Wainwright, however they could not find anyone, whom they felt was God's man for this need. They agreed to make this need a matter of prayer. Reverend A. Dalby was on the Executive at that time. As he prayed, the Lord revealed to him that he was to go to Wainwright.

Human reasoning strongly opposed his going to Wainwright. He had four children. His wife was an invalid. They lived in Claresholm in a comfortable, furnished apartment and had practically no furniture of their own — just a baby's crib and a double bed. As Brother Dalby met with the Executive they, too, believed that it was in the will of God for the Dalbys to go to Wainwright.

Pastor and Mrs. A. Dalby

It was decided that Dalbys open with two weeks of tent meetings. The German brethren of Leduc gave them the use of their tent. Benches were used from the Sylvan Lake Camp. Brother Wilson loaned them his piano.

Two of the Dalby children, Ruth and Allan, went to Claresholm for the remainder of their vacation. Mrs. Dalby and infant son were invited to stay with the Gelin family at Rimbey. Brother Dalby and elder daughter, Doris, went to Wainwright to begin the Pentecostal work. They were guests in the Wilson home.

From a purely human standpoint, the tent meetings were an absolute failure. They had a high attendance of twelve except when a group came from Killam. The hum of mosquitos in the tent was terrifying. The meetings seemed to be ignored by the people of Wainwright.

For eight dollars a month, Reverend Dalby rented a house, complete with outdoor facilities. An old wood cooking stove was bought for five dollars, a kitchen table for one dollar. Several 'chairs' were collected — apple boxes and a pear box. Daughter Ruth said, "The pear box was special for company." Orange crates served as kitchen cupboards. The Killam assembly loaned them another bed.

While Reverend Dalby, Doris Dalby and Harvey (Wilson's teenaged son) were scrubbing the rented house, a man, whose name was Mr. Bear, came to the door and enquired if they would be living there. He said he would supply them with milk. Brother Dalby, thinking Mr. Bear was rather presumptuous, asked how much it would cost. Reverend Dalby was informed there would be no charge. Mr. Bear supplied them with three quarts of milk every day while the Dalbys lived in Wainwright.

It was time for Brother Dalby to bring his wife and baby to Wainwright. He only had one dollar and twenty-six cents and a gallon of gas in the car. Reverend Dalby and Doris prayed that God would supply the need. He hoped that someone would come and give him a ten dollar bill before he started on his trip. This did not happen. He decided he would buy gas for one dollar and twenty-six cents, drive as far as he could, then it would be the Lord's responsibility. The gas station in Wainwright was sold out of gasoline so he decided to buy the gas in Irma, the next town. However as he approached the Thirsk farm, the Lord told him to turn in! The Thirsks were glad to see him, promising him some pork as they had just butchered. As Brother Dalby was driving out the driveway, Brother Thirsk shouted, "How are you fixed for gas?" Brother Dalby replied he planned to buy some in Irma. Brother Thirsk asked him to back his car up to the gas tank and he filled the tank with gas.

When he arrived in Rimbey, he discovered that his wife and son had been invited to the Edwin Morsch home in Bentley. He stayed with the Morsches that night. As the Dalbys were leaving the next morning, with a Toronto couch tied to the top of the car, a donation from the Morsches, Brother Dalby was asked again, "How are you for gas, brother?" Brother Dalby replied he was planning to buy some in the village. Again his gas tank was filled! On the way home, he stopped for the roast of pork. When he arrived home he still had one dollar and twenty-six cents in his pocket and two gallons of gas in the car!

He went to Claresholm to bring Ruth and Allen home. As they were going back, he stopped in Calgary to see Reverend Upton, the District Superintendent. Brother Upton said he had just received a fifteen dollar contribution from Brother G. Hislop for home missions work. Brother Upton gave this to Brother Dalby. He was already planning how he would spend this money. As they went through Wetaskiwin, he stopped to see the Fields, who were pastors there. Brother Jack Field was not at home so he visited a short time with Mrs. Field. They read the Word and prayed. God told Brother Dalby to give the fifteen dollars to Sister Field. This he did. A week later, Brother Dalby received a letter from Brother Field telling him that they had been in need of fifteen dollars. That very morning that Brother Dalby stopped at their home, they had asked the Lord to supply the need. God had used Brother Dalby as the messenger to take the money to meet Brother Field's needs.

Brother Dalby had brought back a pot-bellied heater from Claresholm. This he converted to burn gas and installed it in his home. He needed several lengths of pipe. It would cost about six dollars. That afternoon, he picked up his mail. There was a letter from Sister Mary Simmons in Claresholm. She said, "In prayer this morning the Lord put you folks upon my heart to pray for you." She enclosed six dollars. This paid for the stove pipes.

While scrubbing the wooden kitchen floor, he realized how much easier it would be if he had linoleum on the floor. He asked the Lord if it was His will to supply the linoleum. Before leaving the house to make some calls and pick up his mail, he measured the floor so he would know how much linoleum he needed. The mail that day had two letters for him. Each letter contained some money. There was enough to buy linoleum and three dollars and fifty-five cents left over. His gas bill needed to be paid. It was exactly three dollars and fifty-five cents.

God continued to supply their needs. Mr. Bear supplied them with an abundance of vegetables — ten and one-half sacks plus a squash and a pumpkin.

Mr. Bob Leggit, who operated a machine shop, learned that Reverend Dalby, prior to entering the ministry, had been a machinist. Mr. Leggit asked Reverend Dalby to work for a few hours because he needed help. Afterwards Reverend Dalby worked in the shop whenever he could spare the time. Many months later, as he looked over his congregation of about forty people, he realized that over half of them were there at church as a result of contacts made in the machine shop. Mr. Stan Valleau was among those that Reverend Dalby had met in the shop.

Rev. and Mrs. William Pipke with Bill Jr. and Elaine.

Pastor Opheim and Sunday School in 1945.

Reverend George Upton, District Superintendent, thought that perhaps a special effort, with an evangelist, would help this new work. Reverend and Mrs. Winston Nunes came as evangelists. They stayed with the Dalbys. The Dalby cupboard was somewhat like Mother Hubbards! There was enough for the Saturday evening meal and Sunday breakfast. But what were they going to have for Sunday dinner?

Sunday morning, Doris to comfort her dad, said she would stay home and cook the best vegetable dinner that he had ever had. In the morning congregation, there were less than ten people until the Thirsks came. They were late, as their car would not start. They had come with horses. After the service, Mr. Thirsk said they wanted to attend the afternoon service and could not if they drove home in the wagon — there would not be time. So they invited themselves to the Dalbys for dinner. Brother Dalby hoped Doris had cooked enough turnips. When he arrived home he found a sumptuous feast ready — roast, potatoes, gravy, pickles, pies, home made rolls! The Thirsks had prepared their dinner in the morning so they could quickly come home, eat and go to the afternoon service. Since the car would not go, they had brought the dinner with them. After the afternoon service, the Thirsks returned home not anticipating being able to go to the evening service. Brother Thirsk tried to start the car upon returning home. It started! They were at the evening service! Brother Thirsk could not understand why the car didn't start in the morning but Brother Dalby knew! God was supplying their dinner!

Sister Nunes took over the cooking while with the Dalbys. One day she wanted to make pumpkin pie, but there were no eggs. She prayed, "Lord I thank you for the pumpkins you have sent. I believe you want me to make pumpkin pie. We don't know if pumpkin pie will be good without eggs, but you know, so Lord if we need eggs will you, please, supply them?" As she prayed the sound of milk bottles could be heard. Mr. Bear was bringing their milk. She went to the door and stood shrieking for joy! Mr. Bear had brought one dozen eggs. He had never done it before! She made her pumpkin pie with eggs.

The children were needing books as school started. Again they prayed as there was no money for school supplies. They received a letter from Brother Bob Peel. He had enclosed an offering. It paid for the books with a little left over.

Every home in Wainwright and almost every farm, in a radius of five miles, was visited. The people were most friendly. In almost every home, Brother Dalby was allowed to read the Word and pray.

Christmas was approaching. Doris expressed a wish for a book of poems, however, she said if funds were scarce, get something for the younger children. She could wait until later.

During Reverend Dalbys visitation, he had met a gentlemen, whose name was Mr. Lush. He was a supporter of the Jehovah's Witnesses and was not overjoyed by Pastor Dalby's visit. However, he continued to visit with Mr. Lush and they did become friends but were not agreed on spiritual and eternal values.

Christmas came and the Dalbys had had turkey with all the trimmings. It had been a good day. In the evening, Reverend Dalby decided to visit Mr. Lush, since perhaps he had had no one to visit him that day. Sister Dalby packed a basket of goodies and put in a little gift, also. Mr. Lush seemed happy to have Reverend Dalby's visit. This time he was able to tell Mr. Lush the story of God's love. Brother Dalby was also allowed to read the Bible and pray. He hoped that Mr. Lush found the Saviour. A few days afterwards Mr. Lush passed away.

Mr. Lush's sister and husband came from Saskatoon to make funeral arrangements. Reverend Dalby was asked to conduct the funeral service. The sister was the sole beneficiary; her husband was the executor of Mr. Lush's will. They asked Brother Dalby if he could use some of the books that Mr. Lush had. Among these books was a leather bound book of Tennyson's poems! Brother Dalby was asked to send a dray wagon over after the service to take some other things that they could use. Brother Dalby asked to take the book of poems with him. He ran all the way home to give it to Doris, who had been so willing to let the other children have something!

After the funeral, Reverend Dalby was home when the dray arrived with books, davenport, kitchen cabinet, rugs for the floor, bedroom dressers, chairs and stands, upholstered living room chairs and a host of smaller items. Brother Dalby just sat down and cried — overwhelmed by the mercies of God. Yet it wasn't without regret that he carried the apple boxes, pear box and orange crates out to the yard to be replaced by real furniture.

That first winter passed, the faithful few continued to attend services, the children's church flourished but they lacked teachers to organize a Sunday School.

Early one Sunday evening as usual, Doris and Brother Dalby went to the hall for a season of prayer before the evening service. Some strangers came followed by several groups of people, many of whom Brother Dalby had visited in their homes. Among them were the Valleaus, senior and junior; the Thirsks; the McKenzies; Mrs. McNeely and children; four young men, Bob Lilly, Harold King, Washburn Laird and Allan Dixon. The blessing of the Lord attended this service. Two persons came forward for prayer. From that Sunday onward the number attending began to grow.

In October 1941, Reverend Dalby left Wainwright to enter the Canadian Army. He had laid the foundation and over the years many dedicated workers have continued to build.

Reverend and Mrs. Rourke filled the pulpit for several weeks.

Early in 1942 Miss Lillian Sayer came to shepherd the small congregation. This young lady worked tirelessly to see people saved and built up in the faith. She was joined later by Miss Gladys Halvorsen. They were both good preachers and brought blessing to several people in the area. Miss Sayer left in December 1942.

Services were held for nearly eight years in the Masonic Hall until they were able to build a church.

During World War II Wainwright Military Camp was opened for training soldiers.

Reverend and Mrs. Eugene Opheim were appointed to fill the pastorate. They arrived in Wainwright February 1943. Their daughter, Pat, and son, Mervin, helped to swell the Sunday School. Later their second daughter, Olive, joined the family.

These were busy years for the Opheims as there were many homesick young soldiers, who were hungry for fellowship. Some were christians and added much to the services by their singing and testimonies.

The Opheims were tireless workers and soon had services in outlying areas and were also heavily involved with Youth For Christ rallies in several places.

The Home Missions Department assisted in a financial manner during these pioneer days.

Pastor Opheim realized that it would be well to have an elected official board and this was brought about. A building fund was started about 1945 and slowly grew over the next several years.

The Opheims resigned in late 1946 to take up the work in Claresholm.

Reverend and Mrs. Hubert Rosenke and small son, Keith, were called to pastor the assembly in October 1946. Brother Rosenke was a very energetic young man and soon saw that a church building was a necessity if the work was to grow. Lots were acquired on the corner of Eleventh Street and Fifth Avenue. A building committee was chosen and Brother Rosenke drew up plans for a building thirty feet by fifty feet. During these years building material was not easy to purchase. Finances were very small and they were determined to pay as they built.

An old farm house was purchased and moved on to the lot next to the site of the church. This was remodelled and the Pastor had a home.

A master carpenter was hired and all work on the church was on the voluntary basis thus costs were held to a minimum. The congregation worshipped in the new building the first Sunday in 1948.

Brother Rosenke was a friend to the young people and soon won several to the Lord. Sister Rosenke was a real friend to several young girls and influenced them in a very positive manner. During the three years of their pastorate, the church was built, the parsonage made liveable and two little daughters were born to the Rosenkes.

At Easter time 1949, Reverend C. A. Myhre was called to become pastor. Sister Myhre and son, Wayne, and daughter, Donna, were welcomed into the congregation. Brother Myhre set up a record system for the church that has remained for thirty years and tells the story of the church very well.

December 5, 1950, Wainwright Pentecostal Church became affiliated with the Pentecostal Assemblies of Canada.

The years of Brother Myhre's pastorate were during the time of the Korean war and many young soldiers were reached with the Gospel as the Military Camp was in full operation. Among those who came to assist the Myhres were Selma Komant, the Kanten sisters (Colleen, Carol and Wanda), Edina Harding. Each evening would start with an open air service about eight. This would be followed by a short service in the church. The meetings were informal. New converts were encouraged to publicly identify themselves with the Lord in another street meeting. Coffee would be served in the house, sometimes there would be more singing until the last possible minute before catching the midnight vehicle for camp. Brother Myhre was able to secure an official military vehicle pass for the windshield of his car. He had the privilege of going in and out of camp at will. The effectiveness of this soldiers work was demonstrated as letters returned from the battle fronts of Korea and from other camps to which some men were moved.

A highlight of these years was the Teacher Training course that Brother Myhre taught. This course was spread over many winter months and was a real help in giving several of their people a good basic training in the art of teaching Sunday School.

In 1953 J. Shirley Johnson and Bernice Olson conducted Daily Vacation Bible Schools in Wainwright and Ribstone.

The Myhres gave Wainwright five years of service and left to take up the pastorate in Creston, B.C..

During April 1954 Reverend Bill Pipke started pastoring in Wainwright. Sister Pipke and daughter, Elaine, and son, Billie, were soon filling their places in Sunday School and church. Brother Pipke was young and energetic and soon improvements were made to the building and proper pews were built by a local carpenter and volunteer labor. Water baptismal services were held and several were baptized. Vacation Bible Schools were held. Students from Northwest Bible College were always welcomed and over the years many young people have shared in the services.

During 1956 a former pastor from Saskatchewan, Brother John Larson with his wife and little son, David, joined the congregation and for many years were a help in the work. Brother Larson served on the Board for several terms as well as being Sunday School treasurer. Sister Larson was a good Sunday School worker as well as taking her place with the Womens Ministries.

Reverend A. A. Lewis began his ministry in May 1957. Sister Lewis and twin sons, Bill and Bob, were welcomed to the assembly. The parsonage was not adequate so Brother Lewis soon drew up plans for extra rooms. A basement was excavated and a bedroom, kitchen and bathroom were added. This was a much needed improvement.

During 1959 special services were held with Reverend Don Cantelon as evangelist. These services were a time of spiritual growth. Sister Don Cantelon is the daughter of Brother and Sister Lewis and while they were in Wainwright, their son, Brent, was born.

Brother Lewis co-operated with the evangelical ministers for a Greater Wainwright Crusade in 1960. Reverend Leighton Ford ministered to large crowds in the local arena.

August 1960, Reverend and Mrs. Sandy Johnson with their three sons, Dan, Wayne and Lyle, as well as Aunt Edie moved into the parsonage. During their ministry, new furnaces were installed in the church and several improvements made. New hymn books were purchased. Several evangelists ministered, including Vera Strodle, Sam Jenkins, Reverend Borrows, Reverend Anderson, Evelyn Williams, Reverend Butcher. Daily Vacation Bible School with an enrolment of one hundred and fourteen was held. Sunday School rooms and a nursery were prepared. A new piano was purchased in 1962. The Johnsons served the Assembly until June 30, 1964.

Reverend Wm. Shackleford served the Assembly from July until December 1964.

Reverend and Mrs. Douglas Gaetz and children, Jodi, Jeanine and Mike, moved into the parsonage early in January 1965. Their move from Hay River in mid-winter was quite a trip. During Brother Gaetz' pastoring, a new foyer was added to the front of the church giving much needed room and adding to the appearance of the building. An addition was built on to the south end to serve as a chapel and social room. A kitchen and furnace room as well as a Pastor's study made the church much more serviceable.

A Thirty-Year Anniversary service was held in January 1968 when former pastors were invited to share early experiences. This was a time of renewing acquaintances and letting the younger members know something of the beginnings of Wainwright Assembly. Those sharing included Brother C. Myhre, Wayne Myhre, Brother H. Rosenke and Mrs. Sandy Johnson. Brother A. Dalby and Sister Petry sent written reports which were much appreciated. Others were invited but were not able to be present.

The Gaetzes resigned in August 1969, having given four and one-half years of ministry.

Reverend and Mrs. H. J. Osterhouse took over the pastorate on August 17, 1969. Their four years of faithful service were appreciated. Brother Osterhouse took pride in his little garden, lawns and shrubs. The Osterhouses left in the fall of 1973 to pastor in Drayton Valley.

Dan and Willa Knol began their ministry in October 1973 and served until June 30, 1974.

For the next several months the pulpit was filled by Sister Hazel Opheim and later by several supply speakers — Reverend R. J. White, Reverend Sandy Johnson, Reverend A. A. Lewis, Reverend Charles Barker, Reverend H. Rosenke, Reverend A. Townsend, Reverend D. Gaetz, Reverend D. Hoeppner and others.

In July 1975, Reverend and Mrs. Woods served the Assembly until March 1978.

Reverend A. Townsend became interim pastor for the months of April, May, June and July, 1978.

Reverend Jess Lynn, wife, Virginia, and sons, Regan, Rael and Renard, came to pastor Wainwright Assembly in August 1978. Besides ministering from the pulpit, Brother Lynn took a full share of the work involved in complete renovation of the church basement — new washrooms installed; complete new concrete floor laid; new insulation and panelling; new ceilings and lighting; movable partitions, for dividing the lower auditorium into Sunday School rooms; carpeting on floors and stairways. Under the direction of Brother Ben Kozak this was accomplished with mostly volunteer effort.

Reverend Lynn started the Dial-A-Message telephone ministry.

Among those, who attended Bible College, are Ruby Bakke, Ralph Bouck, Paul Girouard, Judy Hojcska, *David Larson, Gary Sasseville, Marian Valleau, Sheila Wolfe.

Looking back over the years of effort by many dedicated people causes one to thank God for what has been accomplished. Who can weigh the spiritual blessings that have touched so many lives during the time that the Assembly has served the Lord here.

WESTLOCK
WESTLOCK PENTECOSTAL CHURCH

At the 1953 Sylvan Lake Sunnyside Camp Meeting, Mr. Elmer Still challenged the District to start a church in his town of Westlock, which had a population of 2000. The District accepted the challenge; Mr. Still bought the lots for the future church and parsonage. In October 1953, the District Portable Tabernacle was brought into Westlock. The Mueller sisters, Minnie and Hilda, who had recently graduated from Northwest Bible College, came to pastor. Their widowed mother lived with them in the small two-roomed parsonage.

There were six charter members. On October 27, 1954, the Lutheran Church was purchased and moved on to the lot. The congregation began to grow, the church was organized and a local church board elected. At first the girls worked part-time. After a few months they were able to pastor full time. Five years later, the Mueller sisters left Westlock to be full-time evangelists.

A Westlock Service in 1964.

The work became further established under the ministry of Pastor and Mrs. Angus McLean (1958-1961). Under Pastor and Mrs. Dwain Carruther's ministry (1961-1965), a major job of remodelling was carried out on the structure of the church. Hilda Mueller and Loretta Bolman pastored from November 1965 to October 1966. During Pastor and Mrs. R. J. White's ministry (1966-1968), plumbing was installed in the church, cement floors poured and Sunday School rooms built in the basement. Pastor David and Mrs. Hunter shepherded this assembly from October 1968 until sometime in 1969,

when they left to be missionaries to Africa. They were followed by Pastor David and Ruth Townsend (1970-1972), then Pastor and Mrs. Les Howard (1972-1973). After Pastor Henry and Janet Borzel pastored from December 1973 to January 1976, they became missionaries in Hong Kong. Under Pastor and Mrs. Don McNutt's leadership (1976-1978), the small parsonage was enlarged and modernized. In July 1978, Pastor and Mrs. Sidney Ruffo came to minister. They remained until July 1979, when Pastor and Mrs. Kevin Williams arrived. Pastors and people have worked together for the furtherance of the gospel in this area.

Westlock Board 1964 — M. Berezanski, Otto Adam, Elmer Still, Rev. D. Carruthers, Jock Seatter.

People found Christ, sick bodies were healed and people received the infilling of the Holy Spirit. The visitation and even transportation ministry of the pastors was at their own expense. Most ministers had to supplement their salary by part-time work. Perhaps the unsung heroes in this church are those faithful lay people who teach in the Sunday School, serve on the board, give their financial support and encourage the pastor(s).

Among those, who attended Bible college, are Annette Balkwill, Cheryl Berezanski, Marshall Berezanski, *Gerald Adams (entered the ministry).

WHITECOURT
WHITECOURT PENTECOSTAL TABERNACLE

After opening a new work in Mayerthorpe, Mrs. Gladys Prest and Miss Ruth Maser began the Pentecostal work at Whitecourt in 1960. The work started in a small shed with a few christians. Later the services were held in the Legion Hall. This hall had to be cleaned every Sunday morning, as it had been used Saturday evening. Mrs. Prest and Miss Maser worked in offices, but found time to canvass every house in the town. This was the first evangelical assembly here. The congregation at this time consisted of Mr. and Mrs. Burns and family, Mr. and Mrs. Halverson (from Blue Ridge), Mrs. Janet Forder and family, Mrs. Bertha Gibson, Mrs. Adele Gibson and family, Mrs. H. Woolsey.

Part of the Congregation.

Pastor Glady Prest at the Dedication of the basement of the Church.

The folks rallied together. Within three months a building program began. In the spring of 1960, the sod was turned for a new church. It was built entirely by volunteer help. Mr. William Lagore, who worked nights as a fireman in Edmonton, would drive out during the day to help build in Whitecourt. By the fall of 1960, the basement auditorium was ready for use. There was also a three-bedroom suite in the basement. The upper structure with shingles on the roof was still unfinished. All this was done in about two and a half months. Their first service in the church was on Sunday, October 23, 1960. On November 13, Reverend S. R. Tilton, District Superintendent, dedicated the church basement auditorium. Presbyter R. J. White brought the morning message. Mr. William Lagore spoke in the evening service.

In 1961, Pastor and Mrs. William Lagore and family moved to Whitecourt to minister. Under the leadership of Pastor Lagore, the sanctuary finishing work began. Mr. Burns passed away in October 1962. The upstairs auditorium was not quite completed at this time, so the Burns family worked day and night for two days to finish the auditorium. They wanted the funeral service held in the church for which Mr. Burns had prayed and worked.

Pastor Lagore and family left in 1966. Ministers, which followed, were Reverend and Mrs. Len Schmautz (1966-1967), Reverend L. Hale (1969-1971), Reverend and Mrs. D. Shoop (1971-1975), Pastor Jim Barrs (1975-1977). During the year 1976, Pastor Barrs was ordained in the Whitecourt Church. While here, his priority had been to see more men brought into the church. This really took place to the glory of God.

In 1977 Pastor David Nesbitt followed Reverend Barrs. Reverend Darrel Carpenter came to pastor after the Nesbitts. In the 1982 conference, Pastor Carpenter reported a good growth in the assembly, so much so that a larger facility was rented for services. God is continuing to bless in Whitecourt.

Among those from this assembly, who attended Bible College, are Sam Montoya (Blue Ridge), Brenda Sommer and Hazel Wheadon.

Assemblies in the Northwest Territories

ASSEMBLIES IN THE NORTHWEST TERRITORIES (MACKENZIE DISTRICT)
INTRODUCTION

Hay River was located on an island on the south shore of Great Slave Lake at the mouth of the Hay River. It was also across the river from the Hay River Indian settlement, which has been in existence since about the late eighteen hundred sixties. In 1947, there was just this Indian settlement or village. By 1949 beside the Indian settlement, there was a population of fifteen hundred on the island in the mouth of the Hay River, that became known as the town of Hay River. This new town continued to grow due to the fishing industry, metal mining and the new highway from the Peace River District in Alberta. This was the only road into the Great Slave Lake area. Previously a water route had been used and air routes were and still are used.

On Monday, January 3, 1949, Ken Gaetz, a 1948 graduate of Winnipeg's Western Bible College who was one of our Edmonton Pentecostal Tabernacle young men, started for Hay River because he felt that was where God wanted him. At Peace River, Alberta, he was able to find a trucker, who allowed him to ride to Hay River with him. This part of his journey took him two days. He arrived late Friday evening, January 7, 1949. His welcome was a cafe full of men and women, who told him to leave on the first truck out. They were not interested in seeing a church started among them. In the area, there was no professing Christian, outside of an Anglican nurse in charge of the Indian hospital.

Because he was unable to find a lodging place the night of January 7, he spent that night in the cab of the truck. He did not leave on the first truck out.

That first winter was a hard and lonely one for Ken Gaetz. He lived in a little six by twelve foot trailer. He was refused the use of the local hall for Sunday school or church services. He had to look for another way to break into the community. Finally, he obtained permission to use the hall for Boy 'Scouts and Cubs. In the spring of 1949, he built a little two-room cottage. Then he held Sunday school and a Sunday evening service every Sunday in this cottage. This was the beginning of the Hay River Chapel and the Sub-Arctic Mission. A number had received healing in their bodies, which caused a real stir among the people.

On November 12, 1949, in Winnipeg, Manitoba, Kenneth Gaetz was married to Sarah Solomonson. Ken, with his bride, soon arrived back in Hay River.

The Canadian Army Signal Corps provided radio communication with the outside. The Canadian Broadcasting Corporation had granted a non-commercial community radio station, which was run in connection with the Army Signal Corps. Ken and Sarah were granted two radio programs a week. One was a Sunday 10 P.M., half-hour broadcast, Evening Meditation, which caused an interest throughout the northland, as the gospel was heard from week to week. On Friday, they had a children's half-hour broadcast, which interested the children.

In the winter of 1949-50, Ken Gaetz was able to contact different Indian camps. His mode of transportation was dog team and sled. Since that time he travelled hundreds of miles in that manner. It was often necessary to camp out, even in weather thirty degrees below zero Fahrenheit.

In March 1950, after clearing brush and snow away, Ken and his Christians began building the Pentecostal Chapel in Hay River. This was the first church in the town of Hay River. Since it was the only one, services were well attended. Since then, other churches have been built. In 1950, Ken Gaetz was ordained at Sunnyside Camp at Sylvan Lake, Alberta.

In order to reach the Indian villages and camps, which could only be reached by boat in summer, the Gaetzes obained a flat-bottomed river scow. After much repairing and alterations, their boat, The Messenger, was ready for her maiden voyage in July 1951.

Miss Delila Krieger, a graduate of Canadian Northwest Bible Institute, came to assist at the Sub-

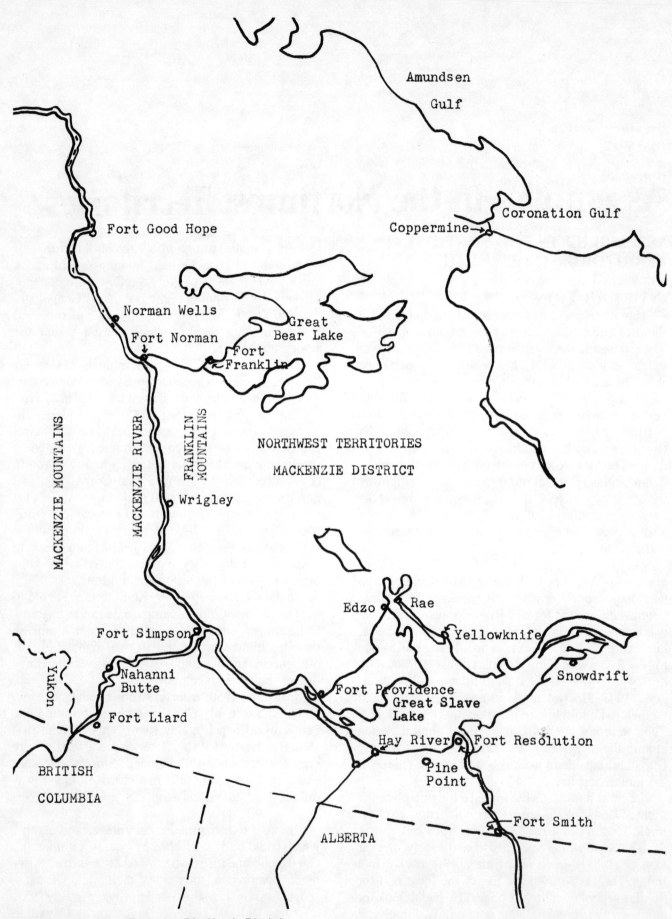

Map of the Northwest Territories (MacKenzie District)

Arctic Mission in 1951. She was in charge of the Hay River assembly, while the Gaetzes were away with The Messenger.

In July 1951, The Messenger was loaded with provisions. On board was an Indian chief, Johnny Lamalice, and their guide, Jimmy Sibbiston, beside Rev. and Mrs. Ken Gaetz. They crossed Great Slave Lake to the MacKenzie River, then down the MacKenzie to the Arctic Circle. They visited as many places along the MacKenzie as they could. What an exciting adventure. They learned much and shared much. Before they returned home, they had travelled one thousand six hundred miles. Through this and later trips, missions were opened in Fort Simpson and Fort Resolution.

In a 1950 report, Ken Gaetz expressed his and Sarah's gratitude to God for allowing them to work among the heathen of the north. Though Indians usually do not speak of the shamans, medicine men or witch doctors, because it is a secret society, there is evidence that the shamans are still active. In 1950, Ken reported what he had discovered: "One does not have to travel to other continents to find heathen conditions. In our vast northland of Canada, we have heathen practices carried on equal to those of Africa, China and India. The following are a few of the practices carried on among the people of the northland. Dead persons are dug up from the graves, the tips of their fingers are amputated and placed into a stream of water. One of the finger-tips will always float; this one is taken and kept for good luck in their gambling and evil doings. The making of love-medicine from herbs, parts of animals and insects, when placed on a person of the opposite sex by various means will cause great affection. The making of bad-medicine, when used against an enemy will cause the person's face to become distorted." Miss Polly Marks reports that the Eskimos have shamans as well. Miss Eva Nicol reported a case of demon possession, where the person was delivered from a number of demons. Our missionaries are thankful for the power of God and the Holy Spirit in dealing with such cases.

In the autumn of 1951, Miss Grace Veale, a graduate of Canadian Northwest Bible Institute, joined the Gaetzes and Miss Krieger. Miss Veale took charge of the radio work in 1952 and later the Hay River Indian work.

The Sub-Arctic Mission has grown to cover a large area.

Pilot Harold Skovmand has flown many a time to take missionaries in and out of the MacKenzie District. He has taken district officials, Work Force men in to build and supplies to most of these places.

By 1960, the Pentecostal message was being preached in Hay River Town; Hay River Indian Settlement; Fort Simpson; Fort Resolution; Fort Wrigley; Norman Wells, where Klaus Scheindl was working and preaching; Fort Norman and Yellowknife.

Reverend and Mrs. Ken Gaetz bade farewell in 1980, though Reverend Gaetz was still involved for sometime after.

By 1982, these were the missions and churches established: Coppermine (Coppermine Pentecostal Mission), Fort Norman (Fort Norman Pentecostal Tabernacle), Fort Providence (Pentecostal Church), Fort Resolution (Pentecostal Church), Fort Simpson (Calvary Chapel), Fort Smith (Bethel Pentecostal Assembly), Hay River (*Hay River Pentecostal Chapel and Hay River Pentecostal Indian Mission), Pine Point (*Pine Point Pentecostal Church) and Yellowknife (*Pentecostal Tabernacle and Pentecostal Chapel, native assembly). The starred ones (*) are self-supporting assemblies; the rest are on mission support from the Pentecostal Sub-Arctic Mission which is unique to the Assemblies.

The Sub-Arctic Mission has gained the respect of the leaders in the Territories. In July 1971, it was reported that Rev. Ken Gaetz was appointed to the Territorial Hospital Insurance Board. This board is composed of three prominent citizens.

In Fort Norman, Pastor Ken Crosby was also elected to the Village Council in 1971. He also served as fire chief.

Evangelism is an important part of the ministry here. It is very expensive to live in the Territories so evangelists are not brought in as often as you would have them in Alberta. Three Indian Evangelists have been a real blessing. Alex Anderson and John Sinclair, Indian Evangelists that travelled as a team, preached and sang under the annointing of the Holy Spirit and were very well received — churches were packed. Quite a number were converted in Fort Norman, Fort Simpson and Hay River. Another Evangelist, Northpeigan, from the Blackfoot Reserve at Brocket, Alberta, was well received and he, too, had good results.

On April 19, 1978, the **Sub-Arctic Mission** Area became the **Sub-Arctic Section with an Elected Presbyter**, Rev. R. Haward.

Up to January 1, 1980, the Sub-Arctic workers were under the Director of the Sub-Arctic Mission. From January 1, 1980, those, on Sub-Arctic Mission Stations, were still funded by the Pentecostal Sub-Arctic Mission. Instead of them being paid directly by the P.S.A.M., the money for their support and needs is sent to the Pentecostal Assemblies of Canada District of Alberta and the Northwest Territories (MacKenzie) District office and those on Mission

Stations are paid from this office. The money comes from the donations from those on the staff of the H. H. Williams Memorial Hospital, who voluntarily go on missionary salary and the balance of their would-be salaries is used to support Pentecostal Sub-Arctic Mission. This type of support has been given for years. Only eternity will reveal the full results of such dedication. Additional funds are available for travel, utilities and more, which are over and above their regular monthly allowances.

COPPERMINE
COPPERMINE PENTECOSTAL MISSION

In 1967, the Sub-Arctic Mission decided to make the opening of the Coppermine Pentecostal Mission, our first Pentecostal Assemblies of Canada Eskimo Pentecostal Mission, their Centennial Project. At that time, Coppermine had about one thousand Eskimos in that area. It was a costly venture, Fourteen Thousand Five Hundred Dollars, to establish this work. Apparently the little combination church and parsonage was built, then shipped to Coppermine by barge. There was a near tragedy, when both the barge and the tug were damaged, while hauling the building, but everything was unloaded in good condition. They were able to set up the building on a very choice location in the town's Eskimo development. A hostile attitude on the part of the English population changed to warmth, friendship and helpfulness in the erection of the building. The building was not yet finished, so that was the next job. Dan and Grace Priest, the founding and first pastors, were happy.

Rev. and Mrs. Dan E. Priest

During this time of working on the building, Dan Priest became very ill. At 3 A.M. that morning, a lady in Calgary awoke with a strong feeling that Dan Priest was in need. So she prayed for him. Her husband confirmed that this happened. It turned out that that was about the time when he was so ill. It was encouraging to know that God cared enough to lay it on someone's heart to pray for him in his hour of need. Dan was taken to a hospital by plane and was back in about a week, feeling much better.

In addition to requiring a place to live and worship, the Priests, also, had to have a year's supply of food (What a list that must have been!) and a year's supply of fuel. This all came in by barge. Food, in the stores there, is terribly expensive.

In 1967, three mining companies had planned to spend about four million dollars for exploration and development that year in the Coppermine area.

Dan and Grace Priest ministered there until the mid nineteen seventies. Among others, who ministered there, were Ivan Gaetz, Wayne, Pastor and Mrs. Dave Shoop and the missionary at the time of publishing, Miss Polly Marks.

Rev. R. M. Argue wrote that he had really enjoyed the roast caribou and the smoked Arctic char that was served in the Shoop home.

Miss Polly Marks reported how happy she was to be able to minister to the Eskimo people. There was quite a culture shock for her, when she came to Coppermine.

Life there in the Eskimo part of Coppermine is very different from the southern part of Canada. She spoke of young people in her church, who remember living, really living in igloos. The Eskimo is having to learn how to live in the southern Canadian style of house, except that water is hauled to the house and sewage is hauled away. Alcohol is a very serious problem. Between the church and Alcoholic Annonymous, some are being helped. Polly's work has included much counselling. Her life was seriously threatened but she was protected. Shamans are very much alive, though they are not often talked about because of the secret society. Shamans are medicine men, whose practices do affect the lives of people. The Christians are so thankful for the power of God to help them live and to be protected.

The price of living is very high. In 1981, a head of lettuce was five dollars and fifteen cents, a cucumber two or up to three dollars, a litre of milk three dollars, a head of cabbage was eight dollars and ninety-one cents. She said that she really enjoyed that cabbage. So you see, when Rev. and Mrs. I. Roset come with a box of apples or oranges, she can hardly wait to open the case.

In 1981, the population was about eight hundred

people, thirty to forty of whom are white. Miss Marks, the Pentecostal missionary, the Anglican priest and his wife, and the Catholic priest all minister in Coppermine and these leaders meet to pray together. These prayer meetings have been very beneficial.

FORT GOOD HOPE
FORT GOOD HOPE PENTECOSTAL CHAPEL

Robert Schneider, a man, who loved God and wanted to help others find the Lord as their Saviour, came to Fort Good Hope in July 1959. From Fort Norman, he went to Norman Wells. There he found an Indian, who took him by canoe down river to an area just south of the settlement of Fort Good Hope. He set up camp in a makeshift tent. He spent the winter camped near Jackfish Creek. There he was often visited by children to whom he told Bible stories and sang gospel songs.

Pentecostal Chapel of Fort Good Hope with good old Shadrach (1979).

In March of 1962, the first Pentecostal missionaries, Pastor and Mrs. Ken Kubryn, and their two children came. They also had one child born in Fort Good Hope. Robert and Ken worked at the old Hudson Bay Store, tearing down some buildings. They salvaged the lumber and Ken built a house with it. Eric Pahl, who later became a missionary to Alaska, helped him build this house. In the summer of 1965, the Kubryns left. An interesting incident was that shortly after their arrival, someone in the settlement circulated a petition in an effort to make them leave. Needless to say, it did not work.

Robert Schneider was the only Christian witness for the next four years. In about 1969, Fred and Yetta

Turner arrived. Fred built the log house, which has served as Chapel and parsonage since. In 1970, Pastor and Mrs. Gary Bennet arrived to take charge, when the Turners moved to Fort Norman. Lynn and Dixie Rosaasen pastored from August 28, 1973 to August 28, 1974, when they went to work in Fort Norman.

Fort Good Hope, looking South in 1980.

Walter T. Anderson, a retired United States Army officer, joined the Sub-Arctic Mission, in September of 1976. He filled in for the Rosaasens, while they were on holidays. When they arrived back in Fort Norman, Walter Anderson assumed the duties of pastor in Fort Good Hope. He arrived on October 19, 1976 and at the time of printing is still there. In the spring of 1981, a new church building was constructed near the home of the pioneer, Robert Schneider, who has been and still is a faithful member of the congregation.

MacKenzie River at the mouth of Skin River.

In December of 1976, Walter Anderson was still new to the North. He decided to walk across the MacKenzie River (one mile wide at that point), so he did, then stopped to see Robert Schneider, crossed to an island. This was a large island, Manitou Island, about ten miles long and probably three-quarters of a mile wide. The river at this point was about a mile and a half wide. On this island the snow was hip deep over willows. It was like walking on bed springs. He crossed the island to about the middle then turned north, with the idea of reaching the ice and then crossing the rest of the river to home. All of a sudden he found himself in Willowbush and up to his armpits in snow and could not seem to get out. At this point, he prayed, "Lord, put it in Robert's heart to phone the R.C.M.P.. Lord, give me a sign." Then the words, Be anxious for nothing, came to him. The dog saw the tiny winking light. Then Walter saw the tiny winking light. The Indian men were ahead so as not to loose his trail. Walter's walking stick left a little hole. Then the Royal Canadian Mounted Police followed the Indians. He could see a whole parade of skidoo lights. They were all out there looking for him and they did find him in all that wilderness. His gloves were frozen stiff by that time. Walter found that Robert had gone to the contractor to use his phone to call the R.C.M.P., which was about the time that Walter had prayed that he would phone for help. When they freed Walter and got him to the fifty feet of bank, Walter could see packs of men ready to search for him. How wonderful in that dark night!

Fort Good Hope is really an old, old settlement. The graveyard dates back to the mid eighteen hundreds. The old timers in this settlement really know how to track and search for the lost. They have had many years of experience.

A native couple, Jack and Adele Charney. Jack is picking up traps and Mrs. Charney is riding in Pastor Anderson's sled.

FORT NORMAN
FORT NORMAN PENTECOSTAL TABERNACLE

Fort Norman is located on an island in the MacKenzie River, where the Bear River runs into the MacKenzie. In 1979, the population was about three hundred — Slavey Indian, Metis and about ten percent white people. The island has about two miles of roads. The MacKenzie River is more than a mile wide at this point.

Dan and Grace Priest, Sub-Arctic missionaries, travelled from Hay River, across part of Great Slave Lake and down the MacKenzie River by canoe to Fort Norman, by July 14, 1959. The reason for such a trip was to pioneer the Pentecostal work in Fort Norman. Dan set up his own sawmill and then proceeded to make an old building into a lovely new church. In a letter dated May 30, 1960, Grace Priest wrote, "We arrived at Fort Norman July 14, 1959. The Indians have told us that this had not been too bad a winter — lowest temperature was sixty-five degrees below zero (Fahrenheit) — not too much snow — not very cold? — we are wondering what it is really like up here. Most of the Indians are on their spring hunt for muskrats and beaver so the village is rather quiet. They will be back the end of June.

Dan is trying to mend an old gas washing machine. It will be lovely if he gets it to go. I will feel like washing everything.

We get our food for the year by boat which comes down the great MacKenzie River during the summer. It is a great day when the boat arrives. This would be the best way for the women to send their Christmas parcels. They would have to mail them the beginning of August as the last boat leaves Waterways (Alberta) August 18th.

We would be glad of some good books. Good used clothing for the Indian work is much appreciated. Food parcels are always welcome.

We are well and rejoicing in the Lord. Pray that God will call and use the Indians to witness to their own people."

Dan and Grace relied largely upon wild-life for their meat. They lived in a small log cabin. Later, once a year by canoe, with a small outboard motor attached, the Priests travelled up the MacKenzie River, and across Great Slave Lake to Hay River to bring out their Year's provisions. Then head back across Great Slave Lake and down the mighty MacKenzie River to Fort Norman. This was a twelve hundred mile return trip.

Travel by canoe, snowshoes or with dog-team was all the same to the Priests, as long as souls were saved and God was glorified. Dan was appointed a Justice of the Peace and was known throughout the whole MacKenzie River area as a prominent citizen of the North. The Priests left Fort Norman in 1967.

In the same year, 1967, Pastor Aaron Cameron took charge. Then Pastor and Mrs. Ken Crosby followed him. Fred and Yetta Turner next served as pastors from about 1970 to 1974. Pastor Turner designed a twelve-sided log church to seat one hundred fifty people. Indian brethren and former Pastor Ken Crosby cut and peeled three hundred trees for the building of the new church. Rev. and Mrs. Harold B. Bradley of Ontario volunteered a summer of service to assist in the construction. This lovely log church, the Fort Norman Pentecostal Tabernacle, was dedicated August 12, 1973, with Rev. Charles Yates (District Superintendent) and his wife, Rev. and Mrs. Ken Gaetz of Hay River, Rev. and Mrs. Dan Priest of Coppermine present.

Rev. and Mrs. L. M. Rosaasen arrived in August 1974 and pastored to about 1977 or 78. Miss S. Smith with Pastor and Mrs. Delbert L. Franklin were the next pastors. Later Miss Smith left and the Franklins carried on. When Rev. R. M. Argue came for a service and in spite of the fact that there had already been large services on Sunday and Monday, there were still more than fifty in attendance, including some fine young men and women. At that time, plans were in the making to convert the old church into a retreat centre for youth work.

September 1, 1979, Barry and Rita Bernhardt arrived to become the new pastors. Harold Skovmand flew them in from Fort Providence. At this time there were about thirty attending services and eight to twelve children in Sunday school. Barry and Rita also taught Religious Instruction in the school, as did the Catholic Sisters. The Bernhardts were still there in 1982.

One fall, a building contractor donated a truck and some building material to the mission. The truck has been used to haul wood and even to pick up people on occasion. Such gifts help the missionaries to do a better job.

FORT PROVIDENCE
PENTECOSTAL CHURCH

Mary Giesbrecht opened this work. In 1967, Miss Eva Nichol was asked to take charge of Fort Resolution and Fort Providence. She accepted the position and used nurses and other hospital personnel in this outreach. It is not known how long this work continued at this time. The mission there was closed until the Ed Garbers and their two children came in August 1977. The whole family was involved in pioneer evangelism there. They left about February 1979. In June 1979, Barry and Rita Bernhardt came and ministered until they were transferred to Fort Norman September 1, 1979. Then Pastor Grace Miller took charge. At this point the only Christians, who attended church, were summer residents. There was still much to be done in this mainly Indian village. It is one of the oldest communities in the

Northwest Territories and has the oldest Roman Catholic school north of the sixtieth parallel.

Miss Miller worked at the H. H. Williams Memorial Hospital from May 1976 to August 1978, then took her third and graduating year of Bible college at Northwest Bible College. During her Pastoral Ministries classes, under Dr. G. Franklin, a desire developed to enter the ministry herself. Fort Providence was laid on her heart and eventually she arrived. She is on Mission salary and works part-time at a local hamburger stand. This part-time job helps her to meet people, especially young people. She allows young people to visit her often. During four months, she entertained sixty different young people (twelve and older). Some are interested in the Gospel and some are not but they know they are accepted no matter who they are. Grace continues at the time of printing.

FORT RESOLUTION
FORT RESOLUTION PENTECOSTAL
CHURCH

Fort Resolution is an Indian community of four hundred, which is situated at the mouth of the Slave River on the south shore of Great Slave Lake.

In 1952 Howard and Wilma Peever came to pioneer this work. Miss Delila Krieger assisted for the winter of 1952 and 1953, then left the North. The Peevers were there until 1955. In 1955, Jim and Doris Tyler became the next missionaries. The efforts of the Peevers, Lily Krieger and the Tylers resulted in the erection of a church and parsonage in Fort Resolution. The Tylers left for Fort Simpson in the summer of 1956.

In 1957, Robert Schneider did some gospel work in Fort Resolution. In 1958, Rev. and Mrs. Gordon Bailey became the next missionaries. They always worked diligently and with a heart for the people. Miss Eva Nichol, a well-known missionary in the Sub-Arctic Mission areas, took charge of Fort Resolution and Fort Providence at the same time, beginning in 1967. She used the nursing staff and other hospital personnel in this outreach. These people worked in the H. H. Williams Memorial Hospital in Hay River. It was a real opportunity to do missionary outreach work.

Later Pastor and Mrs. Henry Konrad came and stayed with this work in hard times and have seen it grow. The new church was built in 1976 and the parsonage in 1977. In 1978, they reached an attendance record of forty-nine in their Pentecostal services. The Konrads served until 1978 or 1979. In 1979, O. Tietz was pastor. Then Tim Acey became the next pastor. It was through the influence of Eva Nichol and others that Tim became interested in the

Pentecostal message. At the conference in Evangel Pentecostal Assembly in Edmonton, Alberta, in 1980, Tim Acey was baptized in water. It caused no small stir, when he received the Baptism of the Holy Spirit as well that same night. He continues to pastor at Fort Resolution. Elizabeth Catholique, a native teacher, taught there for a year or two.

FORT SIMPSON
FORT SIMPSON CALVARY CHAPEL

Fort Simpson is located at the mouth of the Liard River, where it runs into the MacKenzie River. It is about two hundred and twenty miles by road, from Fort Providence. Except for a few hunters and trappers, there is no one for a hundred mile radius around Fort Simpson. The population of Fort Simpson itself is about nine hundred (about half Indian and half white). Fort Simpson's population is quite transient. Alcohol is the cause of many family problems.

Rev. and Mrs. James C. Tyler

The Pentecostal work began there in the summer of 1956, under the leadership of the Sub-Arctic missionaries, Rev. Jim Tyler and his wife, Doris. After ministering here for a while, the Tylers began planning for a church and a parsonage, which were built in 1958.

Among those, who pastored Fort Simpson, were M. Christianson and E. Myhra; E. and G. Pahl; Rev. and Mrs. R. Haward; Pastor and Mrs. V. Munshaw; Pastor and Mrs. R. Wood; Mr. and Mrs. Eschleman; Pastor and Mrs. Jack Hood (early seventies); Pastor and Mrs. Clarence Heyers (March 1978-81); Wayne and Donna Joy Loe (1982-   ).

Because of the transiency of the white population, who on the average stay only two or three years, pastors find it difficult to deal with building a con-

gregation. Those, who move away, are really missed, but missionaries in Fort Simpson have to take the loss and keep on finding others to take their places. Each missionary has done his best to win others for Christ.

FORT SMITH
BETHEL PENTECOSTAL ASSEMBLY

Fort Smith is located on the west bank of the Slave River. It is just inside the Northwest Territories near the Alberta Border. The population in 1978 was about two thousand five hundred people (half native Indian and half white). It was the MacKenzie District Administrative centre of the Department of Indian Affairs and Northern Development until 1968. Fort Smith is an educational point. Young people come there to prepare for their future vocations.

The Pentecostal work at Fort Smith began about 1973 with Missionary F. M. Harvey. About 1974 or 1975, Miss Eva Nichol, well-known Sub-Arctic missionary, took charge of the work there. By 1978, the new church was filled to capacity, so a large lot was purchased on which to build a new church. That same year, the new church was erected by volunteers from near and far. The congregation is not terribly large, but it is an active group. Strangers are soon conscious of the friendly atmosphere in the Assembly. This is a real asset in winning others to the Lord. Eva has told of marvelous answers to prayer. The conversion of Elizabeth Catholique was marvelous. She became a real worker for the Lord wherever she taught school (Snowdrift, Fort Resolution). Eva Nichol has been able to help a number of young people who came there from other points as well as from Fort Smith itself. In her services, Eva may have Indians, Eskimos and white people.

In 1978, Evangelist Don Schellenberg held a crusade in Fort Smith. These services were held in Roaring Rapids Hall and a nearby school auditorium. About thirty were converted (accepted Christ as their own Saviour).

Among Eva's assistants were Nurse Ann Cheeseman and Grace Miller. Miss Eva Nichol is still pastoring (1982).

GREAT SLAVE LAKE CAMP (sometimes referred to as Sandy Creek Camp)

Great Slave Lake Camp at Sandy Creek on the shore of Great Slave Lake, Northwest Territories (MacKenzie District), was a unique camp. Its campers arrived by boat or canoe from Hay River — a five-mile trip. It was interesting to come into camp this way. Sandy Creek was deep enough for even big boats to come in and dock at its steep banks. A plank made the landing from boat to the top of the bank quite easy.

Staking the claim for the Great Slave Lake Camp at the mouth of Sandy Creek.

In July 1960 Reverend R. W. (Bob) Taitinger and Harvey and Genaah Schmautz were the speakers. The sermons and friendship were appreciated. Misses Doreen Thomas and Tews, the Thomas Twins, and J. Shirley Johnson from Edmonton arrived in Hay River about 2:30 A.M. on that rainy Sunday that camp was to start that year. It was so good to be greeted by the friendly voice of Mary Evans as they walked up to the H. H. Williams Memorial Hospital. The nurses allowed them to spend the balance of the night in their beds. Then they had breakfast. They needed a Sunday School teacher at the Hay River Chapel that morning, so Reverend S. R. Tilton volunteered Shirley Johnson to fill in, so she did. After a good dinner with the hospital staff, Ken Gaetz took

1960 Group by an Indian teepee.

us to camp by boat. Reverend and Mrs. Ken Gaetz and Mrs. Ron Mitts (nee Grace Veale) made them so welcome. To add to the childrens services Shirley did a chalk drawing. In order to do this, she bought oilcloth (the type was used on kitchen tables at that time) and colored chalk at the Hay River Hardware Store. Shirley and friends found charcoal (burned log) on the beach near camp. This material plus an easle and board put Shirley in business. Folks and children at the camp provided the musical background for the chalk drawing.

Dads with their babies. The Dad on the left is Rev. Harvey Schmautz.

Shirley was also counsellor for the girls in the girls' cabin (wooden base and sides with a canvass top). She and the girls retired to their sleeping bags, though they could still hear young people singing to guitar accompaniment. It was late, though still quite light — you know how light it is in the summer. It would go to dusk and then to light again.

In the afternoons they quite often played volleyball. One day in spite of the fact, that some supplies had not yet arrived, Shirley remembers the nurse, Miss Purdy, and another lady working to make their dinner a nourishing one.

A Slavey Indian family set up a lovely teepee. A moose had been killed and the Indians were drying moose meat with a fire partway down the bank and moose meat on branches above. The Gaetz children just loved the dried meat the Indians made. It was so nice to see Harvey Schmautz and a young Indian father pose with their babies for a picture. Did you notice the ribbon in the Indian baby's hair?

Shirley also remembers an insect incident or two. A large fly lit on her shoulder blade, bit through her

J. Shirley Johnson, counselor, and girls in front of their cabin.

1960, More Folks at Camp.

dress. She moved, it did not and bit her again. Spray was the only means of keeping them away. She also slept with a net over her face. One night she put it on only to discover she had company. Off it came in a hurry. A similar incident took place in her sleeping bag — that time something bit her. Bugs or no bugs, they had a good time of fellowship and friendship. God was so good, the sermons were good so how could it help but be good.

Ken Gaetz took a number of the "outsiders" on a very enjoyable cruise on Great Slave Lake. Some tried trolling and managed to tangle their lines really well. They caught no fish. They saw a partially submerged stern wheeler. It was so nice of Ken to take them out.

Some of the speakers were Reverend R. W. (Bob) Taitinger (1960), Harvey and Genaah Schmautz (1960), Reverend W. G. McPherson (1963), Reverend C. A. Myhre (1964), Mr. Oya (1965), Evangelist Sam Jenkins (1966), the H. C. McAlister Famiy (1967), Reverend D. V. Hurst (1970), Reverend I. Roset (1973), Reverend R. L. Brandt (1969), Mrs. R. L. Brandt (1969) for the children.

Baptismal service in Sandy Creek, very near Great Slave Lake.

Mode of Travel between Hay River and Great Slave Lake Camp.

Certainly other years were just as good. The camp started in the nineteen hundred and fifties and ended in the nineteen hundred and seventies. Those were years of blessing, encouragement, conversions and people receiving the Baptism of the Holy Spirit.

HAY RIVER
HAY RIVER PENTECOSTAL CHAPEL

The Hay River Pentecostal Chapel had its beginning when Ken Gaetz arrived in January 1949. It was also home-base for the Sub-Arctic Mission. Because he was not allowed to rent the hall for services or Sunday school, he started Boy Scouts and Cubs, for which they did allow him to use the hall.

In the spring of 1949, he built a small two-room cottage. There he had Sunday school and Sunday

First Hay River Pentecostal Chapel

evening services. A number received healing in their bodies, which caused a real stir among the people. The beginning of the Sub-Artic Mission is the same.

Among those, who have been pastors or assisted in the ministry here, are Rev. and Mrs. Ken Gaetz; Delila Krieger; Miss Grace Veale; Rev. and Mrs.

Rev. Kenneth A. Gaetz and his wife, Sarah

James Tyler (1952-1955), who arrived because a new town was expected to be built near Hay River, but it did not materialize. However his assistance at Hay River and in evangelism was much appreciated. In 1955 Tylers left for Fort Resolution. Rev. Charles Howey pastored the Hay River Chapel, while Ken Gaetz arranged for the construction of the first hospital, in 1955-56 (about a year). March 17, 1961, Mr. Ronald G. Mitts married Miss Grace Veale, missionary to the Hay River Indians. In the spring of 1963, there was a very bad flood. It caused some damage to the Gaetz residence, the Hay River Chapel was moved off its lot, and the Gaetzes had a cold wade to safety. The town of Hay River was built on an island at the mouth of the Hay River. After this most of the people relocated on high ground. Though the hospital was not harmed, a new one was built on higher ground, too. The island has since become an industrial area for the most part. Rev. and Mrs. Doug Gaetz ministered well there. Rev. and Mrs. Craig Pitts did a royal job in Hay River, too. Board members at this time were Aubrey Bildson, Dr. Earle Covert, Dr. Jan Gustafsson, Gerry Loewen, Dean Schofield and Ron Mitts. On April 13, 1975, Pastor Pitts and congregation celebrated the paying up of the original mortgage. Doug Schneider came to assist Rev. Pitts. The Pitts left in the spring of 1979; Doug Schneider became the new pastor. In 1982, Rev. and Mrs. Walter Fowke became the new pastors.

Reverend and Mrs. R. G. Veale

request the honour of your presence
at the marriage of their daughter

Evelyn Grace

to

Mr. Ronald George Mitts

on Friday, the seventeenth of March
nineteen hundred and sixty-one
at four o'clock in the afternoon
The Pentecostal Chapel
Hay River, Northwest Territories

Reception 6:00 p.m.   *Please Reply*
School Auditorium   *Box 5*
                               Hay River, N.W.T.

1961 Wedding Invitation for the marriage of Miss Grace Veale and Mr. Ronald Mitts.

111

Al and Lil Goodzeck with Jay Dee and Joy. Lil (nee Freund) was Ken Gaetz's secretary.

Hay River Pentecostal Chapel has a lovely building in the new part of Hay River, a lovely congregation shows that God has blessed the efforts of all, who have labored there.

Among those, who attended Bible college and/or entered the ministry(*), are from Hay River: *Dale Archibald, Bonny Bildson, Val Ellefson, Randy Lee, Louise Sternall, Fred Turner and *Cecil Ross; from Fort Good Hope: Garry Bennett; from Fort Smith: Neil Rempel, Elizabeth Catholique; from Yellowknife: Craig Cooper, Paul Hamilton and Gordon Toppin.

HAY RIVER
HAY RIVER PENTECOSTAL INDIAN MISSION

Ken Gaetz, sometime after coming to Hay River in 1949, met the Indian Chief, Johnny Lamalice and his wife, who became two of the first converts. During the winter of 1949-50, Ken Gaetz used a dog team to visit different Indian camps. By taking Chief Lamalice and Jimmy Sibbiston on board The Messenger to make that long journey down the MacKenzie River to the Arctic Circle, Ken gave the new Christians an opportunity to help win their people for the Lord. Mr. Sibbiston was their guide and Chief Lamalice was Ken's interpreter. Ken took his wife on that journey, too. Ken kept up the work with the Slavey Indians at Hay River. In 1955, Grace Veale came back to specifically work with the Indians. She lived in the back of the Hay River Chapel from the fall of 1955 until the spring or summer, when the

Congregation at the Hay River Pentecostal Indian Mission.

combination house and chapel was finished. In the spring, she planted a garden in the Indian village.

While she was living in the back of the Hay River Chapel, she studied the Slavey language. A Wycliffe Bible Translator couple were a great help. They gave her long lists of suggested conversation. They gave her good advice. Grace used a tape recorder to help her learn. She started using what she learned as she continued to study. Eventually she was able to read stories, carry on a conversation, preach in Slavey both in the Mission and on her radio program. She would include a story for the children by herself or an Indian lady, Mary Norn. She also had services at Indian Cabins, Alberta. She used the Slavey language there, too. She used some of her sermonettes and children's stories. She also did some translation work. In fact, she loved those people. Ruby Martell, an Indian lady, was her bridesmaid, when she married Ron Mitts. They carried on with the Mission, until about the end of April two months before the terrible flood in June of 1963. The combination house-chapel building was moved to the middle of the village by that flood. Ron worked for the government.

Congregation at Hay River Pentecostal Indian Mission.

Pastor Bonk at Work.

One spring, Ron needed to bring the jeep over the river before the ice broke up on the river. Grace remembers watching the ice rising as Ron drove the jeep across the ice. She was a very thankful lady, when he made it across the Hay River. The ice went out a few hours later or maybe it was the next day. During the time she worked in the Indian Village, she took part in the Sunday evening service in the Hay River Chapel. Since the Mission was a branch of the Hay River Chapel, there was always someone to take care of services.

In the spring of 1982, the first wedding of the Indian Mission was performed — the Chief's daughter, Ruth Martell, married the son of the preceding chief's son, George Buggins. Grace Mitts (nee Veale) played for the wedding.

Mrs. Bonk adding wood to the heater.

Grace Mitts mentioned that Marie Villebrun, who helped at Fort Smith for the summer of 1982, reminds her of Marie's grandmother, Mrs. Villebrun, an Indian lady, who was a good Christian.

Rev. and Mrs. Lawrence Bonk are the present pastors of the Hay River Indian Mission. They obviously enjoy their work. Rev. Bonk also ministers in the jail in Hay River. He feels it is a worthwhile ministry.

HAY RIVER
H. H. WILLIAMS MEMORIAL
HOSPITAL

The only hospital facilities were at Yellowknife, one hundred miles across Great Slave Lake from Hay River. Rev. Ken Gaetz was approached about providing such care for the many needy in the area. After much prayer, he accepted this responsibility and was able to contact two fine young women, Miss Beatrice Purdy, a Registered Nurse and a graduate of Bethel Bible Institute in Saskatoon in Saskatchewan, and Miss Adeline Drisner, a graduate of Canadian Northwest Bible Institute in Edmonton in Alberta and a Nurses' Aide, who both accepted the challenge of operating a nursing station. On Monday, January 12, 1953, the Hay River Nursing Station, operated by the Sub-Arctic Mission of the Pentecostal Assemblies of Canada in Hay River in the Northwest Territories, was officially opened.

The first H. H. Williams Memorial Hospital

Early in the morning of January 12, 1953, some fifty miles from Hay River, a lone man entered his fishing shanty on the lake, after spending the night with his brother some distance away. It was around fifty below zero Fahrenheit and everything in the shanty was bitterly cold. He lit the stove but it was slow to drive out the biting frost. To speed up the fire, he picked up a small can of gasoline and poured a little on the fire. There was a blinding flash, flames were all around him severely burning his exposed hands and face. Somehow, he was able to drive his bombadier to his nearest neighbor across the snow and ice. Soon he was rushed over the ice and snow to the Hay River Nursing Station for medical treatment. In the first ten days of operation, the Nursing Station had seventy-three calls and five patients admitted. Homes, otherwise closed to the gospel, were beginning to open. Beatrice Wilson was a Ward Aid at the nursing station from March 1956 to February 1957.

In the autumn of 1957, a new six-bed hospital, the H. H. Williams Memorial Hospital was opened. It was built with funds from the H. H. Williams Trust which was administered by Stone Church of Toronto, the Federal Government and the Pentecostal Assemblies of Canada District of Alberta. This hospital was named after a Christian businessman. May 19, 1958, Dr. Norman Douglas Abbey and Miss Beatrice Purdy R.N. were married in the Hay River Pentecostal Chapel. Dr. Abbey was in private practice but continued to give valuable assistance in the hospital. The Abbeys and their dedicated staff of Christian nurses have done much for the spiritual and physical welfare of both the white people and the Indians in the area. (Beatrice Purdy was the first matron and Dr. Abbey, the first resident doctor.)

The atmosphere in the hospital was lovely. Gospel music could be heard throughout the hospital. Nurses would have devotions with each patient and took time to talk to them.

This hospital was located on the island, where the town of Hay River was built.

Early in 1962, this six-bed hospital was enlarged to a capacity of twelve beds.

In the spring of 1963, Hay River suffered a flood. The Gaetzes had to wade through icy water to safety. Their house suffered some damage and the Pentecostal Chapel was moved off its lot. The hospital escaped harm. As a result many people and businesses moved to higher ground into what might be called the new section. A new twenty-two bed hospital was built with planned growth to eventually fifty beds. This new hospital was opened officially on June 28, 1965, under the chairmanship of Rev. Ken Gaetz, Hospital Administrator.

Among the guests who attended the dedication, were Mr. B. G. Sivertz, Commissioner of the Northwest Territories; Dr. W. H. Frost, Chairman of the Territorial Hospital Insurance Services; Dr. G. Butler, Department of National Health and Welfare; Mr. T. A. Groves of Aberdeen, Groves, Hodgson Architects; and Mayor D. Stewart of Hay River, who spoke of the excellent work of the hospital; Rev. S. R. Tilton, Alberta District Superintendent; Rev. C. H. Stiller, National Home Missions Director; Rev. R. J. White.

On September 10, 1976, the new Hay River Health Centre was opened. This Centre is a complex designed to house Public Health, Social Development and the new hospital. The hospital is now a fifty-bed hospital.

The hospital staff is dedicated to the Lord for the purpose of serving the community of Hay River and environs and ministering to the whole man, both physically and spiritually. On staff, there are four or

Hay River Health Centre (Architects' Drawing)

five Pentecostal Doctors, many nurses and other personnel. They pray before each operation and for each newborn baby. This hospital serves Pine Point as well. Three nurses, engaged by the hospital, provide twenty-four hour medical services for the Town of Pine Point, a mining community of two thousand. Doctors from Hay River make regular visits to Pine Point.

In 1978, the hospital employed seventy-seven people, fifty-five of them opted to go on missionary salary and donated the rest of their would-be salaries to the Sub-Arctic Mission for the support of its missionaries and missions. There are those, who ministered as well.

PINE POINT
PINE POINT PENTECOSTAL CHURCH

In January 1974, Rev. Ken Gaetz, Director of the Sub-Arctic Mission, approached two Pentecostal families (Bill and Darlene Knibb and Hazel and Al Harvey) in Pine Point. He spoke to them about the possibility of starting a Pentecostal Church. There were six Pentecostal families in Pine Point and a number of them had expressed a desire to have a church of their own.

Subsequently, Rev. Ritchie Haward, who was then pastoring in Windsor, Ontario, was contacted to see if he would be available to come to Pine Point as their pastor. After prayerful consideration, he felt this was the leading of the Lord and accepted the challenge.

On April 1, 1974, Rev. Haward, his wife, Beth, and three children, Paul, Ronalee and Robert, arrived. They lived in a rented trailer. There was a bit of a problem with renting a trailer. This trailer was sold a few weeks after the family were settled in. After they had lived for a few months in the next rented trailer, they returned home from a shopping trip in Hay River to find the living room and porch filled with someone else's furniture and boxes. They were surprised and shocked. They discovered that the trailer had been sold. Fortunately, the people were able to complete the parsonage portion of the complex within the next two weeks, so the Hawards were able to move into it in November 1974.

Pine Point is a mining town. There several hundred men lived in bunkhouses with very little to do in their spare time. Several of these fellows helped with the construction of the church.

It was fortunate that Ken Gaetz and Al Harvey had bought property before the Hawards arrived. We wonder how many trailers would have been sold out from under the pastor, if the assembly had not been able to build, when they did. God does go before us;

so He did with the Hawards. Approximately ninety percent of the work on the church-parsonage complex was done by volunteer labour. Work began on this on May 15, 1974. Their first service in the unfinished auditorium was the 1974 Christmas program. What a time of rejoicing! Up to that time, services were held in the Public School facilities. They thanked the Lord for the school but it was good to have their own place. June 15, 1975 was a day of praise, for it was the official opening and dedication of the church. This church was self-supporting from its beginning.

The founding families were Henry and Hulda Perron and family, Judy and Trevor Cook and family, Jim Johnson, Darlene and Bill Knibb, Hazel and Al Harvey and family, Violet and Robert DeLancey and family, Yvonne and Henry Douglas.

The population there is very transient, with numerous families coming and going.

The pastors have been Rev. Ritchie Haward from April 1, 1974 to June 17, 1979 and the present pastor, Rev. Dave Findlay, who arrived August 12, 1979. Rev. Findlay's wife is Elaine.

This church is a friendly church. Three were won by someone taking an interest in them and inviting them to church as well.

YELLOWKNIFE
PENTECOSTAL CHAPEL

In 1963, Reverend and Mrs. G. M. Bailey went to open a chapel in the old section (generally referred to as the Old Town) of Yellowknife. The Baileys rented an old house, built in 1938. This served as home and meeting place. Most, who attend the Chapel are primarily Indian, with some white folk. The house was rented until the Pentecostal Chapel was built.

The Baileys have a heart for the Indian people and the down-and-outers. They were and still are very, very hospitable. Their home was and still is usually filled with over-night guests, who sleep all over the place. They often had and often still have eight or nine at their table with the overflow in the front room. They do what they can to help these people and, all the while, tell how God loves them and how Jesus died for them. Some are saved.

In 1972, the Pentecostal Chapel was built with Work Force help. This certainly gave the work here a boost.

In 1978 Reverend and Mrs. G. M . Bailey received the Citizen of the Year Award. It could not have gone to a more dedicated couple.

These faithful missionaries are still ministering in the "Old Town" (1982). At the 1982 General Conference of the Pentecostal Assemblies of Canada in Winnipeg, the Baileys were honored for over fifty years of ministry.

YELLOWKNIFE
YELLOWKNIFE PENTECOSTAL TABERNACLE

Yellowknife was a town composed of two sections, commonly referred as Old Town and New Town. It is situated on the north shore of Great Slave Lake. In 1958, the population of Yellowknife was about four thousand. Yellowknife became a city in the mid sixties. In 1968, Yellowknife became the Capital of the Northwest Territories and the seat of the Northwest Territories Government, which moved from Ottawa to Yellowknife. This Northwest Territories Government is composed of an elected Legislative Assembly with ministers, similar to a provincial government, except that instead of a premier, it is headed by a commissioner, who is appointed by Ottawa.

In June 1958, a small group, who had been holding Sunday school and church services in the school in Yellowknife, wanted the congregation united in a church with a pastor and a building of their own. As a result, Rev. and Mrs. Geoffrey Veale became their pastors. They were sent a return air fare for Yellowknife, so they flew up, had a week of meetings in June, then were given one hundred and fifty dollars for a month's holiday. After a little holiday, the Veales travelled to Hay River, left their car and utility trailer because there was no road to Yellowknife at that time. They then took a flight to Yellowknife, which arrived June 27, 1958. The Veales were billeted in several different homes for the rest of the summer and services were held in the school until the beginning of November.

The assembly bought a lot on which to build a church. This lot had the remains of a burned house on it, so Rev. Veale, with some help from his wife, cleaned up the mess so that it was ready for excavation. They then began to build. Rev. Veale worked alone, generally six days a week. Most of the men in the assembly worked for the Yellowknife Gold Mine, so they came to help in the evenings and some on Saturdays. Winter comes early in Yellowknife so in the fall it was very cold, when they were working. By the first week in November, all the outside of the building was finished. That first week of November, the temperature dropped to below zero Fahrenheit and never even once touched zero day or night until April 7, 1959. By that first week in November, the wiring was in, the plumbing was in and the pastor, who escaped the extreme cold, had built the parsonage in the basement and had already moved into it. Everyone was so happy.

Beginning the first Sunday in November 1959, services were held in the basement. Even though it was a bit crowded, this happy congregation praised God for what He had done for them and through them.

After installing insulation and gyproc, the congregation moved into the sanctuary. Their first furnishings were planks for pews and a cardboard box for a pulpit. Soon a pulpit and good pews were made.

God blessed the work, some were saved, some baptized in the Spirit, more people attended and the work grew. The Veales, who are the parents of Mrs. Grace Mitts (nee Veale), resigned in August 1962.

Rev. and Mrs. James Tyler pastored from 1962 to 1969. The Tylers were involved in evangelistic outreach and pioneering new assemblies, building churches and left after seventeen years of ministry in the North. For some time, he was Director of the Sub-Arctic Mission. During their time in Yellowknife, a new school principal, who was Pentecostal, arrived in 1967.

Others who served as pastors were D. O. Schneider (1969-   ); A. Craig Gibbs under whose ministry a former United Church was moved next to the existing church, then joined to be a single unit in 1977-78; Rev. Richard Cooper, under whose ministry this building was finished; and the pastor at the time of publishing, Rev. R. Haward. Rev. Haward is also District Presbyter and has been since the Sub-Arctic Mission area became the Sub-Arctic Section.

District Officers and Ministries

THE ESTABLISHMENT OF THE ALBERTA AND NORTHWEST TERRITORIES (MACKENZIE) DISTRICT

In the beginning the groups of believers, who had received the Baptism of the Holy Spirit, were not organized under one or two governing bodies. They were bonded together through having the same kind of experience, though not official, but a loosely knit fellowship of kindred believers.

The Assemblies of God of the United States of America organized a conference of Pentecostal groups. In Eastern Canada, a group of Pentecostal believers, formed The Pentecostal Assemblies of Canada, then applied to the Government of Canada for a federal charter. They received this federal charter in May 1919. This gave them official recognition and the right to own property but, for fellowship and function, they were still under the administration and leadership of the Assemblies of God in the United States of America.

In 1919, the first Western District Council of the Assemblies of God (for the four western provinces) was established with Saskatchewan and Manitoba assemblies co-operating. This Council was organized in Moose Jaw, Saskatchewan, with Rev. J. W. Welsh from the Assemblies of God in the United States of America present.

In 1921 at Montreal, the Conference of the Pentecostal Assemblies of Canada was held. The Eastern churches were the Eastern District Council of the Assemblies of God. This was for fellowship and function. The joining of the Eastern and Western Councils made a single organizational union, though they still had their District Council meetings or conferences.

In 1922, the Western District Council met in Edmonton, Alberta. The executive of three officials was elected — J. M. Cadwalder (Chairman), George Schneider (Secretary-Treasurer), C. O. Benham. In 1922, the special committee from the Eastern and Western District Councils met in Kitchener, Ontario.

They decided that the arrangement with the Assemblies of God and the Pentecostal Assemblies of Canada was not practical. There was some discussion on the situation, with a view to change the situation at some future date. In 1923, the Western District Council met in Saskatoon, Saskatchewan. The new executive was J. M. Cadwalder (Chairman), George Schneider (Secretary), John McAlister (Alberta), P. E. Wills and E. Hoff.

July 2 to 4, 1924, the Western District Council met in Parkside, Saskatchewan. Though in 1923, H. M. Cadwalder was believed to have been elected for a two-year term, he did not serve for two years. Rev. Paul Hawkes discovered that George Schneider was the Western District Council Chairman in 1924.

In the History of Alberta and Saskatchewan, Rev. W. E. McAlister stated that about the year 1924 the Assemblies of Alberta were organized as a District Conference of the Pentecostal Assemblies of Canada.

August 12 to 16, 1925, the General Conference was held in Winnipeg. At this conference, the Western District Council of the Assemblies of God became the Western District Council of the Pentecostal Assemblies of Canada. At this time, a resolution was passed to elect four Western Provincial Superintendents. Rev. John McAlister was elected the Superintendent of the Alberta District.

In 1927, the United Conference of the WESTERN DISTRICTS was held in Saskatoon, Saskatchewan. At this time John McAlister was referred to as the Superintendent of Alberta.

In 1928 at the General Conference held in Montreal, Quebec, the minutes referred to the fact that the (Provincial) District Conferences of Manitoba and Alberta had not yet been held.

In 1929, the first Alberta District Conference was held in Killam, Alberta. The roster included Pastors Bessie Wood and Marge Black of Killam, Superintendent John McAlister, Brother Cobb of Wetaskiwin, Rev. C. Nelson of Lethbridge, Brother Allan S. Ellis of Edmonton, Brother E. W. Robinson of Mayton, Pastor Hugh McAlister of the Pentecostal Tabernacle of Calgary, Brother Posein of Blackmud, Andrew Sorenson, Brother Nash, Brother Still, Evelyn Still, Brother Morgan. Rev. John McAlister was re-elected District Superintendent. Doctrines, approved by the Pentecostal Assemblies of Canada, were read and carried.

If points were more easily accessible to Alberta than British Columbia or Saskatchewan or vice versa, they would be part of the most accessible District. e.g. the Dawson Creek, British Columbia work was part of the Alberta District for a number of years. Cherry Point, Alberta was part of the British Columbia District for a while. Alsask and Hatton, Saskatchewan were part of the Alberta District for a time.

SUPERINTENDENTS OF THE ALBERTA AND NORTHWEST TERRITORIES (MACKENZIE) DISTRICT

The Superintendents of the District of Alberta and the Northwest Territories are highly regarded men of God, who are elected to this chief executive position in this conference. He presides over all the meetings of the District Conference; is supervisor over all the ministers of the District; assists assemblies with advice and ministry as the need may require, at the request of the pastor or local board; keeps accurate records and certifies all candidates for ordination.

The Assistant Superintendent assists the Superintendent and takes his place as needed.

District Office Picture of 1981. Back Row: Ruth Milliken, Secretary; Mrs. Ivar Roset; Mrs. Lee Bell. Front Row: Rev. Ivar Roset, District Superintendent; Rev. Lee Bell, District Administrator.

The Superintendents of this District have been Rev. John McAlister (1925-1933), Rev. Clare Scratch (1933-December 15, 1934), Rev. George R. Upton (December 15, 1934-1943), Rev. Walter Frederick (1944), Rev. Arden A. Lewis (1944-48), Dr. Daniel N. Buntain (1948-1952), Rev. Stewart R. Tilton (1952-1968), Rev. Charles Yates (1968-1974) and our present Superintendent, Rev. Ivar Roset (1974-   ).

Group at the Pentecostal Assemblies of Canada Alberta and Northwest Territories District Conference in Calgary in 1973, when Rev. Charles Yates was District Superintendent.

Rev. John McAlister
(1925-33)

Rev. Clare Scratch
(1933-1934)

Rev. Stewart R. Tilton
(1952-68)

Rev. Charles Yates
(1968-74)

Rev. George R. Upton
(1934-1943)

Rev. Walter Frederick
(1944)

Rev. Ivar A. Roset
(1974-   )

Rev. Arden A. Lewis
(1944-48)

Rev. Dr. D. N. Buntain
(1948-52)

Rev. Kenneth Bunting is the present Assistant Superintendent.

As one recalls the characteristics or incidents concerning these superintendents, many come to mind. First they were men, who truly loved God. Rev. Frederick's knowledge of German was a great help in certain areas in the province. Rev. Upton had a very distinctive voice — very easily recognized whether you could see him or not. Rev. Dr. Buntain loved the moving of the Spirit. He established a Bible school, the Canadian Northwest Bible Institute, in Edmonton in 1946. He, also, published THE ROCK, a forerunner of the District Thrust. Rev. S. R. Tilton was the first full-time District Superintendent. He was well known for his anointed ministry on the Holy Spirit. When having a meal in a home, he was known to say, "This food tastes musty." The hostess would probably reply, "Musty?" His response was always, "Must have more." To date (1982), Rev. Ivar Roset and Rev. Bunting have dedicated about thirty-five churches. At the time of printing, the District has 92 assemblies or missions. Two more have been asking about joining our Fellowship. The end is not yet, for the District is always reaching out to other places.

To assist Rev. Roset, the District Conference appointed a District Administrator, Rev. Lee Bell, who was installed in January 1981. He is very capable.

The District Office has been blessed with some good secretaries — Mrs. Pauline Wynychuk (1975), Mrs. Faye Kublik (1976), Miss Olive Olfrey (1976-1981) and the present secretary, Mrs. Ruth Milliken (1981-   ).

DISTRICT PRESBYTERS

District Presbyters have been a very important part of the District executive. The presbyters in 1982 are Rev. R. Haward, Rev. Mel Jenkins, Rev. Jack Keys, Dr. H. Faught, Rev. Ken Roset, Rev. Keith Running, Rev. Dave Quigley, Rev. George Feller, and Rev. A. Lindoff. These men serve under the leadership of the District Superintendent, Rev. Ivar Roset, and the Assistant Superintendent, Rev. Kenneth Bunting. Each section of this district is led by a presbyter.

MINISTERIAL CREDENTIALS

The following are the categories of credentials:

(a) MEN
- (1) Ordained
- (2) Licensed
- (3) Certificate of Recognition
- (4) Lay Preacher Certificate

(b) WOMEN
- (1) Ministerial License for Women
- (2) Deaconess
- (3) Certificate of Recognition

(c) MISSIONARIES
- (1) Ministerial Missionary
- (2) Lay Missionary
- (3) Associate Missionary

CAMPS

Alberta Pentecostal Camps play a very important part in the lives of Pentecostal People. Taking time apart to worship God and having Christian fellowship is certainly rewarding.

The forerunners of our camps were the tent meetings that were pitched quite near a church. Quite often a district conference was held in conjunction with these camp meetings. This was so with Sunnyside Camp, which had the District Conference there for years at camp time.

Some of our assemblies have a camp meeting of their own or a group of churches in an area have one. Peace River's Pentecostal Tabernacle had one for sometime at Lady Lake and also along the Peace River.

Hatton Assembly of God Pastor, Rev. Norman Labrentz, gathered a number of assemblies together and had a joint camp meeting in the Cyprus Hills. It is understood that more have been held in the Cyprus Hills. A group of Southern Alberta Churches cooperated in having a children's camp in the Crowsnest Pass area. They rented facilities for this. It appears that this camp was held in the sixties and the seventies.

As far back as the 1931 Conference, Rev. John McAlister brought up the subject of a permanent camp or tabernacle, where the annual meetings could be held. After discussion, they decided to look into the matter in regard to the most suitable site for a camp of this nature and it was left up to the District Superintendent and the Field Directors (Presbyters). In 1935 a camp was held next to the Mayton District church. Then in 1936, Czar Lake camp was held in a rented resort. Then in the fall of 1936, Sunnyside Pentecostal Camp Ground was purchased.

The German Conference have a camp at Alberta Beach in the area known as Sunset Point. The English folk in the Westlock, Swan Hills, Barrhead area had a camp in rented facilities at Lake Nakamun, then moved to the German Pentecostal Campground, changing their camp name to Sunset Point Pentecostal Camp. The Slavic Conference camp is Moose Lake Camp, a lovely spot. For a time they had one at Sandy Lake.

CZAR LAKE (NOW SHORNCLIFF LAKE)
CZAR LAKE PENTECOSTAL CAMP

From July 7 to 11 in 1936, the Czar Lake Pentecostal camp meetings were held. This series of camp meetings was born in the hearts of and organized by Reverend Ernie Robinson of Hughenden and Reverend Clifford Nelson of Edmonton. It was held in a summer resort owned by Daniel Gloxene, with a big pavilion for services and a tent for prayer.

The Hughenden ladies cooked and served the meals. All the meals for the whole camp were only two dollars. Farmers provided beef and vegetables and the ladies made the meals (including the baking).

Agnes McAlister remembers that Reverend A. G. Ward was the guest speaker. One day, while he was preaching, he walked down one aisle and up the other. As he walked by people sensed the presence of the Lord, started praising the Lord and some wept. Oh! what a glorious time they had before the Lord.

Because the host church was to pay any indebtedness left after a camp meeting, the profit made was also theirs and, in this case, used to build the Hughenden church. So blessings, spiritual and material, were long felt after the camp meetings were over.

HYTHE
INNER PEACE

In 1981, Inner Peace became our newest Pentecostal Camp, located thirteen kilometres west of Hythe, Alberta, in the Grande Prairie area. This is a wilderness type of camp. The dining hall and meeting place were large tents. Evangelist Otto Kakoschke was the main speaker, whose ministry was enjoyed. Rev. Norman Labrentz was a very busy man caring for the operation of the camp. Rev. Roset attended two days and met with the pastors present.

Inner Peace is a real blessing to the folks in this northern region, rain or no rain.

MAYTON DISTRICT
MAYTON CAMP

In 1935, a large tent was pitched just over the fence from the Mayton Pentecostal Tabernacle, where A. Dalby was pastor. The services were held in this tent. Brother and Sister James Swanson and Doctor Purdie were the speakers. Two to three hundred people attended these meetings. Many were hungry for God's blessing and some curious about the meetings. People were billeted in homes or in road-crew bunkhouses brought in for the occasion. Meals were served in the church. Alberta Morsch, then quite young, remembers looking up to a box of cornflakes on the table. Her brothers remember their family being there, too.

Toward the end of camp a water baptismal service

Ministerial Group at Mayton Camp. Back Row: tenth from the left is Rev. Swanson, the Camp speaker. Row One: from the left is Rev. Clifford Nelson and Rev. Ernie Robinson.

Group at the Mayton Camp.

was held at Revers Lake. A lot of young people were baptized that day. Among them were Emma Hemke, Dorothy Tovell and Martha Maetche.

It was a big undertaking for both pastor and congregation and District.

SUNSET POINT
SUNSET POINT PENTECOSTAL CAMP
(formerly known as Lake Nakamun Pentecostal Camp, when it was at Lake Nakamun)

The Lake Nakamun Pentecostal Camp was held on the Alliance Camp Grounds on Lake Nakamun's shore. The first camp there was held August 2-11, 1963. The tabernacle then had shavings on the "floor" area. However, later they built a lovely lodge. The Pentecostal camp was held there each year from 1963 to and including 1978. In 1979, the name was changed to **Sunset Point Pentecostal Camp**, when they moved to the German Conference Alberta Beach Camp which was rented. It has been held there ever since.

Among the camps guest speakers were Rev. and Mrs. Harvey McAlister, their first guests; Lawrence Aksenchuk; Rev. Ken Bombay; Rev. Don Cantelon; Maralee Dawn; Rev. R. L. Donnelly; Rev. J. Harry Faught; the Forseth Trio; Rev. E. A. Francis; Rev. Gordon Franklin; Rev. J. H. Hazlett; Rev. Laurie Hueppelsheuser; Rev. Milton Israelson; Rev. and Mrs. Mel Jenkins; Rev. E. A. Johnson; Rev. Arnold Kalamen; Evangelist and Mrs. Abraham Kudra; Rev. J. H. Law; the Manntai Sisters; Evangelist Eunice Meyer; Rev. Charles Mooney; Rev. J. C. O'Brien; Rev. Maynard Oss; Rev. William Pipke; Rev. Craig Pitts; Rev. Douglas Stiller; Rev. Clinton Ward; Rev. J. Weller.

This camp has been a tremendous blessing.

SYLVAN LAKE
SUNNYSIDE PENTECOSTAL CAMP

It is believed that Tommy Davies, one of the Bentley Assembly young people, heard that part of the Thomas E. Bigam estate was for sale. This property was on the north-east side of Sylvan Lake. Rev. George R. Upton checked the property and found it to his liking. The District approved the purchase, so Rev. Upton saw Murray Bigam, the executor of the estate, purchased the property (twenty-four acres), less the lots with Dodd's cottage, the Benson Cabin, the W. L. Fraser Cabin (now Edmonton Central Tabernacle's Cottage) and Miller's Cabin (now the speakers' cabin). Those lots that were excluded from the [...] ction were eventually bought by the Camp. [...] gam said that he never met a man that was

Dr. Charles Price, one of the camp speakers.

so honest and straight forward in his business dealing with him as Rev. G. R. Upton.

Murray Bigam sold milk to the camp that first year and for several years after that. He said it was pretty hard not to become Pentecostal, when you've three Pentecostal preachers calling at your house twice a day (morning and evening) for two weeks. It was through Rev. Upton that Murray Bigam and his wife, Laura, were saved. Joyce Shram (nee Bigam) remembers that she was about nine or ten, when the preachers came for milk. She always looked forward to them coming, because they were the happiest

The cabin built by Edwin and John Morsch in 1938.

people she had ever seen. She just stood and listened to them. Among these preachers were Rev. Robert Peel and Rev. Rourke. Joyce was baptized in Sylvan Lake and also was filled with the Holy Spirit there at camp, too.

Edwin Morsch Jr. remembers that in June 1937, his father, Edwin Morsch Sr., worked out at Sunnyside Camp helping to build the dining room. J. J. McLeod, father of our missionary, Miss Sadie McLeod, was hired to be the chief builder at Sunnyside. All the other workers were volunteers. On Saturdays, Mr. Morsch would bring his two teenage sons out to help. John and Ed's first job was to take the nails from the forms that were just removed from the foundation of the dining room. A week or two later, the boys helped with shingling the roof. The men had the dining room ready for camp in 1937.

The road was just a trail through the trees. Edwin Morsch Sr. remembered how he and another volunteer had to clear a lot of trees, that had fallen across the trail during a storm that day, before they could drive out to their homes. A few years later, the road through camp was graded. There was no gravel on it, so when it rained excessively it was impassable. Murray Bigam pulled many a car out of the mud, including Rev. Robert Peel's car that was up to the running boards in mud. Joyce Bigam Shram said that Sunnyside meant you wore the sunshine on your face and boots on your feet. There were sunshiny days, too. A year or two later, sand from the bank at the beach was put on the road, which helped some.

The Camp Steam Engine with Rev. Morris Olson and two of his children.

For the first two years (1937 and 1938), meetings were held in two tents that were joined together. No one sat under the join when it rained. The tents were situated on the sloping ground between the dining room and the present coffee shop (1982). This formed a sort of amphitheatre with the platform at the bottom and the benches situated up the slope. The

third year, the tabernacle was ready. The Tabernacle would hold about a thousand people. Shavings were put on the ground inside the Tabernacle and wooden benches placed inside. The old seats from the Edmonton Gardens were acquired and the best ones installed in the Tabernacle after a floor was put in. Much later a furnace was installed.

Evangelist and Mrs. Lorne Fox

In those early days, accommodations varied from tents and straw ticks (a mattress made of a covering stuffed with straw) to some dormitories with army bunks by 1939. If your tent and bedding became too wet, you could crawl into the straw tent, that was filled with straw for the ticks. Straw ticks were not particularly comfortable. In the late seventies, a little better accommodations were added.

From the very beginning, there were a few cabins, including those mentioned earlier. The Hemkes built the first cabin on the camp property. In 1938, Edwin Morsch Jr. and his brother, John, built a cabin on the lakefront. Many others were built. There are still some of the old cabins in use. The cabin owners just lease the lots from Sunnyside camp.

In the thirties and forties to about 1947, Sylvan Lake was very low. The beach at the west end extended out a few hundred feet from the bank. The campers were instructed to swim out from the west-

Inside the Camp Tabernacle — note the benches.

The weather at Sunnyside varies a lot. Once in a while there is a bad hailstorm. In the summer of 1982, there was a bad wind storm that turned out to be a tornado. Mrs. Helen Gabert saw three funnels sucking up water from Sylvan Lake as it swept down the length of the Lake.

The spiritual impact, on those who attend Sunnyside Camp, has changed many a life. Some accepted Christ as their Saviour, many have been filled with the Holy Spirit, some have been baptized in water, many have been refreshed in their experience, and some have received healing. Usually campers go home with renewed vision and enthusiasm.

ern end of the beach. It was rumored that there was quicksand out from the old Dodd's cottage.

The first factory-built boat was a row boat owned by Mr. Schram from Claresholm. Ted Tobin and Mr. Knight had a fishing boat with a three-or-five-horse motor, which was considered really speedy at that time. Later Edwin Morsch had a plywood boat with a two-horse motor, then another boat, the Sweet Marie, with a fourteen-horse Cayley motor, which he used for pleasure.

In the days when the beach extended out so far, those who were baptized in water had to go a long way out. Those on shore would sing choruses between each baptism, which really added to the spiritual experience.

1944 Water Baptismal Service — Shirley Johnson is shown returning to shore just after being baptized.

Camp Group in front of the Camp Dining Room.

The Family Camp has services for youth and children as well as adults. There are also Childrens and Youth Camps beside the Family Camp at Sunnyside.

Among the special speakers at Sunnyside Camp were the Barrfoot Brothers (1937), Dr. Charles S. Price, the Fox Party, Rev. Russel Olson, Arnie Vick, Rev. Watson Argue, Rev. Don Argue, Rev. Ness, Rev. David Mainse, Rev. McLaughlin, Rev. Walter Rusnell, Rev. Hope Smith, Rev. R. W. Taitinger, Rev. Schrader, Rev. Dale Carpenter, Rev. Sam Buick, Rev. Maynard Oss, Rev. Ken Bombay, Rev. David Tonn, Rev. Peter Youngren, Rev. and Mrs. Laurie Price, Rev. Menaldino, Rev. Murray Dempster, Rev. Ralph Rutledge, Rev. E. W. Robinson, Miss Evelyn Olson, Rev. and Mrs. J. D. Saunders, Rev. Karl Vaters, Rev. Jack West and Rev. C. M. Ward.

Sunnyside Camp has really made a difference in the lives of many, many people.

CHURCH MINISTRIES

This Church Ministries Portfolio covers quite a few ministries — Youth, Sunday School, Crusaders, Child Evangelism and more.

CHRISTIAN EDUCATION AND YOUTH DEPARTMENTS

Originally the Sunday School was a separate department. **Miss Ruth Schoen** was the forerunner of the District Sunday School Supervisor or Director. Miss Schoen was involved with Bible Clubs, taught Christian Education Subjects in Canadian Northwest Bible Institute, was the Bible Truth Crusade Supervisor for Alberta and in 1946 accompanied Rev. and Mrs. L. Honderick on their tour of Sunday School Conventions in Lethbridge, Calgary, Drumheller, Killam, Wainwright and Edmonton. She was not available after 1948. **Miss June Miller** (1949-1952) was appointed Sunday School Supervisor with no salary, except for travelling expenses, a camp meal ticket and camp accommodation. She was a part-time supervisor. She taught in Canadian Northwest Bible Institute, as did the other directors, and was pastor of Jasper Place with a salary there of eighty dollars a month. From her tithe she bought the supplies she needed for the District Sunday School office, for Daily Vacation Bible Schools and other Sunday School materials. **Miss Yvonne McLeod** (1952-January 1955) was on a salary of eighty dollars a month and taught in the Institute as well. Her work involved visiting Sunday Schools in the province, promoting Daily Vacation Bible Schools, Teacher Training Courses, Group Conferences and the establishing of a Circulating Library. Art and Ray Sader built the library boxes that each held fifty books. These boxes were delivered by the pastors to the next pastor about every two months. This gave the children a chance to read good Christian Books. **Miss Dorothy Plastow** (1955) carried on much the same as Miss McLeod. **Miss Mary Shram** (1955 or 1956 to 1959) carried on much the same way, too. In 1959, **Rev. E. C. O'Brien** had both the Sunday School and

Young People's Convention held in Wetaskiwin in the rented Swedish Mission Covenant Church in 1931.

Ministerial Group at the 1931 Young People's Convention. Back Row: , Miss Evelyn Still, Mrs. Gordon Atter, Rev. Gordon Atter, Vera Coulter, Rev. Posein, Rev. Ernie Robinson, Mrs. Ernie Robinson with Donald, Mrs. J. L. Wood, Rev. J. L. Wood. Front Row: Rev. Walter S. Frederick, Rev. R. Martin McCallum, Mrs. A. Dalby, Rev. A. Dalby, Rev. Jack Field.

Youth (Christ's Ambassadors) Portfolios. It was to be a full-time position, but his church was reluctant to let him go, so it remained a part-time position for him. He had both portfolios until conference 1964, when he would accept only the Sunday School Director's position. **Rev. Steve Holomis** was elected part-time Christ's Ambassadors Director. Rev. E. C. O'Brien continued as Sunday School Director until 1966. Rev. and Mrs. O'Brien made a tour through the Sub-Arctic Missions to perform his district duties.

From October 1961, both the Sunday School and Christ's Ambassadors portfolios were combined.

1946 Drumheller Daily Vacation Bible School. Rev. Harvey C. McAlister is front far right.

YOUTH FORMERLY KNOWN AS CHRIST'S AMBASSADORS

Before the Department was established as such, there were youth meetings and conferences. One of these conferences was held in Wetaskiwin about 1931. It was well attended.

In 1941, **Rev. Jim Routley** became the first District Christ's Ambassadors Director and Brother George Baycroft became the first District Christ's Ambassadors Secretary-Treasurer. About 1942, they held a C.A. Rally at Sunnyside Camp. They had young people from different churches taking part. Jim Routley wrote, "One of the first speakers was Bobby Taitinger, who spoke so well. Even Evelyn Olson thought he was great as were the others."

Group in front of the Edmonton Pentecostal Tabernacle Bus. Left to Right: ,   , Max Simmonds, Art Sader, Bob Taitinger, Dudley Bowden. This bus was used to transport the Portable Tabernacle.

Rev. Bob Peel of Wetaskiwin was the next District Director. He made an itinerary visit to Turner Valley, Claresholm, Lethbridge and Calgary in his line of duty. **Rev. Harvey McAlister** (1945-50) itinerated raising money for the building of a portable tabernacle, to be used to open up new assemblies. Plans were obtained from Marshall Ruthven, the designer of this portable tabernacle, which would fold up for transporting. In 1951, the tabernacle was built. The chassis was made in Red Deer, then it was taken to Morsch's Evergreen Farm for quite a bit of work there. Helpers came from as far away as Edmonton to work on this tabernacle. For the next stage it was moved to Buzz Farrel's Shop in Bentley, then hauled by bus to Edmonton for the finishing touches. This portable tabernacle was used in Drayton Valley, Evansburg, Fort Assiniboine, Hinton, Viking and Westlock. One summer, probably 1952, it was used at Sunnyside Camp for children's meetings. In 1952, **R. W. (Bob) Taitinger** was elected District Christ's Ambassadors Director (D-Cap). Under his leadership, the Sunnyside Camp C.A. Tabernacle was built. Many young people helped to build this building too. **Rev. E. C. O'Brien** was both C.A. Director and Sunday School Director from 1956 to 1964. Then **Steve Holomis** was elected District Christ's Ambassadors Director from 1964 to 1966. In October 1966, he became the District Youth Director and the Sunday School Director full time. While he was caring for these departments he built the two district houses which also housed the respective district offices — District Office and the Christian Education and Youth Office.

Portable Tabernacle, when set up at Sunnyside Camp at Sylvan Lake.

Rev. Roy Kemp (1970-74) emphasized youth involvement in outreach programs. **Rev. Jack Hunka** conducted Boys and Girls Camps between Brother Kemp and Brother Lawrence's terms in the month of July 1974. **Rev. Virgil Lawrence** (1974-78) had all the usual seminars, camps, et cetera. He and young people from Alberta were involved in Outreach at the Olympics in Montreal and in the Commonwealth Games Outreach in Edmonton in 1978. **Rev. Darrel Hoeppner** (1978-1982) was always busy with the work of his offices. In the conference of 1982, the Christian Education and Youth Department was renamed Church Ministries. June 1, 1982, **Rev. Allen Downey** became the new director.

CANADIAN MISSIONETTES

In the City of Calgary, Alberta, Elva Garden happened to be the teacher of the Daily Vacation Bible School group which became interested in continuing what they had already done in a Vacation Bible School — study about missions, doing handcrafts and studying the Bible. They approached Brother and Sister Watts. They were thrilled as they had been praying something could be started for girls. The first meeting was in September of 1950 and there were four girls present. The next meeting there were nine. They said, "We want to do something for Missionaries and we want to really do something so let's call ourselves Missionary Action Girls." So the Calgary (Eighth Avenue) group grew until it had to be divided into junior and senior girls. The girls were keen to share their interests with other girls in Alberta and invited them for a week-end conference in 1951. Girls came from Turner Valley, Claresholm, Drumheller, Bentley, Edmonton. The accompanying pastors and interested ladies were convinced that this type of program should go forward throughout the province and appointed Mrs. Elva Garden as the Provincial Director to encourage and care for groups

1951 — First Girls' Conference. From the centre of Row Two to the right are Mrs. John Watts, Rev. John Watts, Mrs. Ernie Peterson, Mrs. Elva Garden, Miss Irene Ashley, Mrs. Evelyn Shedden.

being formed. Reverend R. W. Taitinger, Pastor of Central Tabernacle, Edmonton, was the guest speaker.

Many new groups were formed. The Annual Conference became too large to handle in the Calgary church. The girls were also keen to have a girls camp and the Sunnyside Camp Committee was asked to consider giving the girls some time. The first year they were given two days — such a tremendous amount of work for such a short time! — but proved very beneficial. The camp grounds and buildings didn't suffer and the following year they were allowed one week. Careful supervision and good food were prime requisites. Girls Camp became an annual highlight for girls and counsellors, growing to over two hundred girls. Many girls were saved and filled with the Holy Spirit, made life decisions, saw healings, made new friends and benefitted in many ways.

The National Director, Sister Ethel Bingeman, at that time, became interested in Missionary Action Girls and came to Calgary to interview Sister Watts and Mrs. Elva Garden and persuaded them to draw up the program for printing and making it possible to be a National program. Sister Bingeman added the word "Pioneer" (but the girls preferred their old Missionary Action Girls) and it was approved by the General Conference of the Pentecostal Assemblies of Canada.

In 1962 Mrs. Garden retired as Provincial Director, then Mrs. Sandy Johnson took over until leaving the province. At that time there were over sixty groups. Mrs. T. Boymer followed for a year or two, then the office of Provincial Director was dropped and the Women's Ministries Director of the province was asked to promote Missionettes. The overseas missionaries were also interested in the girls' work and sent for material. Several groups were formed in the West Indies under Mrs. Barker's supervision. Some were formed in parts of Africa.

The first missionary contact the Calgary girls had was the preparation of a parcel sent to Reverend Ken and Sarah Gaetz, in Hay River, Northwest Territories. All items were made from donations of wool and other materials. They received such a thrill, when a letter of thanks was received. "Let's do another one quick!" was their response. An interest in the poor naked babies of India was aroused by letters from missionary Avis Popplewell (from Calgary Eighth Avenue) and a baby layette sent but the shawl was designated for Avis to keep for her first-born!! (Avis was not married then, but she did keep it and did use it.)

Through the years, Missionettes have been involved in all the mission fields at home and abroad through the Women's Ministries. Recently their own

National projects have been a real challenge and the girls have raised money to purchase equipment overseas as well as prepare parcels.

God has blessed through the years and many girls have been saved, filled with the Holy Spirit and grown to take their places as leaders in Missionettes, Women's Ministries, Sunday School, the ministry including being Missionaries. (Rae Garden from Calgary and Virginia Thompson from Edmonton are just two.) Some wives — knitting or crocheting for husbands and children — have been heard to say, "I learned to do it in Missionettes." Their course of study has helped them in many areas. God's Word has been learned and hidden in their hearts to stand them in good stead throughout their lives.

CRUSADERS IN ALBERTA AND NORTHWEST TERRITORIES

In the year 1954, the formation of Crusaders was authorized by the General Conference of the Pentecostal Assemblies of Canada. The Christian Education Department started immediately to plan a program which would interlock spiritual, social, physical and mental standards and activities in the life of the individual child. Bible reading and memorization, badge work, outdoor activities and service to others were all included to make a well-rounded program.

The first Crusader Unit in Alberta to be registered was the one in Turner Valley in February 1956. Hay River, Northwest Territories, has been active since 1963. Some churches have no Crusaders at the present time.

In the 1981-82 term, there were easily three hundred registered members and about eighty officers in seventeen chartered units. However some units are operating without an official charter, so the total number of Crusaders is much larger than recorded. Mrs. Alberta Onciul is Deputy Commissioner of the Crusaders of Alberta and the MacKenzie District of the Northwest Territories.

Every spring Rally Days are a highlight for Alberta Crusaders. Inter-unit competition excitement runs high during the sword drills and Bible quizzes. Unit participation is a blessing and encouragement to other units.

Since our motto is "It is better to build than to mend," we praise God for His faithfulness during the past years of building. We look forward to great days ahead.

WEE COLLEGE

God's Centennial Project began in September 1967, when Mrs. Joyce Shram was standing in her little blue kitchen in Edmonton, Alberta. Her son,

Kendall, was four years old and had been attending a Yamaha music course for four-year-olds. This was a comparatively new course in Edmonton. They learned rhythm concepts of music besides singing and theory. She was delighted with it, for they had a unique approach for the preschool child. They took the serious concepts of music and related them by association, fun and repetition. Each concept was presented for about three or four minutes, depending on the attention span of the class. As soon as their attention began to wane, they were moved to another corner of the room for another teaching activity. During the move their attention was recaptured so the teacher could start on something new.

Edmonton's, as well as the first ever, graduation class of Wee College.

As Joyce stood there looking out of the kitchen window, her mind was bombarded with the thought, "If little preschool children can learn music theory plus other difficult concepts, then why don't we teach them Bible doctrines by the same methods. Our children would then have a foundation for a happy, good life. For a number of days, these thoughts kept coming back so often that she realized it was God asking her to start something rolling in this regard. Speaking to God, she said, "God you can't be asking me to do this. It's too much for me. So many people are more qualified. I'm just a nobody in this great big church (Central Tabernacle) and you want me to try to start this." God replied, "Joyce, I'm asking you to do this. It is a job that has to be done. These children are going to need this fortification because the world is going to get worse and worse. Some of them will need this teaching to stand. Others will be leaders. If you won't do it, I'll get someone else but the job has to be done." She had to believe that God knew what was best. Also, she felt that she had not done much for God. Here was an opportunity for her.

At this point Joyce phoned Jean Mack, a friend from Edmonton Central Pentecostal Tabernacle, who

had taught primary Sunday school children. She was so encouraging. Joyce still remembers what Jean said, "Joyce I can't help you but DON'T LET IT DIE." Those last four words, DON'T LET IT DIE, repeated themselves in her mind for days. A few days later, she approached Pastor Bob Taitinger, regarding beginning this course in Central Tabernacle. Eileen Finnman, another children's worker, accompanied Joyce at this time. Pastor Taitinger said that it sounded like a very good idea but they would have to present it to the Tabernacle Board. They presented it to the Board and received their approval. The course was presented as a kindergarten-type program of an hour per week. It was to be Thursday mornings from 10:00 A.M. to 11:00 A.M..

In the meantime, Joyce and Eileen met with a few ladies to give information and recruit help. Among these was Mrs. Shirley Taitinger. Joyce told the ladies that she felt the name should have the word, college, in it. Shirley Taitinger replied, "How about Wee?" That is how the name, Wee College, was chosen. Shirley Taitinger composed the song, We Believe, for Wee College.

Eileen Finnman, Grace Robinson, Selma Sproule (nee Komant) joined Joyce Shram to be the first staff. In the first class there were seventeen children who completed the course. Those in that first class were Darcy Lynn Carruthers, Loreen Finnman, Dawna Lynn Foley, David Johnson, Gregory Knott, Pamela Kozak, Marlene Martz, Melanie Martz, Darrell Pedde, Donavon Lee Robinson, Jimmie Schroeder, Kendall Murray Shram, Celma Gwen Sproule, Glen Vaxvick, Curtis Walters, Christine Watson and David Wood. That first year was a success.

The staff felt that a one-year course was not enough so in the fall of 1968, Joyce Shram and Selma Sproule outlined the second-year program using the same doctrines but different scripture references. Selma led the second-year course, which she developed from the program outline. She was assisted by Mrs. Lois Foley and Mrs. Lydia Benson.

In the spring of 1969, Rev. Charles Yates gave Joyce permission to present their Wee College Graduation to the conference. In that audience was a delegate from Calgary, Mrs. Eleanor Schmale. She contacted Joyce Shram right away to start a Wee College in Calgary.

Also, at the conference, Mrs. E. C. O'Brien approached Joyce Shram. She asked her to speak and present the Wee College program at the Women's Missionary Council Retreat in Banff, Alberta. The retreat was to be held there in September 1969. Joyce knew that, if she were to present the program to the ladies at the retreat, the first year program would have to be fully written and reproduced for distribution. So Joyce spent the summer writing the manuscripts at their lakeside cottage. In 1968-69, J. Shirley Morsch edited the course and did the art work for the manuscripts. Also, a copy of the first-year manuscripts and the art work were given as a gift to the Pentecostal Assemblies of Canada so that it could be spread across the nation in a shorter time. This way many more children could be fortified with God's Word.

In 1970, the Shrams moved to Calgary. Joyce worked with Eleanor Schmale in the Wee College there for five years.

It was almost impossible to photostat this whole program every time someone wanted the course. It was also very expensive. As a result, Mrs. Shram approached Mrs. E. C. O'Brien about this problem, since Head Office had not yet printed the course. Mrs. O'Brien arranged for Mrs. Diane Megysi to put the program on stencils. One hundred copies were produced. These were enough copies to supply the demand until the first-year course was printed by Head Office about 1973 or 1974. Mrs. O'Brien advertised the course in three issues of the Women's Ministries Bulletin. Consequently more and more people were ordering copies.

Mrs. Eleanor Schmale wrote a second-year course, using the previous course outline, and sent it to Head Office to be available as had the first-year course.

Mrs. Eleanor Schmale felt a need for a third-year course. Joyce Shram and she worked out an outline. Eleanor wrote the third-year course from this outline and submitted it to Head Office for publication, too. Central Pentecostal Tabernacle has had a third year in operation since 1974. They developed the program from the outline mentioned above.

After Wee College was well established in Alberta, Mrs. Shirley Taitinger opened Wee College in the Toronto area. God has spread Wee College around the world. It has gone to the mission field and to the United States of America. Other denominations are using the courses as well. It is God's program; He inspired it.

In Central Pentecostal Tabernacle in the 1980-81 term, there were seventy-three students with a staff of twenty-one in Wee College. In their fifteenth year, 1981-82, Central had fifty students with a staff of nineteen. Over the past fifteen years, eight hundred and nine children have enrolled for Wee college and two hundred and thirty-three have completed the second-year program in Central Pentecostal Tabernacle, Edmonton, Alberta. We wonder what the total enrollment has been in the many other places, where

Wee College is established. The doctrines, on which the courses are based, are the Authority of Scripture; God, His Attributes; the Trinity; Creation; Man and Sin; the Life and Ministry of Jesus, His Birth, Ministry, Death, Resurrection, Ascension and Second Coming; the Holy Spirit; Healing; Heaven; Salvation; Missions; the Great Commission. Since 1970, Mrs. Grace Robinson has been Director of Central Tabernacle's Wee College.

Comments:

Reverend Bob Taitinger and little Darrell Pedde were walking down an aisle in Central Pentecostal Tabernacle shortly before graduation. Reverend Taitinger asked, "Well, Darrell, how is it going with you? Do you feel like you have too much to do?" Darrell replied, "No, Pastor. As a matter of fact, I think I could have taken a little bit more."

A four-year-old child asked, "Teacher, if Jesus was the Son of God, how come He had to carry His own cross?"

Grace Robinson said, "God loves the Indians, Canadians and Eskimos." Little Bradley Lefebvre said, "My dad's one of them." His father, Gary Lefebvre, was a football player on the Edmonton Eskimo team.

One of the teachers asked, "What is a prophet?" One of the children answered, "When you buy a house and sell it."

These preschoolers are so sweet and so eager. Wee College is great for them.

EVANGELISM

Evangelism has played a very important part in the opening of new works in Alberta and the Northwest Territories. These special meetings were held in schoolhouses, tents, halls, theatres, camps, churches, street corners and homes. The early evangelists were preachers and lay people (both young and old), who had a vision of the need. Pastors would encourage their people to reach out. Many young men and women would go out on weekend ministry as did older ones. The individual churches will give you some glimpse of how this helped to establish churches. In some cases, some pastors exchanged pulpits for a week or two for a series of evangelistic meetings. There were unscheduled circuit preachers, who would make the rounds both to churches and to places, where there was no work at all. Many would go into a place have services for a week or more, gather a nucleus of believers and an assembly was started.

Among the ministers, who ministered in evangelism, included Rev. Edward Gaetz, who made unscheduled circuits through Alberta, mainly in pioneer places — Fork Lake, Lac La Biche area, St.

Paul area, Athabasca, Wainwright, Torrington and more, from 1934 to 1960 and then once in a while after that; Evangelist Eunice Meyer, who was known for loving the moving of the Holy Spirit in her services, which were held in many places in Alberta; Rev. Harvey McAlister Sr.; Rev. Harvey C. McAlister, his nephew; Rev. Steve Holomis; Rev. Jack Hunka; Bob and Jean Muir (Jean was from Central Pentecostal Tabernacle in Edmonton); the German speaking evangelists, Rev. Walter Frederick, Rev. Schatkowski, Rev. Posein, also did much evangelizing, especially in the northern areas; Rev. Karp Hrycauk, who established quite a number of Slavic assemblies; and many, many more. There are still folk, including Christians from the local churches, who help with services by singing, playing an instrument or preaching. In the District Thrust, there is always a list of evangelists for full time or weekend ministry. Rev. Jack Keys is the present (1982) District Director of Evangelism.

Over many years, efforts to reach children and young people involved many people in different outreaches — Vacation Bible Schools, children's services, Bible clubs, Sunday Schools, youth rallies, retreats and youth meetings.

Since 1980 one group, Abundance and Wisdom and Love Bug, has worked among children in Alberta, the Northwest Territories, Manitoba and Saskatchewan. No doubt there are and will be other workers to help carry on the outreach to children.

MEN'S FELLOWSHIP

The organization of Men's Fellowship was authorized in 1954, when Rev. S. R. Tilton was District Superintendent. Rev. Eugene Opheim, one of the founders, was the first director for the Alberta District. He was director for seventeen years. Don Hopkinson was one of the founders. Other directors were Les Inkster (for about twelve years), Al Werbiski, Ernie Peterson and the one at the time of publishing is Maurice Glover, who was elected July 1974. All of these men have given good leadership.

Les Inkster, a former Men's Fellowship District Director.

Maurice Glover, Men's Fellowship District Director at the time of publishing.

The purpose of Men's Fellowship is for fellowship (befriending Christians and non-believers, enjoying and encouraging one another), involvement (becoming part of the program and ministry of the local assembly, sponsoring boys' clubs), dialogue-communication-outreach (winning others for Christ, mutual help and growth) and Work Force (donating expertise and labor for the building of churches, parsonages, camp buildings and furnishings as they are able). The Work Force men have worked on many a building. On one occasion, when men took holiday time to build a residence for staff in Hay River, it was noted that the Work Force crew worked about twenty-five percent faster than a conventional crew. They finished the outside of this residence so that the work inside could be done, when the weather turned colder. Many Work Force projects have been done, including building a church in Dominica, West Indies; church-residence complex at Fort Good Hope, N.W.T., pews (built by two members) for the Fort Good Hope church.

The first Men's Retreat in Canada was organized under Eugene Opheim, when Rev. Charles Yates was District Superintendent. Rev. Yates and others cooperated in making this a very rewarding time for the fifty men, who attended. This was marked by the moving of the Holy Spirit and so inspired other retreats in Canada and the United States. These Alberta District retreats are held in Banff, Alberta, a truly beautiful place. These retreats' attendance has increased to three hundred fifty to over four hundred. These men come home refreshed and with a greater determination to be a blessing.

MISSIONARIES FROM ALBERTA

Among those from Alberta, who were/are missionaries, associate missionaries, volunteers in missions (work at some occupation while working on the mission field or go for some special job, such as building churches), served/serve with A.I.M. (Ambassadors In Missions), served with *Y.W.A.M.

Rev. and Mrs. Jess Lynn with Regan.

(Youth With A Mission), or with Mission Boards which are not Pentecostal Assemblies of Canada (*), are *Miss Phyllis Aitcheson (wife of Reverend William Hincks); *Miss Noli Abaya (Y.W.A.M.); Reverend and Mrs. Daniel Anderson; Reverend and Mrs. Joseph Anonby (attended Central Tabernacle, Edmonton shortly before leaving); *Mrs. Gerda Brown (nee Anderson, wife of Reverend Bill Brown); Dr. Mark Buntain (adopted by Edmonton's

Central Tabernacle when his parents were pastors there); Henry and Janet Borzel; Larry Broughton; Miss Mary Edler (Teacher); *Mrs. Mel Friesen (nee Ruth Maser); Thomas and Laura Fodor; Miss Rae Garden; Mr. and Mrs. Garden; Jean Grieves (wife of Reverend Robert Peel); Dr. Pat and Grace Higgins (veterinarian and his wife); Reverend Bernard Hunter; Cheryl Johnson (A.I.M. and Missionary); *Reverend Arthur Lagore; Miss Wilda Lund (Teacher Instructor); Virginia Thompson (wife of Reverend Jess Lynn and also a Registered Nurse and midwife); Lila McAlister (wife of Reverend James Skinner); Miss Sadie M. McLeod (thirty-five years — two years in China, two years in Thailand and the balance in Hong Kong and furloughs); Dan McTavish and wife (Edmonton's People's Church missionary to Mexico); Reverend Robert Peel with his wife, Jean; Mrs. Frieda Regher (Teacher); Reverend and Mrs. Arthur Rosenau (Teacher and his wife); Reverend and Mrs. Clare Scratch; *Miss Beryl Shannon; Paul and Patricia Thunberg (Paul was a teacher in

Rev. and Mrs. Robert Peel

Liberia); *Earl Trekofski and his wife; Reverend Larry Ulseth (lived in Alberta in the earlier part of his life); Mrs. Ruth Williamson; Mr. and Mrs. Arnold Labrentz. We are proud of their contribution to the winning of many to the Lord on foreign soil.

Among our foreign missionary evangelists have been Reverend Mark Buntain, Reverend Robert W. Taitinger and Reverend Steve Holomis. Their ministries have been appreciated. To give you a glimpse of their effectiveness, see the following article about Steve Holomis' ministry.

STEVE HOLOMIS — ALL WORLD CRUSADE

In September 1976, Reverend Steve Holomis joined the ministry of All World Crusade as Associate Director. Reverend Don Schellenberg was Director and Founder of this World Missionary Outreach.

Rev. Steve Holomis with his interpreter on the platform and many at the altar. There were about 1100 at this service in Jaffna, Sri Lanka.

Crusades were held in five areas of Hong Kong as well as out-door rallies in an open-air theatre, in October 1976. This marked the greatest cooperation ever amongst members of the Interdenominational Fellowship of Full Gospel Churches. Over five hundred people made first time decisions for Christ. Counsellors were assigned to visit and shepherd new believers. Many were healed and many filled with the Holy Spirit.

Bangladesh-January 1977. An effective evangelistic thrust was conducted at the Assemblies of God Evangelistic Centre, Dacca, Bangladesh, sponsored by the local churches' Dacca Penetration Plan. A week prior to the Crusade Don and Steve were engaged in a Pastors' Seminar. Over one thousand people were counselled for salvation in the fourteen day period. People from all walks of life came to the meetings, often arriving long before the scheduled time to start, so they would be able to get a seat. From ricksha pullers to high officials, people were eager to hear the word of God and see the power of Jesus Christ demonstrated.

Khulna, Bangladesh. Crowds grew each night until they had to be moved outside under a huge pandel (tent-like structure). There were special daytime sessions for young people. Forty-two came and stayed for four days. Almost everyone of them accepted the Lord, eighteen received the Baptism of the Holy Spirit, thirty-four were baptized in water.

Dominica, West Indies-Grand Bay Crusade. Grand Bay is situated on the southern end of the Island of Dominica. Here the services were constantly disrupted by men who openly opposed the Gospel message. Threats, name calling, shouting, fighting and a demand for protection money showed the mood of many people. Many displayed strong dislike for the nightly services. The Crusade was held in the centre of town. A platform, speakers and lights were erected on the main intersection allowing many to hear the message as they shopped, walked or sat in their homes. As many as four thousand were within hearing range of the loud speakers. It was delightful to see the evidence of the power of God working on the hearts of the very people that opposed the Gospel. Miracles began to happen in the first service. Many were healed and delivered. Over one hundred and ten souls were saved.

Portugal. Crowds increased nightly until some five thousand people jammed the auditorium of the Lisbon Sports Pavilion as Reverend Don Schellenberg preached the Gospel. The final rally was held in Restelo Stadium. Attendance was twelve thousand. Recorded decisions during the Crusade numbered about one thousand. An Evangelism Seminar was conducted for over one hundred church leaders from all parts of Portugal in nine daytime sessions. Follow-up meetings were conducted in two locations as new converts packed the churches following the Crusade.

Catania, Sicily-October 1977. It was impossible to secure a large auditorium or arena for the meetings due to opposition from Anti-Protestant authorities. The services were held in the Central Assembly of God building which was packed for every service. There was standing room only. People arrived early to get a place to sit. One hundred and fifty people accepted Jesus Christ as Saviour. The final service was blessed with a healing love that united the people as one in Christ. Praise poured forth to God.

Bologna, Italy. Posters were placed in apartment buildings, hand-bills distributed, and the meetings were announced by loud-speaker up and down the city streets. A number of people were saved nightly. Many were healed and many baptized in the Holy Spirit.

Sri Lanka-January 1978. For the first time in Sri Lanka, a "Believer's Meeting" was held preceding the open-air Salvation-Healing Crusade. This was unique because of the different churches participating. Believers were encouraged, challenged and their vision enlarged. The crowds increased each evening. Many were healed. Over four thousand five hundred responded to the invitation to accept Christ during two Crusades.

Cordoba, Argentina-March 1978. Evangelist Holomis ministered to the Northwest District Conference of the Union of the Assemblies of God, Argentina. A Crusade followed the Conference. Many decisions were made for Christ and there were several healings.

When not in Crusades overseas, services and seminars were held in the different assemblies in

Canada. Steve resigned in 1978 and joined the staff of Cathedral Developments. He supervised the construction of the church buildings in Napanee, Ontario; Chatham, Ontario and Beddington church, Calgary. Steve resigned in March 1981 and began pioneering the Edmonton Heritage Christian Assembly in June 1981.

NORTHWEST BIBLE COLLEGE
(formerly Canadian Northwest Bible Institute)
DESIRED

From our very first District Conference in Alberta in 1929, there has been an interest in Bible school. In this conference they aimed for every assembly to take up an offering for the Bible College (probably the National Bible College in Ontario).

In the 1931 District Conference, it was "recommended that Bible College students or young workers spend a little time in practical training with some older worker, wherever possible."

In the 1932 District Conference, the District was informed that the National Bible College was closed, at least for a time, because of a financial problem. Rev. D. N. Buntain of Winnipeg extended an invitation to the West to attend the Winnipeg School (later known as Western Bible College).

In the 1937 District Conference, the District was informed that the "Pentecostal Assemblies of Canada requires that all Probationers coming up for ordination must complete a Probationers' Study Course

Canadian Northwest Bible Institute Christmas Party at the Buntains.

before Ordination." (The term, probationers, here referred to new ministers, who had probationers' certificates.)

In the 1933 District Conference, Resolution number fifteen "resolved that the District Executive look into the matter of a short term Bible Training School for this province. Carried. The term to start this year." Because of a shortage of finances, they were not able to begin this school. However, a Bible Teacher was brought in for a series of meetings in Lethbridge, Calgary and Edmonton.

ORIGIN

In 1945, Rev. D. N. Buntain became the pastor of the Edmonton Pentecostal Tabernacle. His vision of

1949 Graduates, the Insuperables, entered Canadian Northwest Bible Institute in 1946, the year this Institute came into being. Back Row, Left to Right: Ole Austring, Paul Cornish, Robert Taitinger, Henry Lindberg, Henry Miller, Edwin Morsch, Gus Wentland. Row Three: Gordon Baillie, Jack Hunka, Kathleen Rubilak, Elsie Johnson, June Miller, J. Shirley Johnson, Esther Vath, Ernie Rachinski, Orville Williams. Row Two: Mary Swekla, Minnie Ziegler. Row One: Violet Nelson, Selma Komant, Deloris Price, Mary Shram, Doris Suprovich.

an Alberta-based Bible School moved him to make plans for it. At the January 19, 1946, Workers' Conference, he received permission to call this school, Canadian Northwest Bible Institute, an Alberta District Bible School. After a dedicated faculty had been hired, Canadian Northwest Bible Institute opened October 4, 1946. This Institute was fondly referred to as C.N.B.I.. The first staff members were Rev. D. N. Buntain, principal; Rev. J. C. Cooke, Dean of Men; Mrs. D. N. Buntain, Dean of Women; Mrs. Ida Cooke; Miss Ruth Schoen; Mrs. Dorothy Plastow, Music Instructor; Miss Lila Dickinson. Though finances were scarce, pioneering spirit prevailed and much was learned. There was a real bond formed between faculty and students. The Institute had two classes that first year — a first year class and a second year class, which had taken their first year in another college. That second year class became the first graduation class in 1948. Quite a number from that first first-year class, plus a few who joined them, became the first class to take all their Bible training at C.N.B.I., graduating in 1949 as the Insuperables. That class has celebrated their twentieth, twenty-fifth and thirtieth anniversaries of their graduation and plan to celebrate every five years as long as possible.

Beside the training in the Institute, the students had opportunity for practical training and ministry — preaching, teaching, musical ministry (instrumental and vocal), conducting services in churches in the District, in jails, in rescue missions and Bible club. Teams would be given assignments for these areas. The Collegaires (a choir) went on assignment, too.

Canadian Northwest Bible Institute had its name changed to Northwest Bible College in 1965.

Though many of our people serve the Lord well without attending Bible college, Bible college education can improve one's sphere of influence for God, no matter what one's vocation may be. Many of our graduates and even undergraduates gained more self-confidence, more knowledge of God's Word, found more avenues of service and more opportunities of leadership in both church and community in different places. Among our graduates and undergraduates are ministers, missionaries, evangelists, ministerial leaders including a General Superintendent of the Pentecostal Assemblies of Canada, Christian Education superintendents and staff, board members, school teachers, writers, lay preachers, nurses, businessmen and businesswomen, and more. Everyone has a ministry. Even the Apostle Paul, in today's language, might have been called a lay preacher because he was a tent maker. We serve God, where He leads us.

Over sixteen hundred have attended our Bible college. Around six hundred have graduated from the

1948-49 Canadian Northwest Bible Institute Orchestra. Back Row, Left to Right: Gilbert Snider, Eunice Clemit, R. W. (Bob) Taitinger at the piano. Row Two: Art Muth, Edwin Morsch, Gus Wentland, Archie Keck, Doris Pohl. Row One: Jack Hunka, Elsie Johnson, Shirley Johnson, Joyce Schram, Margaret Christensen.

three-year program. Most assembly histories show a list of Bible college students and/or those who have entered the ministry. One of the most interesting facts is that the college has had over four hundred students come from outside our District. (Because some students claimed more than one place of origin, it is difficult to be exact down to the last student. However, the numbers of students are as close to being right as possible.) From the Yukon four students came to N.B.C.; from British Columbia one hundred fifty students, from Alberta one thousand one hundred ninety-one, from the Northwest Territories ten or so, from Saskatchewan fifty-nine students, from Manitoba seventy-two students, from Ontario eighty-six students, from Quebec seven students, from New Brunswick nine students, from Nova Scotia five students, from Prince Edward Island one student, from Newfoundland eleven students came to Northwest Bible College. From the United States twenty-six students attended Northwest Bible College. There were also a number from the West Indies, England and Hong Kong, who attended our college.

Among those, who attended Northwest Bible College and became missionaries outside Canada, were and some of whom still are Rev. Gus Wentland, Mrs. Gus Wentland (nee Doris Pohl), Rev. Larry Broughton, Rev. Don Scheske, Rev. Stanley Fitz, Mrs. Stanley Fitz (nee Audrey Rhiel), Mr. and Mrs. Bernard Schellert, Rev. and Mrs. Paul Schellert, Rev. Arthur Lagore, Rev. Mohan Maharaj, Rev. Henry Borzel, Mrs. Henry Borzel (nee Janet Balkwell), Rev. Jack Keys, Missionary Evangelist Rev. Steve Holomis, Mrs. Herman Maschel (nee Elsie

Daase), Mabel Robinson (nee Emde) in foreign children's evangelism, Rev. Eric Pahl and Mrs. Eric Pahl (nee Gloria Sauer), Arnold Labrentz, Mrs. Mel Friesen (nee Ruth Maser), Miss Beryl Shannon, Rev. Ivan Kirsch, David and Sandy Webster, Rev. Jess Lynn and Mrs. Jess Lynn (nee Virginia Thompson), Rev. Rod Harrington and Mrs. Rod Harrington (nee Marge Kerber), Dennis and Leona Kiffiak, and Dan MacTavish.

A Jail Assignment Team with Mrs. J. Boyle, who had been in charge of jail services for years.

As Rev. D. N. Buntain said, "There is no greater work among men than the training of leaders to go forth in full-time service as missionaries, evangelists, pastors and deaconesses, and yet every field of life is honorable. God needs trained, consecrated farmers, teachers, business men and indeed, men and women of every calling to direct in Young People's and Sunday School work, to be leaders in community efforts and to stand by the full-time leader in his efforts to build the Kingdom of God in our land." Northwest Bible College has endeavored to train such leaders.

On October 22, 23 and 24, 1971, Northwest Bible College celebrated its TWENTY-FIFTH ANNIVERSARY. A full schedule of services, banquet and homecoming drew large crowds for the full three days. Friday evening, October 22, the Student Body Choir sang; Rev. R. W. Taitinger, the General Superintendent of the Pentecostal Assemblies of Canada and also a graduate of N.B.C., was the speaker. Saturday morning, the Insuperables had a coffee-get-together; Saturday afternoon, the Alumni had open house at Central Tabernacle; Saturday evening, there was the Anniversary Banquet with Jack Keys as guest speaker. The 1949 Insuperables had the most present of all the classes represented there. The Finale was

the Sunday afternoon home-coming rally at the old Pentecostal Tabernacle (then the Salvation Army church) on 108 Street. Rev. R. J. White interviewed an excited Mrs. D. N. (Kathleen) Buntain. The Collegaires sang. Long-Service trophies were given to three staff members — Lila Dickinson, Rev. John Morsch B.Th. and Rev. J. C. Cooke. The Historical Pageant, Vision of Our Open Doors, was written and produced by J. Shirley Morsch. It was performed by a cast of ninety-nine Alumni members and the Collegaires. The pageant showed the graduates' and undergraduates' spheres of influence for God or ministries. One article referred to it as an impressive historical pageant. Jack Keys, the Alumni President challenged us with the task of ministering. Rev. R. W. Taitinger challenged the overflow crowd to remember that "our primary task is still to go into all the world and preach the Gospel to every creature." The Anniversary was a time of rejoicing, fellowship and challenge.

The Hillerud Memorial Library was founded in loving memory of Mrs. Julia Hillerud, wife of Rev. Martin Hillerud. Mrs. Hillerud endowed the College with a legacy, which made possible the founding of the library, which bore her name. Her son, Professor Sylvan O. Hillerud, became the patron of the Hillerud Memorial Library. This library was a blessing to the College students.

At present, there is a J. C. Cooke Library on the Campus.

On September 1, 1976, was down-payment day for and possession date of the D. N. Buntain Heritage House. Renovations were begun immediately, first to the internal part of the second floor and improvement to the exterior. Later the ground floor was improved. The District Office is on the ground floor, so is the J. C. Cooke Library. The Bible School Office, Staff Offices, District Youth Office, a room that is used for classes and fellowship and an Alumni Office. The last payment for this Heritage House was paid December 1, 1982.

Central Pentecostal Tabernacle has housed the school from its beginning and even after the purchase of Heritage House, most of the classes are held in the Tabernacle. The Tabernacle has been a tremendous blessing to the college and in turn the students have been an inspiration and help to the ministry of Central for many have remained there after graduation.

The College has had five principals or presidents, Dr. D. N. Buntain, Reverend John C. Cooke, Reverend E. A. Francis, Dr. J. H. Faught B.A. M.A. D.Th., and Reverend Marvin Dynna.

The Faculty listed according to years of service are: For twenty-eight years, Miss Lila M. Dickson; for twenty-five years, Reverend John W. Morsch

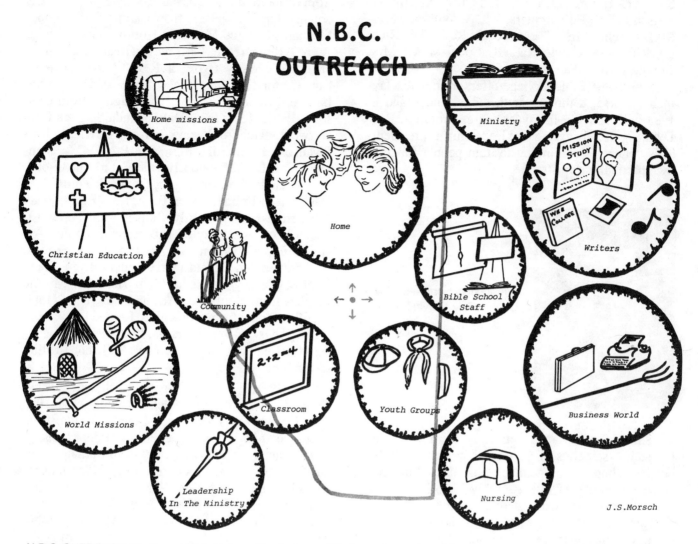

N.B.C. OUTREACH. Northwest Bible College Graduates and Undergraduates found that they could minister in many places and in many occupations.

B.Th., Reverend J. C. Cooke; for nineteen years, Reverend R. W. Taitinger; for eighteen years, D. J. Cooke B.A. LL.B.; for seventeen years, Reverend R. J. White; for sixteen years, Mr. E. R. Shedden B.A. LL.B; for fourteen years, Reverend G. Smith; for twelve years, Miss M. C. Shedden; for eleven years, Reverend Eugene Opheim; for ten years, Mrs. D. N. Buntain, Mrs. G. C. (Barbara) Smith A.R.C.T., Mrs. Anne Eliason; for nine years, Mr. G. Foley, Mrs. E. (Hazel) Opheim, Reverend J. W. Hunka B.A. M.Div., Dr. J. H. Faught B.A. D.Th.; for eight years, Dr. D. N. Buntain, Mrs. C. (Winnifred) McAlister R.N., Reverend E. A. Francis, Mrs. J. C. (Ida M.) Cooke, Dr. G. Franklin B.A. M.A. Ph.D.; for six years, Mrs. E. A. Francis, Rev. L. L. Anderson; for 5 years, Rev. P. Houghton, Mr. D. Hopkinson Dip.Th., Rev. K. R. Ness Dip.Th., Mrs. K. R. (Velma) Ness Dip.Th., Rev. R. F. Olson, Rev. G. D. Giles B.Th. M.Div.; Rev. Ken Bombay

B.Th.; for 4 years, Miss Mary Shram Rev. A. L. Lindoff Dip.Th., Rev. H. W. Eisert B.A. M.Div., Rev. D. J. Gaetz; for 3 years, Miss Jessie Mountney, Mrs. Lillian Petry, Miss June Miller, Miss Mildred McKay, Mrs. Dorothy Plastow, L. W. Vath, Mrs. V. McLeod, Rev. R. J. Smith B.Th. Dip. Th., Mr. B. Fawcett B.A. Dip.Th. Diploma of Library Technology, Mr. J. Telman Dip.Th., Rev. M. W. Dempster, Rev. Robert Muir, Dr. Cherer G. Penny, Rev. R. Kemp; for 2 years, Rev. C. Myhre, Miss Yvonne McLeod, Rev. James Richards B.A. M.Div., Rev. Charles Yates, Colin Wellard, Rev. Steve Holomis, Mr. Louis Harewood; for 1 year, Miss Ruth Schoen, Rev. Lyndon Sharratt, Orville Williams, Rev. T. E. Johnstone, Miss Dorothy Plastow, Rev. J. M. Watts, Miss Norma McLeod, Miss G. Larson R.N., Miss Madeline Rhodes R.N., Miss Mary Evans, Miss Heli Ennis, Mr. B. Derval Dip.Th., Rev. G. Feller B.A. M.Div., L. Berteig, Miss H. Hantke, Professor

Sylvan O. Hillerud B.S.A., Miss Olive Opheim, H. Wilson B.Ed., Ed Summers, J. L. V. Willford, Miss M. Borsheim, Mrs. H. E. Peacock, Rev. Wally Riehl Dip.Th., Rev. Calvin Ratz B. Com. M.A., Mrs. Bonnie Turner, Wayne Walters.

Northwest Bible College offers a one-year laymen's course, a three-year theology course and in 1983 will launch a four-year degree program. Rev. Dynna is already giving fine leadership as president. This college is continuing to train people for their own particular ministry.

President of Northwest Bible College, Rev. Marvin Dynna.

Since all Alberta students came from both Pentecostal Assemblies of Canada churches and independent churches or neither, some names did not come under one of our assembly histories. There were also students, who listed Edmonton or Calgary as their place of origin when they came to college, but it was not possible to find out which churches they attended, so those lists are included here as well. Those Alberta students, from outside our Assemblies, are also listed here.

Among those, who attended Bible college and/or entered the ministry (*) and who listed their origins from points where there are no Pentecostal Assemblies of Canada assemblies, are from Alix, Doreen Rue; from Amber Valley, Winfred Bowen; from Amisk, Marilyn Israelson and *Milton Israelson; from Ardrossan, Helen Komant, Darlene Peredory, Janet Barrie, Beverly Marler; from Athabasca, Bonnie Krawec, Nadine Pasay, Erwin Patz, Lois McCutcheon (wife of Dr. Warren Hathaway), Brett Melton; from Berrymore, Valera Wideman; from Blackfalds, Leonard Rutten; from Bloomsbury, Danny Berg; from Boyle, Wray Naslund, Allen Ness, *Clarence Ness, Henry Wilson, Sharon Hutton, *Kenneth Ness, Erna Ness, Clifford Naslund; from Breton, Nellie Hayes; from Bruce, Edith Froehlick, Nellie Hayes, Gladys Ethel McVige, Edith Mantik, *Rudolph Mantik, *Harvey Schmautz, *Leonard Schmautz;

from Bruderheim, Brian Hauer, Jacqueline; from Cadogan, Sharon Israelson; from Camp Creek, Rodney McClain, *Angus McClain; from Chauvin, Lillian Jean Allen; from Chigwell (near Lacombe), *Mildred McKay (wife of Rev. Charles Howey); from Castor, Ronald L. Pipke; from Condor, *Arthur Lagore, *George Lagore, *Bill Lagore; from Consort, Blaine Kelts; from Delia, Linda Sargent; from Derwent, Richard Yaceyko; from Duffield, Lois Swanson; from Edmonton non-P.A.O.C. assemblies, Carl Back, David Livermore, LaVyne Osbak, Stuart Lamb, Colleen Lamb; from Elk Point, Jean Davis; from Enilda, Karen Berg; from Falun, Brian Jobs; from Flatbush, Lily Radke; from Foremost, Glenn Thompson, Phyllis Thompson; from Fort Assiniboine, *William J. Wulff; from Freedom, Gerhard Engler, Gerald (Jerry) Adam; from Grand Centre, Harvey Lehsner; from Hesketh, Minnie Ziegler; from Hobbema, Arthur Raatz, from Holden, Olga Pipke; from Homeglen, Ronald Petry; from Iron Springs, Wayne Boersma; from Jarrow, *Henry (Lindy) Lindberg; from Keoma, Millicent (Millie) Gerbrandt;

from Knee Hill Valley, Florence Lachman, *Esther Trekofski (wife of Rev. Glenn Rhind), *Earl Trekofski; from Lac La Biche, *David Haimila; from Lacombe, non-P.A.O.C. assembly, Lois Forsberg; from Legend, *Dennis Kiffiak; from Mallaig, Marian Springer; from Meeting Creek, Einar Jonson, Clara Jonson; from Millet, Chris Watson; from Morrin, Vernon Robinson; from New Norway, *Sandy Johnson, *Mrs. Sandy Johnson (wife of Sandy Johnson), Delores Olstad, Marilyn Olstad; from Niton Junction, Herman Andringa; from Nordegg, *Gwen Melnyk (wife of Rev. George Lagore); from Onoway, Irene Eckert; from Paradise Valley, *Dennis Sunderland; from Rich Valley, Jack Super; from Rocky Lane, George Kowal; from Rolling Hills, Gerhard Engler; from Rolly View, Karen Zerbin; from Therien, Mary Anne Talska; from Three Hills, *Lois Wood; from Tofield, Paul Warkentin; from Vauxhall, Howard Connor; from Wembly, Pat Stokke; from Wetaskiwin, Jim Edwards; from Wildwood, Marianne Wiebe; from no address given, Jack Bernard, Henry Barendregt, and Jake Petten.

Among those, who listed Calgary as their origin and their assembly is not known, and who attended Northwest Bible College and/or entered the ministry (*), are Sharon But, *Patty Clark (wife of Rev. William Lewis), Joyce England, Ferne Janzen, Randall Johnston, Cornelius Kuhn, Robert Kuhn, Mel Knutson, Don O'Connor, Alina Patz, Brad Pells, Margaret-Anne Sanders, Bonnie Simpson, Evelyn Sologij, Lorraine Switzer, Barbara Taylor, Tome Waterhouse, Fred Zinck.

Among those, who attended Bible college and/or entered the ministry (*) and which Edmonton church attended is not known, are Martin John Adool, Gladys Arychuk, Darey Bain, Darryl Bain, Paul Benke, Tannis Bishop, Don Bjorgen, Joseph Bogatko, Gloria Bonk, Elaine Breitkreutz, Jim Brown, Lynn Buerger, Gareth Burgess, Lydia Burk, Carol Bushey, Steve Camaschuk, Earl Caswell, Monte Cybruch, Graham Delong, Donald Edgar, Janet Edwards, Joan Edwards, Ron Egert, Ken Elmar, Cindy Ervin, Debbie Graul, Randy Harasyn, Walter Hardy, Sharon Hosteller, Dan Hunter, Linda Husband, Ken Jobson, Eva-Jo Kennedy, Brian F. Klem, Evangeline Krawchuk, Donna Kupchenko, Marie Labots, Lawrence Leflamme, Susan La Pointe, Carol Laskowski, Henry Lauzon, Eunice Lindgren, Janice MacLachlan, Trude MacTavish, Betty Martiniuk, Shane McCarthy, Ruth Mc-Williams, Philip Montgomery, Terry Nother, Earl Pasechnik, Sharon Pasula, Dale Plante, Sheila Prout, Joe Raczkovi, Richard Raglin, Gail Rasmussen, Wilton Rempel, Dennis Rhind, Douglas Rhind, John Richardson, Cnute Riggan, Janette Robertson, Steven Robertson, Ken Rose, Gary Rowbottom, Elaine Sam, Brenda Savelle, Larry Schlereth, Terry Senum, Laurie Shaw, Ruby Shumborski, Van Siemens, *Terry Sproule, Bill Stock, Dennis Strashok, Gary Strohschein, Barbara Styles, Maureen Thomas, Tony Timoshenko, Gordon Toppin, Ruth Vivian, Esther Walker, Larry Warkentin, Rose Werzak, Wayne Wessel, Don Wilson, Barbara J. Wisniewskie, Carol Wispinski.

WOMEN'S MINISTRIES
(formerly known as Women's Missionary Council)

At the 1944 Alberta District Conference, Mrs. Ida Cooke, wife of Rev. John C. Cooke, was appointed District Secretary of the Alberta Women's Missionary Council. The term, District Secretary, was later changed to District Director. Mrs. Cooke was the first District Secretary of Alberta. Her main work was to organize Women's Missionary Councils in Alberta. At her request, Rev. A. A. Lewis drew up itineraries for her — one for the fall of 1944 and one for the spring of 1945. The first Women's Missionary Council (W.M.C.) formed was in Lethbridge, where the Cookes were pastors. Under W.M.C., the older women there formed a prayer group and the young married women formed a work group.

On her itinerary tours for organizing W.M.C. units, she contacted ladies in the assemblies of Killam, Wainwright, Hughenden, Bentley, Calgary (who were very happy to form a unit), Claresholm and Turner Valley. All these assemblies formed units.

Claresholm Pentecostal Assembly's Women's Missionary Council in 1958.

Another assembly, on her tours, did not form a unit. Local pastor encouragement helped to form a strong local W.M.C. unit. The prayers and parcels from these units were much appreciated.

The first project, of the W.M.C. work units, was a bedroom parcel — one pair of sheets, one pair of pillow slips, one blanket and one quilt. If the group was too small then they made one quilt. These parcels were sent directly from the local unit to the one or ones in need.

The Lethbridge W.M.C. gathered old woolen garments or blankets, washed them then took them to a McLeod factory, where this material was made into blankets. A certain number of pounds of this old woolen material plus three or four dollars was the price of one blanket. The Lethbridge W.M.C. realized that their own pastor's wife had need of blankets, so presented Mrs. Cooke with three blankets, for which she was very grateful.

The projects became more varied as needs were recognized and the groups were able to provide them. Their ministry, beside the parcel ministry, included prayer for local people, pioneer workers, home missions and the Sub-Arctic Missions and foreign missions.

The parcel ministry was increased to include food parcels; clothing; for a time, bandages for the H. H. Williams Memorial Hospital; quilts for each graduate of Northwest Bible College for quite a few years; linen and other things for the missionary cabin at Sunnyside Pentecostal Camp. The penny fund projects have benefited a number of assemblies or missions. Overseas missions and missionary projects include contributing to the Missionary Outfit Fund and the missionaries' outfits; parcels or money for these missionaries as assigned by the Women's Ministries Director at Head Office and the District

Women's Ministries Director, so that each one is remembered at Christmas time; correspondence with missionaries; literature and money for literature; parcels for District pastors and home missionaries.

Under Mrs. Morris (Lillian) Olson and at her request, the Women's Missionary Council District Director was elected in the District Conference.

Under Mrs. Iva O'Brien, the W.M.C. Retreats were first organized. All the early ones were held in Banff. Others have been held at the Alberta Beach Camp Lodge and Caroline. At the time of writing, two retreats are held each fall — one at Alberta Beach and one in Banff. These retreats are marked by the moving of the Holy Spirit and blessing of God. All come away feeling it was good to have come.

At the General Conference in 1978, the WOMEN'S MISSIONARY COUNCIL name was changed to WOMEN'S MINISTRIES because their area of service had broadened.

The Women's Ministries Directors have been Mrs. J. C. (Ida) Cooke (1944-45), Mrs. Jim Routley (9 months in 1945-46), Mrs. Flemming May (3 months), Mrs. Morris (Lillian) Olson (1946-63), Mrs. A. A. Lewis (1963-66), Mrs. E. C. O'Brien (1966-76), Mrs. Kenneth (Sybil A.) Bunting (1976-82), Mrs. Kay Carbert (1982-   ). Their efforts to help units be of service to others have been much appreciated.

Dedicated women have and will continue to work for the Lord.

Nursing With a Message

Nursing is more than a smile, and "Hello"
"Here are your pills", "Lets take it slow".
It's more than the bedside comfort and care;
Food on a tray, a cap that we wear.
Our patients are special, so we add to their orders,
A warmth and uplifting to be found in these
    corridors.
For us at the 'Williams', we do our best,
A love and a message to each to express.
It's not learned in textbooks or some school of art,
But rather — an experience in yours and my heart.
We're concerned for each one, more than you
    know,
In ways that are many, I'll tell you so.
You say you're in pain, yes I see that you are.
A warm friendly hand, and help mend a scar.
You seem to be troubled; things aren't looking
    good,
To talk and be friends — maybe we should.
Now, those hurts of life, sure, they come to us all.
The brave and the shy; the big and the small.
But the God of great wisdom knew thus it would
    be,
So to heal these and more, He died on a tree.
Ay "Why?" you may ask, "What good could that
    do?"
I reply, rather simply — "I tell you 'tis true."
They say it was love that caused such a deed,
There was no other way; yes list to His plead.
You need more than a helping hand,
    more than a friend,
You need Jesus, the Savior, to His strength
    there's no end.

— Joan Andrews R.N.

140

Former Assemblies and Home Missions

FORMER ASSEMBLIES AND HOME MISSIONS
INTRODUCTION

A number of churches, home missions or outreaches were closed for various reasons, including too many members moved away, not enough pastors were available, a few joined other groups.

The Turner Valley area had a number of points, where services were held at one time — Little Chicago, where Rev. Kenneth Bunting pastored; Royalties, which was opened by Sister Holdsworth, later pastored by Brother Stronstad, then was pastored from Turner Valley; Black Diamond opened by Morris Olson, while he was pastoring Turner Valley. These places were born in the oil boom, however, when the oil business there slowed down, most of these places closed. Most of these are now serviced by the Turner Valley Pentecostal Church.

Corbett Creek and Fort Assiniboine were open for some time. The Portable Tabernacle was used in Fort Assiniboine, too.

In Fort Vermilion, Pastor Charlie Howey and his mother opened a work. About a year later, after Brother Howey married Mildred McKay, Mildred came. Charles was there for two years. Keg River, Paddle Prairie and Kathryn were three other places where services were held for a time.

Following are histories of other former assemblies and home missions.

ALLIANCE
PENTECOSTAL CHURCH OF ALLIANCE

The Pentecostal Church in Alliance was organized in October 1935 when Mrs. Florence Webster and daughter, Joyce, arrived. The first services were held over the Chinese restaurant. There was not one Pentecostal believer in this whole community at the time but God opened hearts to receive the Word and a fine assembly was started. In August 1938 Pastor Webster and Joyce left for Eastern Canada and now reside in Ottawa.

Mrs. Helen McLeod

Pastor Stronstad and his wife succeeded Mrs. Webster and remained here for over two years until October 1940 when they moved to Edson. Between 1940 and 1945, the following ladies were in charge of the assembly — Miss Emma Hemke and Miss Jean Grieve (now married to Robert Peel, who was a missionary to Africa), Miss Marion Malloy, Miss Lucy Hardy, Miss Esther Sorenson and Miss Jean Dinsmore, Miss Mabel Hysop. Mr. and Mrs. C. E. Warkentin arrived in 1945 and pastored until August 1946.

In May 1947 the congregation purchased the property and Music Studio of Miss E. B. Payne and began holding services in the part of the Studio, where the Anglican Church services had been formerly held. The living quarters were used as the parsonage. Pastor and Mrs. S. R. Tilton arrived from Oyen to minister. They remained until August 1949. During Brother Tilton's ministry, Evangelist Eunice Meyer conducted two weeks of meetings. Many people were saved. Among the first families in Alliance

141

were the Paul Paulson family, Mr. and Mrs. T. H. Royer, Mrs. Helen McLeod, the T. Rancier family, the Searle Wills family. After the meetings with Eunice Meyer, the Chris Reister family, John Reister family, Stewart Heffel family, Walter Heffel family, Jack Bullee family attended.

Reverend and Mrs. Morris Olson pastored from 1949 to 1955.

Alliance Pentecostal congregation, 1970.

Reverend and Mrs. Steve Holomis arrived in August of 1955 and resigned in 1959, when they moved to St. Paul. During their ministry there were between twenty-five and thirty young people who faithfully attended the church. A new gas range for the parsonage was given by Bruno Lehman of Edmonton. A new furnace was installed. Their salary was two Sunday evening offerings a month. The folk were good to bring in food items.

Reverend and Mrs. Leonard Schmautz followed Pastor Holomis. Reverend and Mrs. D. L. McNutt came to pastor about January 1963. Reverend and Mrs. V. Lawrence and family arrived in October 1965 and left June 1970, moving to Kavanaugh, Alberta, where Virgil and his dad bought a dairy farm.

Mr. and Mrs. Jim Smart went to Alliance December 1970 and left July 1972 when they moved to Hay River, Northwest Territories. In January 1973 Mr. and Mrs. Dale Archibald arrived and stayed until August 1973 when they moved to Forestburg. After the Archibalds left different ministers came each Sunday until October 1973. At this time since no one was available to pastor Alliance it was decided to close the church. The folk from Alliance began attending the Forestburg assembly and still do.

Among those, who attended Bible College and/or entered the ministry (*), are James Bullee, John Bullee, *Joyce Bullee (married to Reverend

Mel Dietrich), *Shirley Heffel (married to Reverend D. Schneider), *Stewart Heffel, *Evelyn Olson, Dale Wills, Richard Wills.

BENTON
BENTON ASSEMBLY

George and Phil Hawtin were Bible students who lived in Alsask, just over the border into Saskatchewan. Alsask was near Oyen, Benton and Sibbald, Alberta. George and Phil Hawtin held some special meetings in the Benton Hall. Phil and George picked up Mrs. Janet Thom and her daughter, Anne (now Cornell), and took them to their services. Both of them accepted the Lord as their Saviour. A younger daughter, Jean (now Mrs. Al Dittman), was converted in Sibbald under the ministry of Kenneth Bunting and his father, who were having special services there sometime later.

In the early thirties, P. M. (Todd) Cantelon held services in homes in Benton, including Dan Mac-Donald's home just outside of Benton. Later the services were held in Wavy Plains School, north of Benton. Different ones carried on services here as part of a sixty-mile-circuit of services which were held in Benton, Sibbald and Oyen on Sundays. Among those, who preached on this circuit, were Rev. and Mrs. J. R. Allen and Andrew Wek. During Pastor Allen's time the services were held in homes in the Benton area.

Some of the early families in these services in Alsask, Sibbald and Benton Districts were the Speers, Collins, Hislops, Nash, Switzer, Halverson, Othens, Dittmans, Thoms, Cornells, Bessy Mac-Donald. The people of Benton have been and still are welcome to attend Glad Tidings Tabernacle in Oyen.

BOWVILLE DISTRICT
BOWVILLE PENTECOSTAL TABERNACLE

Bowville is a country district about twelve miles east of Carmangay. In the early nineteen hundred and twenties, Mr. and Mrs. Marvin Green, Mr. and Mrs. John Olson and Hazel from Bowville attended evangelistic meetings in Claresholm. Here they accepted the Lord as Saviour. They invited the evangelists, Reverend and Mrs. Reynolds and her son, Cyril Brooks, to come to Bowville for meetings. These were held in a dance hall. Crowds came, people were saved. During the day, prayer meetings were held in the Olson home, where many were gloriously filled with the Holy Spirit. After the evangelists left, these new Christians continued to meet together for worship. Rev. and Mrs. Clare Scratch, Lucy Hardy and people from Lethbridge would come to assist this new assembly in services.

Rev. and Mrs. R. Drisner in front of Bowville Pentecostal Tabernacle, 1955.

Reverend and Mrs. Fred Willis came to be their first pastor. An old dance hall was bought for a church. This was moved with horses for one mile across a field to a parcel of land donated by Mr. Olson. Pastor Willis and the men of the Assembly renovated this hall into a church with two rooms at the back as living quarters for the Pastor. The men also built seats. A piano was donated by Mr. Jack Patey of Lethbridge. In the summer of 1927 the church was dedicated.

In the fall of 1927, a missionary convention was held in the Bowville church. Even though it was harvest time, the convention was well attended. Among those who took part in this convention were Reverend George Chambers, General Superintendent of the Pentecostal Assemblies of Canada; Reverend Elmer Morrison, missionary to China; Mrs. Lindsey, missionary to India; Reverend R. Spence, Sophie Nygaard.

In the summer of 1928, two young men, Robert Parkinson and William Ball, ministered in Bowville before returning to the Bible School in Winnipeg. Among the ministers, who pastored in Bowville, were Reverend and Mrs. Robinson, Reverend and Mrs. Cecil Cobb, Reverend and Mrs. Arden Lewis, Reverend and Mrs. Alder, Mr. and Mrs. Gene Peretti, Bill and Effie Warkentine, Mr. and Mrs. Chester Ansley, Reverend and Mrs. Kenneth Bunting, Reverend and Mrs. James Robertson, Reverend Charles Howey, Reverend and Mrs. John Morsch, Reverend and Mrs. Reuben Drisner.

During the ministry of Reverend Arden Lewis, an old house was torn down, the lumber was used to add a kitchen and an upstairs bedroom to the suite at the back of the church.

While the Warkentines were in Bowville, they held successful Daily Vacation Bible Schools.

In the nineteen hundred and fifties some families moved away and eventually the church was closed. When the church was opened in Vulcan those of the Bowville Assembly, who were still in the vicinity, attended the Vulcan Church. The Vulcan Assembly obtained the piano from the Bowville Church. The old church was sold and moved away. Funds received from this were divided between the Vulcan and Lethbridge Assemblies.

During the years of the existence of the Bowville Church, many souls were saved and filled with the Holy Spirit.

Among those, who attended Bible College and/or entered the ministry(*), are *Laureen Schneider (Mrs. Bill Drury), *Donald Schneider and the *Olson daughter, who married Reverend Cyril Brooks.

God's Kingdom has been extended and glorified by the influence of the Bowville Full Gospel Church.

BROCKET
INDIAN FULL GOSPEL MISSION

In 1948 Henry Clausen and Ed and May Sinclair of Lethbridge became concerned about the opening of the Peigan and Blood Reserves to receive the Gospel. God opened the way for them and they were able to minister on the Reserves. Mr. and Mrs. Maynard Anderson also helped in this ministry. Andersons were assisted by Ray and Ruby Lindgren. The first baptismal service on the Peigan Reserve saw some fifteen candidates baptized. Some were filled with the Holy Spirit at that service also.

The Sinclairs went to the Blood Reserve. Mr. and Mrs. Maynard Anderson volunteered to look after the work at Brocket.

Early 1950 Mr. and Mrs. Ole Austring returned to Lethbridge from Northwest Bible College in Edmonton. They began to help in the work at Brocket. When the Andersons moved away from Lethbridge, the Austrings took over the ministry on the Peigan Reserve. They met each Sunday in a log house, which was later converted into a church. One night a week, Bible Studies were held in private homes. God moved and many were established in the Word.

After the home going of Ole Austring, Reverend Watts, Reverend S. R. Tilton, Mr. William Fraser, accompanied by Mr. and Mrs. Maynard Anderson, held a business meeting in the home of Mr. and Mrs. Big Swan in 1960. The board of Indian brethren were present. The future of the work was discussed. The

Board voted in favour of Mr. and Mrs. Maynard Anderson continuing as pastors of the Indian Full Gospel Mission in Brocket. All voiced their deep appreciation of the late Ole J. Austring. The Board thanked Mr. and Mrs. Crow Eagle for their kindness in letting them use their former home for services. They were then considering moving a schoolhouse into Brocket to be used as a church.

In 1964 Pastor Labrentz of Pincher Creek was called occasionally to conduct a Sunday afternoon service in Brocket. Then the Labrentz family started to drive out on Thursday evenings. Sister Labrentz would conduct a children's church as Brother Labrentz led in a Bible Study. On January 18, 1965, an organizational meeting saw Brother Labrentz put completely in charge of the Brocket Assembly. In the fall, Pastor Labrentz appointed a local brother to be the pastor while he continued to supervise the work. The first was Brother Ernie Villebrun, followed by Brother Freddie Northpeigan in March 1966. Roderick and Fay Northpeigan were placed in charge of the Sunday School.

In January 1966, a new ministry was begun. Evangelist Hartwell Northpeigan and Brother Labrentz started twice-monthly Worker Training Classes for the leaders of house-type prayer groups throughout the Blood Indian Reserve. Meetings were held in Cardston, St. Mary's Dam, Stand-Off, Glenwood, etc.. One particular service at Chief Harold Moon's home of Glenwood saw Brother Labrentz share the Word for five hours. Such was the intense hunger for the Scriptures.

Every summer, an Indian Camp meeting was held by the river at Glenwood. Teepees were set up and the meetings were held on the grassy slopes of the river bank. Brother Labrentz was one of the speakers at these meetings for three years — 1962, 1963, 1964. One day he spoke five times. He taught Sunday School and spoke in the morning service at Pincher Creek, then rushed to Glenwood and preached at the afternoon service. Later, after dedicating a lot of babies and praying for all the sick, Brother Labrentz was again asked to teach the baptismal candidates at the river's edge. Then he rushed back to Pincher Creek to conduct the evening service.

The Blackfoot people had difficulty pronouncing Brother Labrentz' name so nicknamed him "Pastor Norm of the Whitefoot Tribe." Those were precious days which saw many answers to prayer. One extra-special experience was a message in tongues by an elderly Indian grandmother. She also brought the interpretation, but the whites didn't understand. After a pause, she brought a third utterance, this time in English, fresh from the Lord. Brother Hartwell Northpeigan got very joyously excited. He ex-

plained that the first was an unknown tongue, the second was in the Blackfoot language, the third in English. The miracle was that this aged sister could not speak a word of English and her third utterance was in perfect grammar in English. The Lord saw the few whites present and questioning. The Lord didn't leave them out.

The work in Brocket is still progressing. A good church has been built on the Reserve. Many gather each Sunday. Many special meetings are being held there. On April 12, 1982, Pastor Nash of Pincher Creek was invited to go to Brocket to lead Bible Study and prayer meetings. The Lord worked mightily baptizing in the Holy Spirit and meeting many needs.

COALDALE — eight miles from Lethbridge
GLAD TIDINGS TABERNACLE

It is thought that the Coaldale Assembly may have begun with Reverend and Mrs. John Erhardt around 1951. The Erhardts sang duets and Reverend Erhardt was referred to as a dynamic preacher.

In the late fifties Pastor and Mrs. Rueben Drisner ministered. The T. Texas Tyler meeting was a real blessing in 1958. Pastor and Mrs. Gunnar Gulbransen came in 1959. About 1965 Pastor Mike Bernadsky came. In June of 1965 this young pastor married Julie Remple. They were happy with God's blessing. Many improvements were made on the property.

The work here was closed and in 1968 the church building was moved to Claresholm. A number of the folk there then attended the Lethbridge Pentecostal Assembly about eight miles from Coaldale.

Among those, who attended Bible College and/or entered the ministry (*), are *Verna Buhlin, *Vivian Buhlin, *Arnold J. Dyck, Helen Harmes, Elsie Harms, Jake Hubert, *Peter Hubert, Ken Jenkins, *Mrs. Joy Jenkins, *Mel Jenkins, Bernie Knelson, Elizabeth Knelson, Mary Knelson, Linda

Glad Tidings Tabernacle

Martens, Suzanne Otten, *Sandy Otten (wife of Reverend Don Eshelman), Hilda Roever, Verna Roever. All of these young people attended the Lethbridge Pentecostal Assembly.

Early in 1967, Peter Hubert, Bernice Knelson, Mary Knelson, Suzanne Otten and Sandy Otten — all Mennonite Brethren young people from Coaldale — came to Lethbridge to hear the Collegaires from Northwest Bible College. These young people were so impressed by the students' sincerity that they attended Northwest Bible College that fall. They also attended the Lethbridge Pentecostal Assembly until time for College.

EDMONTON
IDYLWYLDE PENTECOSTAL TABERNACLE

In 1956 and 1957 in the Mill Creek School of Edmonton, Pastor and Mrs. Jack Keys held Sunday School for one hundred people and Morning Service for about thirty-five to fifty adults. This was so encouraging that the Pentecostal Tabernacle folk put up the money to build a church. Brother Keys located the property and the Tabernacle folk paid for it. A Mr. Baker from the Tabernacle became the Superintendent of Construction. Mr. Baker's son and Brother Keys helped to build the church, too.

Wee College Graduation Program 1970. From Left to Right: Blaine Mack, Brenda Sloboda, VerLynn Carruthers, David Lasner, Kevin Fitzgerald and Scott Morsch with Mrs. Helen Lasner.

Among those, who formed the nucleus for this new church, were Bob and Phyllis Swaffield, Wes and Faye Klassen and Mr. and Mrs. R. Henderson. Pastor Keys did not pastor in this new church, which was called Idylwylde Pentecostal Tabernacle.

In 1957, Rev. and Mrs. P. Houghton arrived. Rev. Houghton enjoyed a fruitful ministry as the first pastor in the new Tabernacle. Six years later, Rev. and Mrs. Houghton became missionaries in Kenya, Africa. The next and last two pastors were Rev. William Pipke and Rev. Lyle Anderson.

During the school term of 1959-60, Shirley Johnson conducted children's church services during the entire morning service. During these services, children would take part — sing, give object lessons, usher and more. Many children gave their hearts to the Lord and were encouraged to tell what the Lord had done for them. It was a very rewarding time to see spiritual growth among the children.

In 1969-70, Mrs. Shirley Morsch conducted the first Wee College in Idylwylde Tabernacle. Mothers played a very important part in this college. Mothers, who helped, were Mrs. Helen Lasner, Mrs. Vivian Sloboda, Mrs. Marie Mack, Mrs. Alice Fitzgerald, Mrs. Mary Hirsch. The graduates' names are listed with their picture. There was another special student, Mark Hirsch, who could not finish because he moved away.

In 1974, Idylwylde Tabernacle became two assemblies — Evangel Pentecostal Assembly and the other one was called Calvary Temple, when they moved into their new building in Mill Woods.

ELLSCOTT
ELLSCOTT CHURCH
(Neighbour of Newbrook and Begun by German Ministers)

Ellscott was north of Newbrook. Mr. E. Drisner, who with his family had escaped from Siberia, borrowed ten dollars from his brother in Bruderheim, Alberta, for a homestead. In May or June 1931, Mr. Drisner walked all the way from Bruderheim to Newbrook. His homestead was about half way between Newbrook and Ellscott. This was to be an important position. Once he had a little log house built, he brought his wife and family out to the homestead. It was very primitive because there was little to do with. He cut down trees to the right height so that certain stumps would serve as chairs, the ground was their floor. A cellar was dug for keeping vegetables. Since at first there were no boards on the roof, rain would bring water into the house, root cellar and around the house. Adeline Emde (nee Drisner) remembers running through the water. Eventually, Mr. Drisner was able to shingle the roof. In those days you did what you could with what you had. During those rain-soaked days, Mrs. Drisner would have to hang the wet bedding out to dry as best she could. I am sure she was very thankful for the shingles on the roof after all she had been through. The roads were very

Mr. and Mrs. Ewald Bresch and little Rita, who later married James Berteig. Rita is the mother of Laurey Berteig.

1933, Group gathered for service at the Drisner Homestead.

poor zig-zag roads. The countryside was very wet — lots of muskeg.

About November or December 1931, Rev. J. Schatkowski started meetings in the Proaknow home. This preacher was one who had received the Baptism of the Holy Spirit. The folks, mainly, were German Baptists, who attended the services. The early families were Mr. and Mrs. Ewald Bresch, Mr. and Mrs. E. Roller, Mr. and Mrs. Belert, two Molson families, Mr. and Mrs. E. Drisner. They all had families. Mrs. Bresch, Mrs. Roller and Mrs. Belert were sisters from the Grapentin family.

Adeline Emde remembers those days quite well. At the age of 8 years old, she accepted Christ as her Saviour. Once she and her mother rode to service on horseback. In one particular muskeg they had to cross, the muskeg was so deep that she was so afraid her mother would not make it to the other side. She did make it and then it was Adeline's turn to cross on her horse. She made it too.

They never had a steady pastor, however Rev. Schatkowski had an irregular circuit and would return as often as he was able. Rev. Posein gave the same type of service. Rev. Schatkowski was well remembered by the children. In those days treats were in short supply. He always carried candy for the children. They just loved him. One day, as a special treat when the pastor came to their home, Mrs. Drisner served cornflakes. It was so new to them that they did not know how to eat them. They wondered if you were to pour boiling water over them or not. Anyway it was a treat.

There were times when the Ellscott group and the Newbrook group (both Pentecostal) would meet in the Drisner log house usually in the winter time because it was not such a busy time and on the whole the route was more easily traveled then, that is by sleigh. One occasion, Adeline remembers well. She, about ten years old, and her brother, Seffren, two years younger, walked six or seven miles north to let the Ellscott folk know there would be a service at the Drisner home for both the Pentecostal groups. That time in particular, the snow was so soft and deep that Adeline had to keep pulling Seffren out of the snowbanks. What a trip! The first family would let the others in the Ellscott group know. Adeline and Seffron stayed overnight. Then the next morning while the snow was firmer, two big sleighs of folk made their way to Drisners. Mr. Bresch and Mr. Roller both played trumpets. They would play them on the way to service, sometimes walking behind the sleigh and sometimes on. What a lovely thing to hear! The Drisners would hear them coming, probably before they could see them coming, because of the lovely trumpet playing. Other times, Adeline remembers times when she and her dad would stand out on the road listening and looking for the Ellscott group to arrive. Meanwhile the Drisners were busy dismantling beds to make room for benches (blocks of wood with planks laid on top). The beds were put outside for the service. My, how they all enjoyed those times of fellowship. One time after service Mrs. Drisner had made tea, which she usually did. These were hard times, so they did not have any sugar. However, there was a jar of white granules on the table, which the guests mistook for sugar and put some in their tea. You should have seen the look on their faces when they tasted their tea "sweetened" with salt. Rev. W. Frederick came on a circuit type of basis, though not on a regular time basis. These circuit preachers would have services in quite a large part of Alberta. Student pastors would come to Newbrook and area. Evangelist Edward and Bertha Gaetz came to Gamefield School, north of Drisners about three miles. The services were well attended and quite a number saved. This would be around 1945.

After the Gaetzes left, Miss Leila Busenius, who was pastoring Newbrook, would walk out for services in the Gamefield School area.

The group from Ellscott would come to service in Newbrook, too. Because the area was so wet, people would walk on the railroad to come to church. Adeline remembers walking to church with her father. She carried her shoes. Then about a half mile from Newbrook, she would wash her feet, put on her precious shoes and walk to church. She also remembers going to some of these combined Newbrook Ellscott meetings, which would be all-day trips, because it was too far to go home and come back for service again. They would walk home by the light of the fireflies.

The Roller children included Irma, who married Rev. Arvin Sorge; Egan Roller, who became a minister; Alfreda, who married Rev. Posein's son. The Bresch children included Rita, who married James Bertieg and whose son, Laurie, is Music Minister at Central Pentecostal Tabernacle in Edmonton. It is believed that some of the Belert boys live in Barrhead. The Drisner children included Adeline, who married Walter Emde and they have a Bible Book Store, Light and Life, in Edmonton; Seffron, who attends Evangel; Reuben, who is a minister and has a son who is a minister; Ben, who attends Central Tabernacle in Edmonton; Freda, who is married and living in Barrhead; Rheinhold, who married a Miss Bigam and lives on the home place. The Drisner children are all living for the Lord.

Eventually, as transportation and roads improved they came to church in Newbrook or moved away.

EVANSBURG
PENTECOSTAL ASSEMBLY

The original minister was Arthur Lagore, who came to Evansburg because Herman and Elsie Walters asked for a preacher. The preacher was invited to stay with the Walters. Arthur got around to visit folks by walking. The next preacher was Larry Broughton. Both these young men became/are missionaries to Africa. Rev. S. R. Tilton asked Lay-Preacher Robertson L. Howatt and his wife, Elsie (nee Johnson), to pastor. They began pastoring in 1956. They had a daughter, Deanna, and a newborn boy, Laurie, at that time. The services were held in the Portable Tabernacle. Elsie remembers teaching Sunday School, while having to hold her new baby. On Saturday evenings, Mr. Howatt, after commuting from Edmonton, would leave his wife and children at the small shack, which was next door to the Portable Tabernacle. Then he would pick up young people for his Saturday evening young people's meeting in the Park Court Baptist Church. After this was established, the Bap-

tists decided to call their own pastor. During the three and a half years that Howatts commuted to Evansburg, there were a few highlights. Seven-year-old Deanna Howatt gave her heart to the Lord. In the summer of 1959, a girl was converted. Rev. Jack Hunka held special meetings in the community hall. John Morsch was guest speaker, twice. Shirley Johnson came out a time or two to assist, especially in music. An older girl played the organ for a while, then Mrs. Howatt played after she left. Pastor and Mrs. Paul Slemming followed the Howatts; then Pastor McGhie followed the Slemmings. Pastor and Mrs. James McAlister served the assembly, while they pastored Stony Plain.

Among those, who attended Bible college, were David Krawchuk and Ruth Krawchuk.

Although there is no church in Evansburg at the time of writing, there were lives that were enriched because of those, who passed their way in Evansburg.

GRASSLAND
GRASSLAND PENTECOSTAL
SERVICES

J. Shirley Johnson, a lady minister and teacher, came to Grassland in 1957 after receiving her teaching certificate. She mainly taught English and Music in the junior high school section. During her second year there, she held Bible club for boys and girls in her teacherage, then taught religious instruction to elementary and junior high students at noon once a week. This was called the Sunshine Hour. Shirley

Religious Education — Sunshine Hour.

involved other teachers (Miss Roberta Edwards, Mrs. Ruby Edwards, Mrs. Elsie Zembal and Miss Joyce H. Elgert) in this. Shirley, also, had Theolog Club for the senior high school students. She also held Sunday school and services in the community hall. An evangelist, who had been to Amber Valley for a series of meetings, came to Grassland for some meetings.

Religious Education — Theolog Club.

Some of the Grassland folk, who were converted at Amber Valley, attended these services.

Shirley left Grassland at the end of June 1959 to teach in Edmonton and also to conduct children's church for five-year-olds to fourteen-year-olds at Idylwylde Tabernacle. After Shirley left Grassland, an independent work was established with Rev. Clarence Ness and his wife, Ann (nee Twerdochlib).

KEG RIVER
PENTECOSTAL ASSEMBLY

Pastor Harry Nettleton and the Pentecostal Assembly of Peace River were concerned about the unchurched communities in other areas around them. In the summer of 1958 Reverend and Mrs. Nettleton along with two other ladies went to Keg River. They visited the homes and held outdoor services. Several families showed an interest in the gospel when they were contacted.

In autumn of 1958, a family moved into Keg River district to begin holding Sunday School and to continue visitation. In the summer of 1959 Joyce Sinclair and Beryl Berg conducted services in Keg River.

In August 1959 Reverend and Mrs. Floyd Schwindt came to Keg River to take charge of the work. The Alberta District purchased a building. This was located on a fine piece of land owned by a farmer, who had been recently saved.

Later Reverend and Mrs. Paul Slemming came to pastor. Pastor Slemming worked as a carpenter and drove a school bus to help with finances.

The church and house at the time of writing have been dismantled. Most of the people have moved elsewhere.

May Lou Vos of this assembly attended Northwest Bible College in Edmonton and, also, has received her Bachelor of Education degree from the University of Alberta. She is now Mrs. Yanch. Mrs. Yanch was a Sunday School Department Superintendent in Central Pentecostal Tabernacle in Edmonton.

MAYTON DISTRICT (East of Olds)
MAYTON PENTECOSTAL
TABERNACLE

In 1924, Mr. Calvin Peterson held services in the country Baptist Church in the Mayton District. Among those, who attended these meetings were Mr. and Mrs. David Hemke. Mr. Hemke, still living at the time of publishing, gave a report of what happened during the time of these early days. Mr. Calvin Peterson's ministry had a power dimension that was new to Mr. Hemke. He wanted that spiritual power in his own life, so he invited Mr. Peterson to his home. Mr. Peterson arrived in the morning that had been agreed upon. Mr. Hemke did his morning chores, shaved and dressed in his Sunday best. Then he said, "Now I want to receive the Baptism of the Holy Spirit." He presented himself to the Lord and the study of God's Word. Seeing that Acts 2:4 was for him, he asked the Lord to fill him before noon. The Lord graciously filled him with the Holy Spirit with the evidence of speaking in other tongues. Close to this time, two other men, who received the Baptism of the Holy Spirit, were Daniel Gill and Edward Maetche. Mr. Hemke's wife received this experience a few days after her husband. It was glorious and so new to them, who had never seen or heard of this experience before. Many received this special experience which is certainly Scriptural. Persecution followed but the revival spread. There was good fellowship and they cared for one another. Homes and schoolhouses (including Schmouse Creek School) became too small for services.

Among the early families were Mr. and Mrs. David J. Hemke with Emma, Esther and Ruth; Mr. and Mrs. Edward Maetche with Otto, William, Elsie, Martha, Ida, Bertha; Mr. and Mrs. Daniel Gill with Alfred, Kaleb, Rueben; Mr. and Mrs. R. E. Miller with Mildred, Robert, Donny; Mrs. Mauk; Mr. and Mrs. Dave Thoman with Samuel and Ruth; Mr. and Mrs. Herb Lachman with Mildred, Gladys, Helen, Hazel, Ruth and Charles; Mr. and Mrs. Alex Erhardt with Marion, Leah, John, Dave, Jake and Rachel; Mrs. Catherine Gaetz with William Gaetz, Emma, Selma, and Edith; Luella Boettger (now Mrs. William Gaetz); Mr. and Mrs. Ben Gaetz with Wallace, Alvin; Agatha, Martha, Ella and Lily Knecht; Lily Boettger; Mr. and Mrs. John Schuechner; Mrs. Crowell with Edgar, Bertha and May (who became Mrs. Gusella); Miss Ida Riley (now Mrs. Alfred Gill).

A church building was essential, so in 1926 the Mayton Pentecostal Tabernacle was erected to the glory of God. The church was a real lighthouse in the community.

During 1924-27 various ministers and laymen

conducted services. Then resident pastors came. They were Rev. E. Robinson (1928-32), Rev. A. Dalby (1932-37), Rev. W. Frederick (1937-41), Rev. V. Graham (1942), Rev. G. Hutchinsen (1942), Miss Lucy Hardy and Miss Emma Hemke (1943), Rev. Howard Cantelon (1944-46), Rev. Homer Cantelon (1947-50), Rev. Fred Hunter (1951), Rev. Hubert Rosenke (1952-54), Mr. Smith (a good layman) (1955-56), Rev. Gordon Bailey (1957-58), Rev. Krassler (1959).

The Lord answered many of their prayers, people were healed, saved and filled with the Spirit.

In 1959 a number of families moved away and some had died, so Rev. Ernie Peterson, District Presbyter, and Rev. S. R. Tilton, District Superintendent, moved the location of worship to Olds, Alberta, where some of the Mayton people had taken up residence.

Twelve or more of the young people had gone into the ministry, also some from the next generation. Among those, who attended Bible college and/or entered the ministry (*), are *Emma Hemke (wife of Rev. Ernie Peterson), *May Crowell (married Mr. Gusella), *Earl Trefkoski, *Esther Trefkoski (wife of Rev. Glenn Rhind), Mrs. E. Gaetz (Bertha Crowell).

METISKOW
PENTECOSTAL CHURCH
(formerly Swedish Assembly 1922-1944)

Reverend Elof Lindquist was pastor of the Wetaskiwin Baptist Church in 1912 when Victor Nystedt arrived in Canada. Through Victor's testimony of his own recent receiving of the Baptism of the Holy Spirit in Sweden, both Reverend Lindquist and Reverend Holm, pastor of the Metiskow Baptist church, received their own personal "Pentecost," too. Reverend and Mrs. Holm moved to Wetaskiwin later.

About 1915 Mr. O. H. Sellin came from Wetaskiwin to Metiskow. He, a Lutheran, had had a new

Metiskow Pentecostal Church, built in 1938, with an annex which was added later. It still stands on the same lot.

experience with God. He, with other christians, began holding meetings in various homes, where they sang, prayed and studied the Word of God. Often they would walk to these services along sandy trails. Several of them carried their guitars and other instruments. Mr. Sellin carried a small Johnson's organ which he played. Among these early christians was Victor Nystedt. At a prayer meeting in Victor Nystedt's home, a Mr. O. Quist received the Baptism of the Holy Spirit. He became so dedicated to the Lord that he allowed them to use his newly constructed barn for special evangelistic meetings during the summers. Many homesteaders were saved in those services. Baptismal services were held in Sandberg's Lake and Metiskow Lake.

By 1922 these early christians had organized an Assembly with a church board. Since the majority of these people were of Scandinavian origin, their services were conducted in the Swedish language. Mr. August Hellquist was the secretary for the church for many years. His records were beautifully written in the Swedish language.

Mr. O. H. Sellin pastored this assembly from 1922 to 1946. Many laymen contributed to the ministry as well. Some of the early founders of the Assembly were O. Quist, Axel Setterlund, Johnson, Pearson, V. Nystedt, E. Olson, C. Olson, Lindbech, N. P. Olson, Sandberg, V. Israelson, O. Carlson, C. Carlson, A. Carlson, Ada Carlson, A. Hellquist, Holmquist.

From about 1922 to 1938, the meetings were held in the O. H. Sellin home. Donations and offerings were received toward a church building. In 1938 this became a reality. On June 25, 1939 the Pentecostal Tabernacle was dedicated. Reverend C. O. Nordin spoke in the morning in a Swedish service. In the afternoon Reverend Harvey C. McAlister brought the dedication message; in the evening Reverend G. Gulbransen spoke. A large crowd gathered from the surrounding areas for these services.

Until 1944 this assembly had been known as a Swedish Assembly, then it was organized as an English Assembly.

In 1947 Reverend D. McNutt came as pastor. A house, donated by Mrs. Ada Carlson, was their parsonage. In 1950 Reverend and Mrs. Ray Lindgren became the pastors. They were followed by Reverend George Corris. He also had services in the Little Gap School about twenty miles southwest from Metiskow.

After George Corris, Mr. and Mrs. Stan Christon took charge of the work until Pastor Rhind could come. The Christons, who were missionaries from the Ivory Coast in Africa, did much carpentry and electrical work in the church.

In 1954 Reverend and Mrs. G. A. Rhind came to pastor. During their ministry, the Hartlip School was purchased. It was moved on to a foundation to the rear of the church building. This gave them larger church and Sunday School facilities.

In 1958 Reverend and Mrs. Reuben Drisner followed the Rhinds.

In 1960 the Assembly became affiliated with the Pentecostal Assemblies of Canada. The property is held in trust by the Pentecostal Assemblies of Canada for the local assembly.

Others who ministered here were Reverend and Mrs. Arthur Lamb (1961); Miss Violet Nelson (1962); Miss Alice Olsonberg (1963); Reverend Eli Fricker (1964), who also served the Provost church; Reverend Bill Bridle (1965), while Provost's pastor; Reverend and Mrs. Glen Murphy (1967), while Provost's pastor; while Hughenden's pastor, Reverend Asselstine (1973); Reverend A. Townsend (1976), while pastoring Provost; while Hughenden's pastor, Reverend Delbert Pierce (1978).

In 1978, Allan Lindskoog became the pastor. He commuted from Hughenden, where he was engaged in carpenter work. He assisted in Christian Fellowship services in the Community Hall as well.

Others who held services in the absence of pastors were Reuben Kvill, II. Osterhouse, Stewart Heffel, O'Coins, R. Woods.

From about 1947 to 1972, there was an active Sunday School. Mrs. Josie McPherson taught the adult Bible Class for many years. She also acted as Secretary-Treasurer for the Assembly for several years.

In 1945 the ladies formed a Mission Band. They helped support Sadie McLeod in China and Hong Kong, other missionaries in Haiti and Africa. They also contributed to missionaries in the Northwest Territories and the Hay River Hospital. This group was active until November 1975.

Among the early founding families were the Israelsons. There were twelve children in this family. Some are in the ministry while others are serving in various Assemblies. Among other families, who came later and were very active in the church, were Mr. and Mrs. James Hughes, Mr. and Mrs. Dave McPherson, Mr. and Mrs. Vern Downing.

The blessing of the Lord has been upon the Metiskow Assembly. Many of its adherents have moved to other places where they are serving the Lord. Many have been promoted to higher service.

Among those, who attended Bible College and/or entered the ministry (*), are Erling Forsberg, Ernest Hamre, Daniel Hughes, *Velma Hughes (wife of Reverend K. Ness), *Alvin Israelson, *Lily Israelson (now Mrs. Maynard Anderson), George Israelson, *Sharon Israelson (wife of Reverend Stan Lagore), Victoria Israelson (Mrs. R. Cassidy), *Raymond Lindgren, *Ruby Lindgren (nee Israelson), *Leroy Larson, Jean McPherson, Kenneth McPherson, *Gordon Setterlund, Fern Stewart, Doug Widmer (Walsh, Alberta).

Rev. Del Pierce, while pastoring Hughenden Pentecostal Church, held Sunday afternoon services in the church of the Metiskow Pentecostal Assembly for a year and a half to two years (1976-77). Allan Lindskoog held Sunday morning services for about a year (1977-78) following Rev. Pierce. Then the church was closed. However, at the time of writing, a Lutheran Sunday School is held in the church. The Pentecostal folk now attend the assembly in Provost.

NEMISKAM
NEMISKAM ASSEMBLY

In the summer of 1936, Rev. and Mrs. A. A. Lewis ministered and there, for six months, they stayed. Miss Edina Harding assisted Rev. Lewis. That first summer, there were only a few who attended. They held their meetings in a renovated butcher shop. The attendance increased to about eighty on a Sunday night. The Harty Clan (John, Jake and Fred) were converted. Andrew Wek was converted. His father, Carl Wek had a General Store in Nemiskam. Rev. and Mrs. Harvey C. McAlister pastored three or four months in the summer of 1937. Basil Leonard pastored there, too. Unfortunately, it was depression time. People left because they could no longer make a living there. Larger farms were formed. Soon there were no longer enough people left in the church to support the work there, so the church was closed. The pews and piano were acquired by the Burdett Full Gospel Church in 1947 or 48. Nemiskam is practically a ghost town. There is no longer a store or post office.

However, all was not lost. John Harty became an Apostolic minister and Andrew Wek became a Pentecostal Assemblies of Canada minister. Lives were changed, because those, who loved God and knew the power of the Spirit of God, passed their way.

PERRYVALE
PERRYVALE CHAPEL

On December 7, 1949, Deaconesses Elsie B. Johnson and Selma Komant came to the hamlet of Perryvale. Their first services were held December 18, 1949. That morning, twelve children came out to Sunday School and, in the evening service, seven children and one adult came. The two deaconesses were encouraged. Weather permitting, the services and Sunday School were held in the little Anglican church on the east side of Perryvale. If it was too cold, Sunday School and services were held in the ladies' two-room suite, which was behind Dorothy Waffle's Variety Store. Among those, who then attended Sunday School, were the Ward children, the Holmes children, Donald Lewis, Bobby Silverthorne, Joan Zygash and the Watt children. On January 10, 1950, Elsie and Selma started Bible Club. In a letter, that Elsie wrote in January of that year, she stated that the children there appreciated Sunday School so much. Mid-week service was held in the Watt home.

J. Shirley Johnson as a Deaconess.

Elsie and Selma taught Religious Education in the Rochester School. They would take the bus to Rochester in the morning, teach in the afternoon, then, as soon as school was out, they made a mad dash to catch the Blueberry Special (train), as it was locally called. If they missed the train they would have to wait for the bus. They also held a week of special meetings in Rochester. Another time, they held a service there. A Miss Maida Vale came along to play the organ for them. All went well except that they had a long walk back to Perryvale. That nine or ten miles seemed very long to them. They were very happy to hear Mr. Craswell's St. Bernard bark, for they knew they must be nearing home.

Living in Perryvale was quite an experience for Elsie and Selma. Part of the time, Elsie drove the 1927 Chevrolet coupe that the District Superintendent, Rev. D. N. Buntain, purchased for their use at Perryvale. Elsie's father and brother, Bud, repaired and painted it. Elsie and Selma used it occasionally.

It had to be cranked, so it was rather hazardous, when it back fired. Their outdoor freezer for food was a box nailed up in a tree not far from their door. The bush came up quite close to the building. During the very cold weather, they would take turns sleeping and keeping the fires going in the cook stove and the airtight heater. If they did not, the water would freeze in the pail and both fresh and canned food would freeze. There was no plumbing in their suite, so the only way they had running water was to run up the hill with it. A scrub board, tub and elbow action was their "washing machine." Those were the days.

Perryvale Chapel Sunday School Group with guest, Mrs. Ethel Tarbuck, at far right of Row Two.

While the ladies were there, they each received twenty dollars a month from the Home Missions Fund. From this they paid the rent on their suite and their expenses. The offerings helped, too.

Deaconess J. Shirley Johnson arrived shortly before her sister, Elsie Johnson, and Selma Komant left in May 1950. Shirley carried on with the services, Sunday School and Bible club as already established. Shirley was in the area full time until August 1953. During this time she had three co-workers for varying lengths of time. These ladies were Miss Mary Readner; Miss Doris Tarbuck, one of the young people from the Red Deer Gospel Mission, who stayed until she became ill; and Miss Bernice Olson, daughter of Rev. and Mrs. Morris Olson. They each contributed to the ministry there.

To the ministries already mentioned, Shirley added a teenage girls' club, Religious Education in the Perryvale School and outstations (combination service and Sunday school in the Willow Ridge Schoolhouse, Sunday school on a farm south-east of Perryvale for a time, Sunday school in the old Caribou Ridge Schoolhouse and later in a house, plus more services in Rochester).

Shirley remembers taking some Perryvale area young people caroling on Christmas Eve. That was a highlight for them and to some folks, who heard them sing. Then she and her co-worker, if there was one at the time, would catch the last bus home for Christmas. They caroled at least two different years.

A number of the young people (Wards, Holmes, possibly Joyce Clark) went horseback riding with Shirley. Someone loaned Shirley a horse. They all enjoyed themselves, both times.

In the summer of 1951, when Doris Tarbuck was Shirley's co-worker, Sharon Johnson came to visit her big sister. One afternoon just north of Perryvale, a beautiful wolf crossed the road, just a short distance away from Shirley, Doris and Sharon, who were walking out to visit some folks, perhaps Wards, Granny Ward or Clarks. The wolf did not seem the least bit interested in them, for he took his time with steady gait and soon disappeared into the bush. On the way home from mid-week service, Shirley remembers hearing coyotes as she walked that mile in the dark with bush on both sides of the road, except for the cemetery. She was never harmed. Not too long after Shirley had moved back to Edmonton, she was told that a mother cougar and her cub were sighted down the valley in the Meanook area. It is a little difficult to explain the feeling that went through Shirley, when she heard that choice bit of information.

Shirley remembers one of her first visits to a home in the Perryvale area. The Tawatinaw River Valley is a very pretty, deep and rolling valley. She was nervous as she walked about a mile and a half to reach a farm just above the valley. She wondered how she would be received. As she entered the yard, dogs announced her arrival. Then the lady of the house came to the door and invited her to come into her home. That lady was Mrs. Violet Rein. She was so nice. She knew just how to make a person feel welcome. Her children came to Sunday School after that. Through her, Shirley learned about Benhams in the Willow Ridge District. After meeting the Benhams in the summer of 1950, she started to conduct a combination service and Sunday school in the Willow Ridge Schoolhouse.

Driving a 1927 Chevrolet coupe, provided Shirley with an opportunity of visiting quite a way from her home base at Perryvale. It was an old car and there were some exasperating moments. One afternoon, she drove up the steep incline to the Holmes farm. One little piece would not stay put on the motor. Part way up this incline, that piece bounced off again. So she just left the coupe facing up the incline, went to the Holmes home, acquired a piece of wire and went back to the car. She was the only one in the area, who drove a 1927 Chevrolet coupe, so when anyone saw the coupe, they knew that she was somewhere around. When she arrived back at the car, she found that someone had turned the car around so that it was facing downhill. She wired the piece in place and was on her way. Shirley never did find out who turned the car around for her.

One Sunday afternoon, a dear, elderly lady handed Shirley an envelope containing a note (which Shirley still has) and ten dollars. The very next day, the starter went on the 1933 Dodge Sedan. The bill for the repairs was nine dollars and some cents.

Some very nice things happened to or for Shirley. Her co-workers were a great help. After Shirley had been in Perryvale for a year, an anniversary celebration was held in the community hall in May 1951. This was organized by Mr. Holmes. There were gifts from the clubs, which Shirley had for the children and young people. Mr. Aloisio, the Reeve for the Municipality of Athabasca, spoke some kind words of appreciation, then presented a gift of money from Mr. and Mrs. R. Aloisio and family; Mr. and Mrs. F. Rein and family; Mr. and Mrs. T. Golonka and family; Mr. and Mrs. L. Banack and family; Mrs. Waffle and family, including Betty; Mr. and Mrs. Clark and family; Mr. and Mrs. P. Ward and family; Mr. and Mrs. Art Lewis and Donald; Mr and Mrs. L. Silverthorne and Bobby; Mrs. McClusky; Perryvale Ladies Club; Mrs. A. Aloisio and family; Mrs. B. Aloisio and family. This celebration was such an encouragement to Shirley.

In the spring or summer of 1951, Shirley moved into the white house, next door to the Variety Store. The living room became the chapel. While there, Mr. W. Craswell, who owned the house, donated wood for fuel as he had when Elsie and Selma lived in

Allyn and Helen Splane. Mr. Splane gave Shirley an accordian and a car for the work at Perryvale in 1952.

Perryvale. The house had a heater that was made to burn coal, so it could be banked to keep the house warm even at night. That was very much appreciated. In the winter of 1951-52, Mary Readner and Shirley had to dig the coal out from under the snow but were very glad to have it.

Mr. Allyn Splane of Redcliffe, Alberta, found out that Shirley Johnson and Bernice Olson were ministering in Perryvale, through a child, who had been given a Sunday school paper at a religious instruction class in Perryvale. When he came, he left his accordian for Shirley and in July 1952 brought a 1933 Dodge Sedan because by this time a car was needed. What a generous person! That summer, Mr. Splane married a lady from the Lake Baptiste area. Shirley and Bernice prepared a string of tin cans to attach to the Splane's car, when they came through. They did not stop, so the tin cans were not used. One day when Shirley started to drive the Dodge away, she noticed that those tin cans were attached to the car she was driving. Somebody had a sense of humour.

On May 5, 1952, J. Shirley Johnson was granted her Ministerial Certificate from the Pentecostal Assemblies of Canada.

© Copyright owned by J. Shirley Morsch 1982.

PERRYVALE
CARIBOU RIDGE DISTRICT

From about the spring of 1951, Caribou Ridge Sunday School was held in the old Caribou Ridge Schoolhouse, weather permitting. There was a lovely weeping birch tree in the yard.

Among those, who attended, were Mr. and Mrs. Arthur Gerlach's children (Lawrence, Charlie, Joyce), Mr. and Mrs. Adam Janczyn's children (Alice, Gordon, Donald), Mr. and Mrs. Lawrence Morrell's children (Shirley, Loretta, Lorraine, Hazel, Lorna) and Jean Anderson. Folks from this district attended the Willow Ridge services, too, from time-to-time.

Later this Sunday School was held in the Gerlach house, across from the Jack Anderson farm home. Shirley Johnson and Bernice Olson lived there from the spring of 1953 to August of that year. The hospitality in Caribou Ridge was heart warming. Mom Anderson provided them with lots of milk and eggs. The Howards and Shirley spent one New Year's Eve with the Morrells. Mrs. Morrell really knew how to make potato soup. Mrs. Cherry Gerlach was a gracious hostess. Shirley stayed with Ruth Janczyn and her children for a month or two early in 1953. Ruth was good to Shirley, even tried match-making but Shirley felt that in her position she had to play it cool.

When the car, Shirley drove, was not worth fixing

Sunday School at the old Caribou Ridge School. Shirley Johnson's relatives were guests. Doris Tarbuck, Shirley's Assistant, is far right.

any more, she and Bernice made the difficult decision to leave, conduct Daily Vacation Bible School in Wainwright and Ribstone and then on to work in Edmonton. However, in the June or July of 1954, Shirley Johnson began commuting from Edmonton for services at the Willow Ridge Schoolhouse. A number of these folk attended services there.

© Copyright by J. Shirley Morsch, 1982

PERRYVALE
ROCHESTER

© Copyright by J. Shirley Morsch, 1982

Besides giving religious instruction in the Rochester School, Selma Komant and Elsie Johnson held occasional services in Rochester. Shirley and her co-workers later held regular services as part of their circuit ministry. These services were held in the United Church. In the fall or early winter of 1952, Shirley and Bernice Olson moved their home base to Rochester. The large living room in the Smith house, where they lived, became the chapel for a few months. Then early in 1953, the ladies moved into the United Church Manse and again held their services in the United Church.

One winter day, early in 1953, the temperature dropped to fifty or sixty degrees below zero by about five o'clock in the afternoon. A married daughter of Mrs. Waffle invited Shirley and Bernice to spend the night because the manse was so cold. How the ladies appreciated her kindness! That night the thermometer at the railroad station registered seventy-two below zero Fahrenheit. Late winter or early spring 1953, Bernice went home and Shirley stayed at the

Janczyn home in the Caribou Ridge District for a month or two. Then in the spring they moved into the vacant Gerlach home. Thanks to the Gerlachs, they had a house in a good position for their ministry.

PERRYVALE
WILLOW RIDGE DISTRICT
© Copyright by J. Shirley Morsch, 1982

In the summer of 1950, shortly after Shirley Johnson's visit to Mrs. Rein, Shirley visited the Benhams in Willow Ridge. The Benhams made her feel so welcome. Sheila Benham was especially encouraging. The whole family became very good friends with her. As a result of that first meeting, Shirley decided to start services at the Willow Ridge Schoolhouse. She tucked some Sunday school in the middle of each service there. In the beginning Shirley was song leader, soloist, musician (on autoharp or accordion), teacher and preacher. She used a few of the young people to lead in action choruses. There were others, who assisted in other ways. When she had a co-worker, the co-worker would take part, too. These services were held in the schoolhouse unless the weather was too cold, then they were held in homes.

Willow Ridge and Caribou Ridge Folk after service. Guests were Bill and Bertha Lagore, Joan Anderson (nee Benham) and her husband, Irvan Anderson. Shirley Johnson is standing in front of the tallest man.

Shirley also had a boys' and girls' club in this schoolhouse. The Caribou Muskeg stretched for miles. At one point, it is, perhaps, half a mile from the Willow Ridge Schoolhouse. One year there was a bad fire that swept over this muskeg. Spruce trees would go up in flames, just like huge torches. One day during this time, Shirley had her children's club, but she had to keep a close watch on this fire because it was too close for comfort. It was very dangerous for the farmers in the district, especially those, who owned part of the muskeg or land bordering it. One family, the Lawrence Morrells, lived on a knoll right

out in the middle of this muskeg in the Caribou Ridge area. Another time after this club, when Shirley was driving the Kostiw children home, the lights went out on the 1927 Chevrolet. There was not anything she could do but hold a flashlight out her window and drive. She made it safely to Kostiws and to Perryvale. Louis Silverthorne, a mechanic who had a garage in Perryvale, fixed the light problem. It was good to have a mechanic nearby to service her car.

Each year at Willow Ridge, they had a Christmas program. They tried to involved as many as they knew wanted to take part.

Shirley and her co-workers continued services until August 1953. It was a difficult decision to make to leave the area. Many were so kind to them. Shirley Johnson and Bernice Olson did leave, conducted Vacation Bible School in Wainwright and Ribstone, then worked in Edmonton. In May 1954, Shirley Johnson began commuting from Edmonton to Willow Ridge for Sunday services, twice a month. Benhams met her when she came by bus. Later Ruth Maser became her co-worker in these services, the same type held, when Shirley lived in the area. During the school year, 1956-1957, Bob Kostiw, a fine young man who had attended the services from the first year, was living in Edmonton. He brought Shirley and Ruth out for the Sunday services. The Kostiws often had them stay over Saturday night.

Shirley attended the University of Alberta to obtain her teaching certificate, so that she could teach school in the Perryvale area, if a position was available. Then she would be able to continue holding services in Willow Ridge. However, the Athabasca School Division Superintendent placed her in the junior high section of the Grassland Consolidated School. There she mainly taught English and Music. She, also, conducted a children's club, Sunday School, services, and religious instruction in the Grassland School.

Ruth continued the Sunday services at Willow Ridge until she had an accident on very, very icy roads. Mr. and Mrs. Orn, though not from the Pentecostal Assemblies of Canada, were good people, who held services for some time after Ruth left.

Shirley Johnson married Edwin Morsch and has resided in Edmonton for quite a few years. She was able to be of comfort to two cancer patients from the Willow Ridge area. Derril and Bev Benham took care of little Scott Morsch one time, so that Shirley could visit one of them. Shirley sang at the funeral of John Kostiw. It was a privilege for her to be of comfort to the family. Once in a while Shirley is able to see some of the folks in the Perryvale and Willow Ridge areas.

Though the Pentecostal Assemblies of Canada no

longer have a minister in the Perryvale or Willow Ridge areas, the time spent in the ministry here was not in vain, for there were those who learned to trust in God and that God really cares about them.

Among those, who attended services in the Willow Ridge Schoolhouse, were Robert and Sheila Benham with Joan, Derril, Dale; Mr. and Mrs. John Kostiw with Bob, Dorothy, Bill, Betty, Patsy (Pinkie), Joy, Jean; Mr. and Mrs. Bill Speers with Ross and Darlene; Mr. and Mrs. Howard with Alvin and Alva; Mrs. Roy Speers with Don, Neil, Larry, Marcella, Gladys, Sharon and possibly Shirley; Granny Speers; Mr. and Mrs. Ray Smith with Patsy, Gloria, Jeanette, Bernice, Kenny; Mrs. Jack (Mom) Anderson and Jean; Mr. and Mrs. Arthur Gerlach with Lawrence, Charlie, Joyce; Mr. and Mrs. Adam Janczyn with Alice, Gordon, Donald; Mrs. Janczyn Sr., Mr. and Mrs. Lawrence Morrell with Shirley, Loretta, Lorraine, Hazel, Lorna and possibly Rocky; Arnold Newman (Proctor's grandson); Wilfred and Hazel Lehto with Gordon and Myrna; Bert and Louise Nicol with Barbara and Don; the Yarish boys — Gordon and Murray; Bert, Tony and Betty Bandola; Ethel; Shirley R.. Some attended more often than others. Usually there was good attendance. They are still very special people.

PONOKA
ENGLISH PENTECOSTAL ASSEMBLY

About 1941 Mr. and Mrs. Rudolph Pohl and family moved to a farm near Ponoka. They held services in their home. In 1942 or 1943, Ransom Wagar came to minister. Near this time, Reed hall, above the Co-op Store, was rented for services. Others who ministered were Fred Hunter, John Martens and Mabel Hyssop.

During the ministry of John Martens, in 1945 a Daily Vacation Bible School was held in the district. Miss Anna Neilson (now Mrs. Gordon Donaldson) and Miss Jessie Gross (wife of Reverend Ernest Hawtin) of Red Deer were in charge.

In March 1946 Evangelist Edward Gaetz held an evangelistic campaign. At that time the Assembly was worshipping in the same hall.

Several German people had settled in the area. Reverend Schatkowski had services in some German homes before Reverend Schultz conducted German services in the homes on Sunday mornings. Shortly after, the English Assembly asked Reverend Schultz to preach in their evening services. He continued to do so until and after the church was built. If German speaking people were present, the service was bilingual.

In 1947 or 1948 the assembly men and boys cut logs. These were made into lumber from which they built their church in Ponoka.

About 1949 the church became part of the German Conference.

Pastor Schultz ministered for seven years. Others who pastored were Paul Schellert, Art Sader, Otto Kakoschke, Gus Wentland (1966-1969) and Ron Posein. Since no pastor was available after Ron Posein left, the church and parsonage were sold. Ponoka has no Pentecostal Assembly of Canada church at time of writing.

SIBBALD
SIBBALD ASSEMBLY

In the early thirties, Peter Mervin (Todd) Cantelon, Lawrence Holdsworth and others held services in the Community Church in Sibbald. In 1939, Rev. and Mrs. J. R. Allen held services there as part of a circuit ministry.

On March 21, 1940, Sybil Speer was united in marriage to Kenneth Bunting. Rev. Allen officiated.

Other Oyen ministers held services in Sibbald. Among them was Andrew Wek. People from Sibbald area are welcome to attend Glad Tidings Tabernacle in Oyen and have been welcome for a long time.

Among those, who attended Bible college and/or entered the ministry (*), is *Sybil Speer, who married Kenneth Bunting, who was/is a minister.

STONY PLAIN
PENTECOSTAL ASSEMBLY

Virgil and Nina Lawrence started meetings in a hall in June 1957. They commuted from Spruce Grove and Edmonton for one year. They bought the Glory Hills Baptist Church in the country and had it moved on to a basement in Stony Plain. The church

The Stony Plain Church

was renovated and a suite built in the basement for the pastor. During the summers they conducted Daily Vacation Bible Schools in Stony Plain. Shirley Johnson helped in these for two summers.

Some of the early families are Richard and Fred Ratz; Grandma Sonnenberg, Ed, Fred and Artia; Mr. and Mrs. Heiman; Mr. and Mrs. Wesley Lawrence; Mr. and Mrs. Zyg Fermaniuk; Evelyn Schmuland and children, Byson and Dan; Allan Schmuland; Earl and Irene Hudson, who came to the Lord.

Keith and Rhelda Evans moved out to Stony Plain to help the Lawrences. It was from here that Keith felt God was calling him to full time ministry. He filled in for Reverend Jack Keys in Lacombe for about six months. Then he went to Mayerthorpe where Virgil Lawrence helped build the church.

The Lawrences left Stony Plain in 1962. Mr. and Mrs. Ken Mervyn followed them in 1964 and 1965. Mr. R. Thomas ministered for a time in 1966 until Mr. and Mrs. Jim McAlister came to pastor in September 1966.

In 1967 Evangelist Eunice Meyer had a tent crusade, with good results in Stony Plain. The tent was set up near the church.

For some time Pastor and Mrs. Jim McAlister ministered in Evansburg, while still pastoring at Stony Plain. On Saturdays they would go to Evansburg for visitation. They also made the church building ready for Sunday afternoon service. In June 1968 the McAlisters left to pastor Edson.

Rev. and Mrs. Virgil Lawrence with Sharolyn and Carolee (1962).

On July 1, 1968 Bob and Gisela Eckstrom came to minister in Stony Plain for one and one-half years. They were followed by Pastor and Mrs. Ken Eburne and assistant pastor Don and Mrs. Eshleman. Keith Agrey helped the Eburnes, too.

In 1970 the church in Stony Plain closed. At the time of writing, Pentecostal people from this area, who wish to attend a Pentecostal assembly, attend the Spruce Grove Community Church.

TABER
TABER OUTREACH

In 1968, Terry Law had an evangelistic campaign in the Legion Hall in Taber for one week. After this campaign, services continued in the Legion Hall for a while. Then the services were held in the rumpus room of Nick and Marion Kiffiak. Rudy Mantik was pastor for the two and a half years of Pentecostal Assemblies of Canada services in Taber. They had Sunday school and Sunday services plus a Wednesday prayer and Bible study meeting, during that time.

Among those, who attended, were the Puticcis and Kiffiaks.

Among those, who attended Bible college, was Diane Puticci.

TORRINGTON

Services were held in Torrington as an outreach of Mayton. In 1939, Rev. Frederick reported good attendance and interest. In 1947, Rev. Edward Gaetz reported a great revival for three weeks. Even the largest buildings were filled to capacity. Many were saved and some were healed. This was one of the greatest stirs in the area for over twenty years.

VIKING
PENTECOSTAL ASSEMBLY

Pastor and Mrs. Daniel Anderson, who were pastoring Killam, helped to start this work. Rev. Paul Olson, an outstanding evangelist, had special meetings in Viking. He was very well received. The Stans came to pastor.

In the early days of this work, the Portable Tabernacle was used there. This Tabernacle was built by the Christ's Ambassadors of the Alberta District, with the help of some older folk, too. One Saturday, when this church was without a pastor for a certain weekend, Rev. D. N. Buntain had sent J. Shirley Johnson out to preach for the Sunday service. Somehow, plans had changed and someone forgot to let Rev. Buntain know, so when Shirley arrived, there was no one to meet her. She did not know anyone there and was short of money. Since the Tabernacle was not locked, Shirley slept on one of the narrow

Viking Vacation Bible School, July 1955.

benches. She was nervous but no one bothered the Tabernacle.

In May 1954, Pastors Art and Lucille Sader arrived. The Andersons, from Killam, helped. The Saders built up the Sunday school. In the fall of that year, the Yukes gave them one week of special services — children's services after school, which were well attended, and evening services for the whole family. At one meeting, they pretended to auction off a boy to show the value of a child.

While the Saders were there, Art drove a school bus to add to their twenty-five dollars a month from the District Home Missions Fund. They also fixed up the church building.

In 1956, a Missionary Action Girls group was started.

Rev. and Mrs. Poierier followed the Saders. Then Violet Nelson (1958-1961) ministered. While she was there J. Shirley Johnson came for Vacation Bible School. Shirley remembers Violet lived in a small suite in the basement of the church. Pastor Larry Broughton followed. He later became a missionary to Liberia, West Africa. A couple, who provided a home for quite a few Indian children, were interim pastors. Fred Murphy pastored from 1964 to 1966. Pastor Lorne McAlister (1966-67) pastored this home mission work, next. Many supplied Lorne with cookies, the McVeighs faithfully supplied him with milk and the Macks supplied him with meat. In 1967, Pastor Milton Israelson commuted from his parents' home in Amisk to pastor. Beryl Shannon (May 1970-July 1971) was the next pastor. She was assisted for six weeks by Donna Baker. Beryl became a missionary to Zaire, Africa. Miss Olsonberg came next.

A tornado came through Viking and almost wrecked the church. The church was then closed and sold. It became a furniture store.

Among the folks who attended this church were Mrs. Arychuk and David, Mrs. MacPherson and Bonnie, Mrs. Bailey, The Mantiks, the Froehlichs, the McVeigs, Mrs. Sather (pianist) and Glen, Alex and Marg Wilson, Robert and Helen Snider, Metro and Lena Arychuk, the Munces (parents of Bertha Lagore), the Tom Newleys.

Among those, who attended Bible college, were Gladys McVeigs and Joan Gommeringer.

WETASKIWIN
THE WETASKIWIN FULL GOSPEL FELLOWSHIP

In 1918-19 a Swedish itinerant Full Gospel minister, Rev. C. O. Nordin, visited the Wetaskiwin district. Cottage prayer meetings were held. Many were saved and filled with the Holy Spirit. A church was built on A. Leverth's farm in the Wang district, about eight miles north-east of Wetaskiwin. Here Full Gospel services were held in the Scandinavian languages as well as in English. Tent meetings were conducted when Scandinavian people from Central and Eastern Alberta would meet for fellowship under the leadership of Full Gospel evangelists from various parts of Canada and the United States.

In 1924 in the City of Wetaskiwin, Mrs. George Owens, wife of a local auctioneer, heard of the outpouring of the Holy Spirit. She invited Reverend Hugh McAlister from Edmonton to conduct a series of meetings in Wetaskiwin. Some were held in the Ebenezer Baptist Church. At that time a tent meeting with some Scandinavian Full Gospel preachers was being held in the city. They invited Reverend Hugh McAlister to minister in the services. The Lord truly blessed. Many were saved and filled with the Holy Spirit. Since the Pentecostal message was new, many believers suffered persecution from their families and friends. The group that formed the Assembly held services in a hall above the local Co-Op Store. Later they moved to an old Blacksmith Shop on Main Street, about a block east of the C.P.R. Station. During this time the church was pastored by Reverend and Mrs. Swanton, who made their home with the Owens family. Reverend and Mrs. Jack Knight also pastored during those early years.

In 1926 a young man from Victoria, B.C., Bert Robinson, came to minister. He married a local girl, Alma Kaiser. In 1929 a country school house (the Lucas School) was purchased. This was placed on a lot near the Anglican Church on fifty-first Street. Pastor and Mrs. Parker were shepherding the flock at that time. Later in 1929, Reverend and Mrs. Cecil Cobb accepted the leadership of the Assembly. Pastor Cobb painted the church inside and out, varnished floors and woodwork and replaced the old benches with comfortable chairs.

During this time, several families from the little country church in the Wang District had added their

Church Picnic during C. R. Cobb's Ministry.

support to the work in the town. Pastors and Evangelists would conduct a Sunday afternoon service in the country as well.

In 1931 Pastor and Mrs. John L. Wood came to minister. A Young People's Convention was held during the Easter break, when ministers and young people from Central Alberta gathered for a time of fellowship. Services were held in the Swedish Covenant Church to accommodate the crowd. The women of the church served meals in the Baptist Academy, which was rented for that purpose. While the blessing was being said at one noon meal, the Holy Spirit moved upon those present. Eating was postponed for a time of worship.

In 1935 a young man from Edmonton, Harvey C. McAlister, became pastor. He was assisted for a time by Douglas Jones, also, Marjorie McAlister came to play the piano. Souls were saved and filled with the Holy Spirit. Street meetings were held in front of the local hotel bar room. The police asked them to move to another location, as the large crowd blocked the sidewalk and entrance to the bar room. In 1936 a tent meeting was conducted in a vacant lot across from the church. Reverend Asa Miller from Kalamazoo, Michigan was the evangelist. Even though no public address system was used, the neighborhood was greatly disturbed by the services in the tent. Many who didn't attend still heard the gospel.

Pastor McAlister married a local school teacher, Agnes Leverth, in 1936.

In 1938 Pastor and Mrs. Jack Field came to minister. They were followed by Reverend and Mrs. T. E. Crane in 1941. The church was renovated, a full-sized basement for Sunday School rooms was added. In 1944 Reverend and Mrs. Robert Peel came as pastors. Reverend M. Kirkpatrick pastored for a few months in 1945-1946, followed by Miss Marion Cornish in 1947-1948. About 1948 the church became an independent assembly. Other pastors which followed have been Reverend and Mrs. Raymond Lindgren, Reverend and Mrs. Victor Graham, Reverend and Mrs. Jake Toews, Reverend and Mrs. R. Jacobson, Rev. and Mrs. T. E. Crane.

On April 27, 1980 a beautiful new church, The Wetaskiwin Full Gospel Fellowship, was dedicated to the glory of God. It is situated at the site of the old Outdoor Theatre, one mile west on Highway Thirteen. Some of the early founding families were Mrs. George Owens, R. Wagars, C. C. Nelsons, Wm. Kaiser, A. Leverths.

The little church in the country was eventually sold to a neighboring farmer, Mr. P. Lindahl. He built his home as an addition to the church. Sunday School was conducted in the church hall in the Wang Community for many years by his daughters. Miss Annie Lindahl is still conducting a Sunday School there.

Among those, who attended Bible College and/or entered the ministry (*), are *Alma Kaiser (married Reverend Bert Robinson), *Agnes Leverth (married Reverend Harvey McAlister), *Reverend James McAlister, Rodney Finnman, Ben Kellert, Mardell Peterson, *Ransom Wager.

WINFIELD
POPLAR VALLEY CHURCH (Four Miles West of Winfield)

During the winter of 1938, The Shamp brothers (Lionel, Fred, Clem, Ray), their father, Orrin Day and his son, Don, "got up" lumber for a church building. They did this because Fred Shamp, who was converted in a meeting in British Columbia, wanted services in the Poplar Valley area.

In 1939, Albert Grimes built a small prayer room building. It was often crowded.

Poplar Valley Church

Land across from the Poplar Valley cemetery was donated to the church by Mr. and Mrs. Charlie Clemmer. By volunteer labour, a church was built there. In 1939, it was finished enough for Mrs. Orrin Day to organize and conduct a Sunday School there. In 1939, Orville Williams became their first Pentecostal Assemblies pastor. Orville Williams worked in the Shamp Mill to support himself. By the spring of 1940, they reported they were finishing the church.

In December 1940, Brother Williams married Marjorie Day. Because World War II was in progress, Orville Williams joined the Signal Corps of the Army in 1942. From that time on, Mrs. Orrin Day carried on Sunday School until a pastor was found. As often as there were preachers, there were services. Among those, who came, were Arthur Schindel (for some months) and John Morsch, who commuted from Bentley for Sunday services in the fall of 1944 and spring of 1945. Jack Whitesell took John's place, when he was ill.

The congregation was without a regular pastor until 1949, when Rev. and Mrs. Olaf Haug became the pastors. Under their ministry in 1951, the church was organized under the Pentecostal Holiness Church (Canadian Branch). They have experienced growth.

Among those, who attended Bible college, was Orville Williams, who also taught in Northwest Bible College while it was still Canadian Northwest Bible Institute.

DAWSON CREEK, B.C.
PENTECOSTAL ASSEMBLY

David Faust, a young man in Manitoba, shared his desire to go to the Peace River country with Reverend D. N. Buntain. David had attended the Winnipeg Pentecostal Assembly of Canada Bible School and had sat under the ministry of Reverend D. N. Buntain in Wesley Pentecostal Church in Winnipeg.

In the spring of 1930, Reverend D. N. Buntain gave David a railroad ticket to Hythe, Alberta plus ten dollars spending money. Brother Buntain said, "Launch out and trust God."

Noreen Duncan and her younger brother

By 1932 David Faust was married and lived on a homestead twenty-five and one-half miles west of Dawson Creek. Here they had Sunday School and services in school houses. God blessed and souls were saved.

Mr. Irvin Wenzel spent a year with the Fausts helping in the ministry.

By the year 1936, Dawson Creek was experiencing steady growth. The Fausts felt that this town needed a Full Gospel Church. They contacted Reverend George Upton regarding this need. Brother Victor Graham came to take charge of street meetings which were held every Saturday night in Dawson Creek.

In the spring of 1937, the Fausts bought a lot in Dawson Creek. They built a house with squared timbers. In this house they held Sunday School and church services. During the summer they held tent meetings, where the police station is now built.

Later they were able to buy two lots where the Sears store is now situated. They bought a tract of spruce timber, had logs cut and made into lumber. From this they built the church. Among those, who helped in this enterprise, were George Gullackson, Duncan Smith, Ronald Benterud.

Wes Duncan

Reverend and Mrs. H. M. Graves and family came to minister here in mid June. They lived with the Fausts until the church building with living quarters was ready to use in October.

In 1944 while Reverend Graves was pastor, Miss Spycher and Miss Helgeson held a two-week Daily Vacation Bible School in Dawson Creek. Among the young people at this time were Wesley and Noreen Duncan.

About 1945 a new road was completed linking Prince George, B.C. with Dawson Creek. In June 1945 Dawson Creek Assembly became part of the British Columbia District of the Pentecostal Assemblies of Canada.

Noreen Duncan attended Northwest Bible College, when it was known as Canadian Northwest Bible Institute.

HATTON, SASKATCHEWAN ASSEMBLY OF GOD

In 1959 Reverend Norman Labrentz was Youth Director in Medicine Hat. In the summer of that year Vic Widmer, a member of the Medicine Hat church living in Hatton, requested that meetings be held in the village of Hatton.

In August 1959 Reverend Labrentz drove out to Hatton every Sunday afternoon to conduct a Sunday School in the school house. Meetings continued on a Sunday afternoon basis until January 1960, when Labrentz's moved to Hatton to pastor there. Reverend Labrentz obtained a job on Ed Stahl's ranch. The meetings were then changed to a morning Sunday School and morning worship.

The ranch community, some fifty miles east of Medicine Hat, had a population of approximately seventy. That first year in church the average attendance was thirty eight with an occasional attendance of seventy.

In 1961 the church was transferred from the Saskatchewan District into Alberta, as there were no neighboring Saskatchewan churches.

The summer of 1961 (July 4-9) a camp was organized in Cyprus Hills with Norman Labrentz as Director. Reverend Marvin Forseth was camp speaker to the five denominations that co-operated together from Medicine Hat to Maple Creek. The Labrentz family left on May 15, 1962 to go to Pincher Creek.

Harold Cain, a graduate of the Bible School in Eston, Saskatchewan, and his wife, Ruth, continued the ministry in Hatton for three or four years. Harold was an accountant in Medicine Hat. They would drive to Hatton for Sunday morning services. Several people from First Assembly in Medicine Hat, who shared in the ministry, were Edina Sponholtz, Fred Rattai, Don Scott and Alvin Gill.

Under Harold Cain's leadership the congregation in Hatton purchased and relocated a small church from Walsh, Alberta in Hatton. It was moved on to a basement. Sunday School rooms were developed in the basement. There was good attendance for the area and was packed for special occasions.

Eventually part of the ministry of the Medicine Hat Assistant Pastor included pastoring Hatton. Among those Assistant Pastors were Terry Law (1966-1967), Lorne McAlister (1968-1970), Ross Olson (1970-1972), Ted Bonk (1972-1974).

When Reverend and Mrs. Paul Slemming moved to Maple Creek, they attended the Hatton Assembly of God.

Under Ted Bonk, the Hatton congregation decided to relocate in Maple Creek, Saskatchewan. At this time the Maple Creek Assembly became part of the Pentecostal Assembly of Canada Saskatchewan District. Pastor Bonk pastored for some time after the relocation. He was followed by Reverend John Dobroski, Brian Hall and Randy Nolan.

Among those, who attended Bible School after relocation in Maple Creek, are Louise Kramer, Bob Stewart, Lorraine Siegle, Judy Siegle, Darrel Widmer, Douglas Widmer, Sharon Widmer.

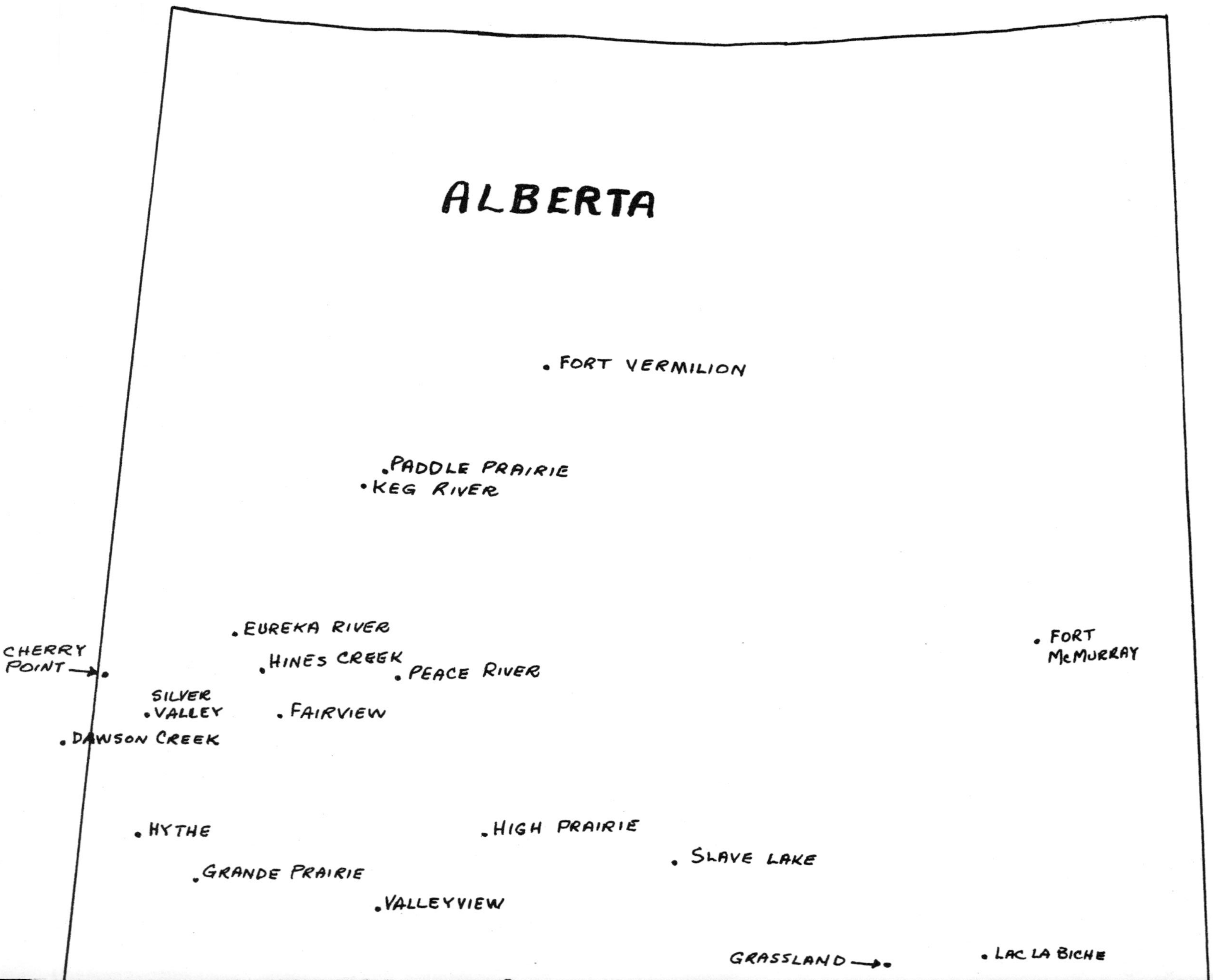

ALBERTA

- FORT VERMILION

- PADDLE PRAIRIE
- KEG RIVER

- EUREKA RIVER
- HINES CREEK
- PEACE RIVER
- FAIRVIEW

SILVER
- VALLEY
- DAWSON CREEK

CHERRY
POINT →•

- HYTHE

- GRANDE PRAIRIE

- VALLEYVIEW

- HIGH PRAIRIE

- SLAVE LAKE

GRASSLAND →•

- FORT
  McMURRAY

- LAC LA BICHE